PSYCHOLOGY TEACHER'S RESOURCE BOOK

First Course

Margo Johnson and Michael Wertheimer, Editors

Published by the
American Psychological Association
Washington, D.C.

Library of Congress Cataloging in Publication Data

Main entry under title: Psychology teacher's resource book.

    Published in 1970 under title: Program on the teaching of
psychology in the secondary school.
    1. Psychology--Study and teaching. 2. Psychological
literature. I. Johnson, Margo. II. Wertheimer, Michael.
III. Program on the teaching of psychology in the secondary
school. [DNLM: 1. Psychology--Education. 2. Teaching.
BF77 P9746]

BF77.P764 1979   150'.7   79-19143

ISBN 0-912704-10-1

Published by the American Psychological Association, Inc.
1200 Seventeenth Street, N.W., Washington, D.C. 20036.
Copyright 1979 by the American Psychological Association.
All rights reserved.

Contents

Preface

This Resource Book is a third edition of Program on the Teaching of Psychology in the Secondary School: Final Report, published by the American Psychological Association in December 1970. The original Resource Book was prepared by participants in a 1970 summer project at Oberlin College (Ohio) funded by the United States Office of Education. Much credit is due those participants for that initial effort. They were:

John K. Bare, Carleton College (Minnesota)
Charles Brader, then of St. Charles High School (Missouri), present
  whereabouts unknown
Al L. Cone, then of Lynchburg College (Virginia), now of Interbehavioral
  Consulting, Inc. (Maryland)
Donna M. Cone, then of Lynchburg College (Virginia), now of the Rhode
  Island Department of Mental Health, Retardation and Hospitals
Robert Dixon, then of Oberlin College (Ohio), now retired
David K. Hogberg, Albion College (Michigan)
Richard A. Kasschau, then of the University of South Carolina, now of the
  University of Houston (Texas)
Frank M. Lackner, then of Chatham College (Pennsylvania), present
  whereabouts unknown
Bernardine McPherson Novak, then of Arundel High School (Maryland), not
  teaching at present
Barry S. Markman, then of Indiana University, now of Wayne State
  University (Michigan)
Patricia O'C. Milkowski, then of State University College at Buffalo (New
  York), present whereabouts unknown
Ralph H. Turner, Oberlin College (Ohio)
Irvin S. Wolf, then of Denison University (Ohio), now retired

From the time the first Resource Book was published, it was apparent to us that such an evaluation and compilation as the Resource Book represented ought to be a continuing responsibility of the Association. We called on Oberlin project participants and others whom we knew to be interested in high school psychology to become a network of reviewers for APA's Clearinghouse on Precollege Psychology, evaluating introductory texts, books of readings, and lab manuals on a continuing basis for publication in Periodically, the Clearinghouse newsletter (now High School Psychology Teacher), and in revised editions of the Resource Book. Following is a roster of persons who have served as reviewers for some or all of the eight years since the first edition:

Virginia Andreoli, James Madison University (Virginia)
Eileen Brown, a graduate student at the State University of New York at
  Buffalo
Barbara Benedict Bunker, State University of New York at Buffalo
Samuel Cameron, Beaver College (Pennsylvania)
John M. Christiano, McQuaid Jesuit High School (New York)
Stephen Davol, Mount Holyoke College (Massachusetts)
Jan Duker, Teachers College, Columbia University, and Spence School (New
  York)

Delbert G. Eberhardt, Greenwich Public Schools (Connecticut)
Stephen Epley, Wartburg College (Iowa)
Robert S. Harper, Knox College (Illinois)
Charles W. Hill, Louisiana State University at New Orleans
Gloria Hill, Largo High School (Maryland)
Raymond G. Hunt, State University of New York at Buffalo
Paul D. Jones, University of Louisville (Kentucky)
Robert H. Koff, Roosevelt University (Illinois)
Linda Meador, formerly of McGavock Comprehensive High School (Tennessee),
    now of Metropolitan Nashville Schools (Tennessee)
Margaret Miller, formerly of United Nations International School (New
    York), present whereabouts unknown
Henry S. Pennypacker, University of Florida
Charles Peyser, The University of the South (Tennessee)
Meredith Platt, United Nations International School (New York)
Janet Price, Knox College (Illinois)
Judith J. Plows, formerly of Montgomery County Public Schools (Maryland),
    currently a graduate student
Oakley S. Ray, Vanderbilt University (Tennessee)
Louis Snellgrove, Lambuth College (Tennessee)
Robert J. Stahl, Mississippi University for Women
Kathleen White, Boston University (Massachusetts)
Peter Wolff, State University College at Potsdam (New York)

We are indebted to all of these persons as well as to most of the original
Oberlin project participants for their contributions, which are the substance
of Chapters 1, 2, and 3.

For revisions of Chapters 4, 5, 6, 7, and 8, we asked persons with special
expertise to assume editorial responsibilities: Ivan N. McCollom, formerly of
San Diego State University, now retired; James B. Maas and Carol M. Howe of
Cornell University (New York); Richard A. Kasschau; and Joseph Sidowski of the
University of South Florida. All four chapters required substantial over-
haul. The respective editors took on the task willingly and executed it
ably. We are very grateful to them.

We are grateful too to Maxine Warnath (Oregon College of Education) for
authorship of what is virtually a new chapter--10. Chapter 10 in the first
and second editions contained, among other things, a collection of exercises
and demonstrations for classroom use. With many more such exercises and
demonstrations available, APA is considering separate publication of
them--hence the decision to drop them from the Resource Book. The new Chapter
10 retains the idea of what remained of the old one, broadening it in some
respects, narrowing it in others.

The old Chapter 11 was judged expendable. In its place we have presented
the texts of three sets of ethical guidelines pertaining to the teaching of
psychology in the high school.

Revision of the remaining chapters was largely accomplished by APA staff.
Special recognition and thanks go to Natalya Krawczuk-Ayers, who doggedly

tracked down and verified the numerous details of a report such as this and who patiently proofread successive drafts of the manuscript. Thanks are also due Harriet Parks, able operator of the automatic typewriter, and Janet Neale, who backed us up on many tasks--mailing, proofreading, and typing.

Finally, thanks go to Brenda Bryant and Shelley Hammond, who managed the production of the report and did the technical editing.

Impetus for preparation of the third edition came from APA's Committee on Psychology in the Secondary Schools, which also advised the editors on modifications of content. Members of the Committee during the period of revision were: John K. Bare, ex officio as director of the Human Behavior Curriculum Project from January 1974 through November 1977; Evelyn Frye, then of McGavock Comprehensive High School (Tennessee), now a clinical psychologist; Frank B. W. Hawkinshire, New York University; Linda Meador; Mary Margaret Moffett, then of Murray Road Alternative School (Massachusetts), no longer teaching; Paul R. Munford, University of California at Los Angeles; Philip Newman, ex officio as director of the Human Behavior Curriculum Project from December 1977 through December 1978; Mark O'Dowd, New Madison Park High School (Massachusetts); Norman Sprinthall, University of Minnesota at Minneapolis; Maxine Warnath; and Michael Wertheimer, University of Colorado at Boulder.

The American Psychological Association is pleased to be able to provide this Resource Book as a service to teachers. So doing, however, does not constitute endorsement, implied or otherwise, of the views and recommendations that are contained herein. Any omissions that may have occurred are deeply regretted. We note that from 1974 through 1978 the APA was the recipient of a National Science Foundation grant to develop modules for use in high school psychology instruction.

Margo Johnson
Director of the APA Clearinghouse
    on Precollege Psychology, September 1969-June 1978

Michael Wertheimer
Chair of the Committee on
    Psychology in the Secondary Schools, June 1976-December 1978

Chapter 1

Reviews of Introductory Textbooks

The reviews in this chapter cover only a sample of the texts appropriate for an introductory course in psychology. Lowman (1979) presents a fairly comprehensive listing. In addition, the teacher may want to consult Chapter 2, "Reviews of Books of Readings," for selections that conceivably could be used as texts.

Wide ranges of emphasis, content, and level of reading difficulty are represented. Some effort has been made to show where each text falls on these continua. Because the amount of the teacher's undergraduate training in psychology and the types of students enrolled in a class vary, the final decision on the suitability of a particular text must be left to the judgment of the individual teacher.

The reviews are of necessity short and represent a single reviewer's judgment. Thus, teachers should obtain a copy of the text they are considering and examine it personally before making a decision concerning its use. Usually a complimentary desk copy or examination copy can be obtained from the publisher through a request written on school letterhead. If there is a college or university nearby, it also may be possible to borrow a text from the library or from a member of the department of psychology.

The entries contain as much information about each text as was available through library sources. The codes IM, TF, SG, and BR refer to materials that accompany the text. The codes translate as follows: IM--instructor's manual; TF--test-item file (sometimes separate, sometimes combined with the instructor's manual); SG--study guide, workbook, or a combination of the two; and BR--book of readings. Initials appearing at the end of reviews are those of reviewers, whose full names are listed in the Preface. The designation O.P.P., for Oberlin project participant, has been used for all reviews done during the Oberlin project in summer 1970; we are unable to identify individual authors of those reviews. The references given at the end of some entries represent other reviews of those entries. Addresses of publishers appear in Appendix A.

Belcher, D. M. <u>Giving psychology away</u>. San Francisco: Canfield Press, 1973. 369 pp. $11.95 cloth. IM, SG.

This text is intended to present "humanistic behaviorism" to the general student. The author also attempts to give due credit to scientific theory and research, but they definitely play a supporting role. The text is quite readable and complemented with many illustrations, graphs, and references to related studies and anecdotes.

There are 12 chapters, beginning with the development of personality, extending through learning, perception, and motivation, and closing with several applied areas in adjustment, prejudice, group dynamics, and behavior modification. A bibliography and index are placed at the end, but no glossary.

The text would be appropriate for a high school curriculum in the social sciences or for an adjustment course at the college level.--C.W.H. See also Rubinstein (1975) and Turner (1974a).

Bourne, L. E., Jr., & Ekstrand, B. R. Psychology: Its principles and meanings (2nd ed.). New York: Holt, Rinehart & Winston, 1976. 540 pp. $14.50 cloth. IM, TF, SG, Unit Mastery Workbook. (Now available in a 3rd ed.).

This text is clearly for the college-level student, and perhaps the high school teacher should read no further. However, advanced students in a science-oriented course and even the teachers of such a course could benefit from this book, as a reference if not as the main fare.

The approach is scientific, emphasizing the biological bases of behavior. There are 12 chapters, which should fit nicely into the typical semester. Three appendixes delve into statistics, neurophysiology, and tests and measurements. Completing the package are a glossary, a bibliography, a name index, and a subject index.

For some teachers, there will not be enough history and systems; for others there will be a deficit in scientific methodology; for still others the applications of psychology to the problems of education and industry will be given short shrift. Everyone should agree that the text is relatively easy to read, and that there are plenty of pictures, graphs, and examples. This book should be in every high school library, regardless of the courses offered or the specific uses of the book within such courses.--C.W.H.

See also Fuchs (1977), Sexton (1977), and Turner (1976a).

Brennecke, J. H., & Amick, R. G. Psychology: Understanding yourself. Beverly Hills, Calif.: Benziger, 1975. 337 pp. $5.68 paper. IM, TF.

Designed for the introductory student who is unlikely to take another psychology class, this text is intended to be "student-centered" and "experience-oriented." Although the chapter titles are popularized (e.g., "Growing into Being," "How Come? and What for?", and "Can You Believe Your Eyes?") much of the traditional subject matter of psychology is covered, albeit in a superficial way. Some of the material is misleading--for example, the implication that boys and girls reach puberty at the same age, and the treatment of the Freudian view of "fixation." Also, in some chapters there are a lot of personal opinions and very little psychology; Chapter 5, on emotions, is a case in point. In addition, the authors have a tendency to state that "most psychologists believe . . ." without attributing the belief to any particular psychologists or admitting to the amount of controversy actually present.

On the other hand, the material is easily readable at the high school level and probably adequate for the audience at which it is aimed. Each chapter has suggested readings "for further exploration" and study exercises. The teacher's manual provides suggestions for expanding the text's coverage ("particularly for more capable students") and conducting study exercises and supplementary activities. There are also annotated lists of audiovisual resources and both objective and short-essay test questions.--K.W.

Bruno, F. J. Psychology: A life-centered approach. New York: John Wiley, 1974. (Originally published by Hamilton Publishing Co., Santa Barbara, Calif.) 496 pp. $10.95 paper.

This text is designed for college students. It is decidedly human-istic in its approach though the author does present both the behavior-istic and psychoanalytic viewpoints where appropriate. Bruno organizes the book around major themes or problems of general interest to stu-dents: childhood, motivation (or more globally, what gives purpose or direction in life), emotions, sexual behavior, defense mechanisms, and psychotherapy. Learning, perception, thinking, and social behavior are also treated. Each chapter is divided into sections presenting high-in-terest topics (e.g., biofeedback, punishment, and sex before marriage) and discussing psychological principles appropriate to them. For in-stance, in probably the most extensive chapter in the book, Bruno describes the theories of Freud, Jung, Adler, Frankl, and Maslow as they apply to motivation. Each chapter is followed by a section of true-false questions, discussion questions, and references.

The book is quite interesting though somewhat superficial. Bruno does a good job of presenting the humanistic view of psychology, and in that respect the book is quite helpful. However, some high school stu-dents and teachers would have difficulty in dealing with the chapter on sexual behavior, which discusses masturbation, sex before marriage, or-gasm, and how marriages fail. Although the discussion is both informa-tive and nonjudgmental, teachers, and adolescents who are still concerned with their own sexual identity, may find these topics difficult to dis-cuss objectively in a classroom situation.--J.J.P.

See also Popplestone (1975) and Turner (1975a).

Cox, F. Psychology (2nd ed.). Dubuque, Iowa: Wm. C. Brown, 1973. 680 pp. $12.95 paper. TF, SG.

This text is a potpourri of contemporary psychology arranged into 16 chapters and 2 appendixes (statistics and drugs), complete with paren-thetical definitions in the text, 88 short insets amplifying or expound-ing on points, and one or two readings (of about six pages each) appended to most chapters. There are also a glossary and an index, both rather short for a book this large. The book is intended for a terminal course that will stimulate the students' "interest and curiosity as well as in-troduce them to the field of psychology" (p. xv). It is a respectable introduction to psychology, including discussions of such current topics as biofeedback and the invasion of privacy, but it is probably not a good text for a high school course because of the language level. Although some of the readings are from newsmagazines, more are from professional journals and upper-level texts. The remaining few were written especial-ly for this text. These latter readings, along with the insets and tex-tual material, are clearly written with the typical college sophomore in mind.

The student guide, in addition to containing the usual self-examination questions, identifies the major concepts in each chapter and provides summaries and group projects for each chapter.--R.S.H.
See also Abma (1974).

CRM/Random House. Understanding psychology (2nd ed., high school version). New York: Random House, 1977. 558 pp. $10.96 cloth. IM, TF, SG.

The publisher calls this book "the most successful high school psychology text" and it is easy to see why the book may enjoy a good deal of success. It is, indeed, both readable and engaging. While covering the traditional areas of psychology, it also presents the student with direct practical applications of psychological principles--for example, how to improve study habits, how to improve memory, and techniques of self-management. Each chapter begins with an outline and ends with a summary, a glossary, a set of activities for use in and outside the classroom, references, and suggested readings.

Although some areas of psychology--for example, Freudian psychology, the role of instincts in animal behavior, and Piaget's theory--seem to be covered in an unnecessarily abbreviated and/or oversimplified manner, the text is on the whole a rich and enjoyable introductory book. It is too comprehensive to be covered adequately in a one-semester high school course, but individual units could be selected. Use of the exercises and recommended readings should provide a valuable experience for both students and teachers and compensate for any shortcomings inherent in the Psychology Today style of presentation.--K.W.
See also Gerow (1978b) and Kasschau (1978).

Dallett, K. It's all in your mind: Understanding psychology. Palo Alto, Calif.: National Press Books, 1973. 244 pp. $10.50 cloth; $6.50 paper.

Although its contents are similar to those of most introductory texts, in format, style, and presentation this text is not typical. Its purpose is to acquaint students with issues likely to survive the current knowledge explosion in psychology. Dallett challenges students to discover psychology as a personal experience, through the narrative and personal observations. The book focuses on providing the basic concepts and ideas on which these observations--hence, experiences--can be based.

The unusual format of the narrative accents the author's lively and clever writing style. However, this format often makes it difficult for the reader to follow the flow of the narrative, offsetting much of the impact of the unique writing style. The format would create problems for students who struggle with the traditional pattern of printed-page layouts. More highly verbal students would probably be attracted to both the author's style and the novel arrangement of the narrative.

Student-oriented exercises and activities designed to help students "discover and invent" psychology for themselves are included in the various chapters. Although not available to most high school psychology

teachers and students, the few references cited are not necessary to understand the text. The unusual illustrations scattered throughout the
volume attract one's attention at first, but they quickly lose meaning
because they have little relationship to the accompanying narrative.

Teachers who desire a structured, fact-laden, encyclopedic text will
find this book inadequate. The book would be especially adequate for
courses enrolling highly motivated, discussion-minded students or courses
with a more casual, relaxed approach highlighted by frequent discussions
of student ideas about psychology and short lectures containing related
factual material. The reading level is that of the good high school
senior. The text could be used in a one-semester course that focuses on
understanding the major concepts and vocabulary of psychology. It would
be most useful as a springboard for in-depth studies and activities in
the areas suggested by its 15 chapters.--R.J.S.

See also Review of Dallett (1974), Rubinstein (1975), and Turner
(1974a).

Davidoff, L. L. Introduction to psychology. New York: McGraw-Hill,
     1976. 560 pp. $14.95 cloth. IM, TF.

Davidoff's thorough text could be covered in a one-semester high
school course. The writing style, content, and organization make it very
well suited for high school students. The vocabulary is professional but
not overly difficult to comprehend. The writing style allows for smooth
enjoyable reading and facilitates understanding. In terms of content the
text covers the traditional topics of an introductory course as well as
current areas of student interest. In particular, the last chapter
directly relates psychology to social issues such as urban problems,
work, and the prison system. Davidoff does not overwhelm her readers
with research; she presents enough to demonstrate the scientific nature
of psychology. The research is used to provide examples and clarify
theories. The text also contains many case studies, photographs, drawings, and diagrams that complement the written material.

The most impressive features of the book are its organization and the
inclusion of a study guide in the text itself. The fact that the main
points are reiterated several times will undoubtedly aid the high school
student. Each chapter begins with a list of four to nine objectives to
help guide the student. At the end of each chapter (or at the end of
major sections in the chapter) there is a brief summary of the major
points. The study guide following each chapter provides an excellent
review of the material. First, there is a list of key terms, important
research, and basic theories. The list is followed by a 15-item multiple-choice self-quiz and, in some chapters, a fill-in-the-blank exercise. Also included for each chapter are thought-provoking questions, a
data-collection project, and a list of suggested readings. At the end of
the book is a 15-page glossary of important terms and a chapter-by-chap-
ter bibliography.

The instructor's manual contains a bibliography, exercises, demonstrations, titles of recommended films, and multiple-choice, true-false,
completion, matching, and essay questions for each chapter.--V.A.

See also Sexton (1977) and Turner (1976a).

Dustin, D. S., & Johnson, J. M. Explaining behavior: An introduction to psychology. Encino, Calif.: Dickenson Publishing Co., 1974. 273 pp. $8.95 paper. TF.

This incisive, stimulating text does just what its title suggests: It introduces the reader to the explanations that professionals offer for behavior. After an initial chapter (with a confusingly brief foray into statistics appended to introductory material), eight chapters focus in turn on types of explanations: developmental, learning and cognitive, social, physiological, perceptual, motivational, personality, and clinical.

The writing is admirably concise--a mixture of general principles, examples, and questions (with suggested responses in the back of the book). The excellent layout of pages complements the carefully selected material although there is insufficient space to answer some questions. About 50 suggestions for further reading are provided. They have been carefully selected for the beginning student, but too many come from Psychology Today to suit this reviewer. Test questions are available from the publisher.

Teachers overwhelmed by the encyclopedic monsters that masquerade as beginning texts will welcome this book--probably to find that the students overwhelm them with searching questions. That would be a refreshing change--provided the teachers have at least a moderate background in psychology. Dustin and Johnson have produced a very readable, flexible, application-oriented, one-semester text that should challenge student and teacher alike, to mutual benefit.--C.P.

Edwards, D. C. General psychology (2nd ed.). New York: Macmillan, 1972. 466 pp. $14.50 cloth. TF, SG, BR.

This second edition is a classical treatment concentrating on historical issues and experiments. The chapter on sensation and perception and the chapter on emotion and motivation are the most comprehensive. Chapters on animal and human learning are well written but somewhat dated. Missing are such topics as behavior modification, sensitivity training, racial attitudes, sex roles, and drugs.

An outstanding feature of the book is a glossary that contains almost 500 definitions. The many headings and subheadings will help students outline and review material. On the other hand, the book contains few illustrations and explanatory charts. Another drawback is that chapters on the nervous system and statistics are out of context, in the back of the book. Also, the writing style would be difficult for high school students, and the experimental and traditional nature of the text make it suitable only for students already committed to studying academic psychology.

The study guide would be more appropriately referred to as a readings book. It contains a collection of historical and theoretical papers by key figures in the history of psychology such as John B. Watson, Charles Darwin, William James, Eleanor Gibson, Nicholas Tinbergen, and J. P. Guilford. A few current readings such as Verhave's "The Pigeon as a

Quality-Control Inspector" and Gardner's "Teaching Sign Language to a Chimpanzee" are provided. There are also a vocabulary list and 15 self-study multiple-choice items for each chapter in the text.--P.W.
     See also Van Krevelen (1973).

Engle, T. L., & Snellgrove, L. Psychology: Its principles and applications (6th ed.). New York: Harcourt Brace Jovanovich, 1974. 535 pp. $7.95 cloth. IM, TF, SG. (Now available in a 7th ed.)

     The names T. L. Engle and Louis Snellgrove as authors should be sufficient recommendation for a high school text in psychology. This text is the sixth edition in a series dating back to 1945. The material has been kept up-to-date, and nothing in the text offsets for the reviewer the favorable impressions generated by the authors' names.
     The text is organized into seven units, each unit including three chapters, except Unit 1, which is also Chapter 1. One might quarrel with the ordering of this material: "What is Psychology," "Learning," "Understanding Human Behavior," "Patterns of Behavior" (physiological bases), "Emotional and Behavioral Adjustments," "Small Groups," and "Psychology and Society." However, as the authors point out, the units may be taught in any order with no problems created thereby. Each chapter concludes with sections on (a) Terms to Know, (b) Topics to Think About, (c) Suggestions for Activities, and (d) Suggestions for Further Reading. Each unit concludes with a special feature on such topics as extrasensory perception, intelligence, and love and aggression; the special features cover only two pages each and could be easily integrated into the appropriate chapter. The text concludes with a glossary and a very detailed index. The book is easy to read, contains an adequate number of relevant illustrations, and is quite successful in keeping the principles of psychology in touch with the everyday world. Although it is more appropriate for use in an introductory course, it might be partitioned into meaningful modules for more general courses in behavioral or social science.
     The teacher's manual contains a host of aids: suggested objectives, methods, and techniques; sources of films, tapes, and apparatus; demonstrations, exercises, and experiments; and a variety of objective test questions. The student workbook provides instructions for do-it-yourself experiments and demonstrations, including the construction of simple apparatus.--C.W.H.
     See also Kasschau (1977a), Meador (1977), Popplestone (1975), and Turner (1974b).

Fincher, C. A preface to psychology (2nd ed.). New York: Harper & Row, 1972. 149 pp. No price available.

     This book emphasizes the importance of a scientific and systematic approach to the study of human behavior. In eight chapters the reader explores historical attempts to explain behavior, ranging from mythology to science. The lively reading of the first four chapters, in which are described the characteristics of science and the development of psychology as an empirical science, slows slightly in the next two chapters. However, "The Experimental Approach in Psychology" (Chapter 5) and "The

Statistical Approach in Psychology" (Chapter 6) build on the first four chapters and provide the teacher with many teaching options. The last two chapters deal with the individual. "The Clinical Approach in Psychology" exposes the reader to the role of psychology in the study of individuals. "The Dual Role of Psychology" examines the broader implications of psychology as a profession and as a science, concluding with a discussion on the importance of the mind-body problem. "Bibliographical Notes" serve as a resource index for the interested teacher although the references included are a heady collection.

The reading is challenging but not overwhelming. A junior or senior in high school should be able to comprehend the material without difficulty--C.L.B.

See also Turner (1973).

Gallup, H. F. <u>An invitation to modern psychology</u>. New York: Free Press, 1969. 252 pp. $3.25 paper.

This is a short, eclectic text obviously written for a one-semester introductory course. It manages to squeeze all of the usual areas into a readable, concise piece of work. Uses of examples are liberal and interesting. Also included is an appendix consisting of a program on probability.

While the book ostensibly was meant to deal with human behavior, it does so only in an anecdotal way. Most data cited come from animal studies.

The book is not recommended for use in a four-year program but might be appropriate for community college and/or high school students.--O.P.P.

See also Cytrynbaum (1969).

Gardiner, W. L. <u>Psychology: A story of a search</u> (2nd ed.). Monterey, Calif.: Brooks/Cole, 1974. 343 pp. $9.95 paper.

Gardiner's text is more appropriate for use at the college level than at the high school level. The light, breezy, often witty style in which the author writes creates a deceptive impression of the text's reading and conceptual level. Both are beyond the abilities of all but the brightest high school student.

Although the traditional content areas of the introductory course are covered, some very advanced topics are also discussed. For instance, within the author's specialty area, cognition, there are extensive discussions of advanced topics such as linguistic analysis, logical operators, and TOTE units. Within the area of social psychology there is a detailed description of Bales' interaction process analysis, a sophisticated means of studying small-group social interactions.

Most high school students are interested in the areas of mental health and abnormal psychology. Yet these areas receive little weight relative to the areas of learning, motivation, perception, and cognition. Even within the sections devoted to mental health and abnormal psychology, the high school teacher might find Gardiner's choice of topics debatable. For instance, in discussing psychopathology he spends two pages on a cogent but esoteric discussion of the difference between organic and functional illnesses. Little attention is given to more "relevant" topics such as the kinds of neuroses and psychoses.

Instead of a glossary, the author presents a table classifying the terms used in the text. The usefulness of such a table to the student is debatable. Some aspects of the classification scheme are also questionable. Multiple personality, for instance, is classified as a psychotic rather than a neurotic disorder.

The publisher does not provide any accompanying materials such as a student workbook or an instructor's manual. Some teachers may feel that this is a disadvantage.--S.C.

See also Turner (1975d) and Sexton (1977).

Geiwitz, J. <u>Looking at ourselves: An invitation to psychology</u>. Boston: Little, Brown, 1976. 600 pp. $13.95 cloth. IM, TF, SG.

This is a good, academically oriented text. The prose is clear, straightforward, and readable. The material is presented with thoughtful objectivity, attractively formatted, liberally illustrated, and supported with research results. The first two-thirds of the text introduce the student to a wide array of topics, including memory, learning, emotion, language and thought, biological bases for behavior, personality, human development, and moral development. The last third is concerned with "Psychology at Work in the World," represented by psychological testing, abnormal psychology, and social psychology. Throughout the text and in the accompanying student guide the reader is presented with a variety of helpful study questions and laboratory exercises. At the end of each chapter a summary and a suggested reading list are provided. The student guide is divided into four sections: behavioral objectives, terms introduced and defined in the text, multiple-choice items and answers, and laboratory exercises. It is designed to help students master ideas and information presented in the text. It tends to emphasize information to be memorized (e.g., definition of terms) and may therefore be viewed by some as rather narrowly focused. This deficiency is corrected, however, by a manual and a multiple-choice question booklet available to the teacher.

On balance, this text and its accompanying instructor's manual and student guide contain a good overview of information that should be covered in a beginning psychology course. The book is modest. It breaks no new ground, but the research reported is current and well documented. Its limited scope and goals are a strength as well as a handicap. It teaches a reasonable amount of psychology and hence should be a highly useful book for the beginning student. Teachers who adopt this book as a primary text should probably supplement it with original readings. No matter how the text is used, it should be held in high regard by students.--R.H.K.

See also Fretz (1977), Langsam (1977), Popplestone (1978), and Turner (1977c).

Gilmer, B. V. H. <u>Psychology</u> (2nd ed.). New York: Harper & Row, 1973.
    646 pp. $12.95 paper. IM, TF, SG.

Gilmer set out to present psychology as a science, as a profession,
and in terms of its applicability to day-to-day situations. The text's
organization and content are based on the premise that students learn
best those things that are closely related to their own lives. Gilmer
has achieved all of his objectives through a more or less traditional
presentation of psychological content and examples. However, it is
doubtful that many high school students could or would wade through this
646-page text.

One can find few complaints with the scope, sequence, organization,
and content. As an all-encompassing introductory text, it is excellent.
It is well suited for college introductory courses--its prime audience.
No high school psychology text approaches it in total information. However, its content and vocabulary would be difficult for the average high
school student (who reads several grades below grade level). Sub-
ject-matter information in nearly every area of the discipline is presented in concentrated--not condensed--form. The text is basically too
difficult, bulky, and encyclopedic for most high school psychology students. Even if teachers do not buy or use the text, they should consider
the instructor's manual. It is an excellent source of compacted lecture
and discussion information, examples, and student activities.--R.J.S.

Goodale, R. A., & Goldberg, E. R. <u>Experiencing psychology</u>. Chicago:
    Science Research Associates, 1978. 768 pp. $9.45 cloth. IM, SG.

<u>Experiencing Psychology</u> represents the effort of a major publishing
firm extensively to sample high school psychology teachers prior to, during, and following the development of a text exclusively for the high
school psychology course. Included in the editing process was rewriting
the text narrative to meet the reading level of the present-day high
school student.

Goodale and Goldberg served as final editors for a series of manu-
scripts by a number of psychologists who reviewed the literature in their
area of expertise. From these reviews the editors took the psychological
content they believed was relevant for adolescents and infused it with
the latest research findings in an orientation toward practical application. The narrative attempts to personalize the content so that students
find it easier to become attracted and attentive to the text.

Each of the short 48 chapters begins with a brief introductory outline of the major ideas to be addressed and concludes with a special section entitled Extending Yourself, which focuses on personal and practical
considerations related to the psychological content just provided. Visuals, including numerous pictures, charts, diagrams, and cartoons, illustrate important points covered in the narrative. The book includes a
glossary and two appendixes, entitled "Research Methods in Psychology"
and "The Biology of Behavior."

In spite of the publisher's effort to apply a readability formula to
the text, the book seems best suited for solidly average or above-average
sophomores through seniors who can master an extensive new vocabulary in

a relatively short time. The narrative, in stressing the generalizabil-
ity and applicability of psychological knowledge, and an inductive
methodology, sometimes goes to the point of excess.

For teachers who know the kinds of contents and concepts they want to
include in their course, this book gives ample choice from a great range
of topics and psychological content areas. In this reviewer's opinion,
Experiencing Psychology is one of the three best books available to the
high school psychology teacher.

The teacher's manual is adequate, but the accompanying student workbook is extremely cut-and-dried. The workbook stresses memorization activities, overemphasizes fill-in-the-blank procedures, and is in sharp
contrast to the personal and application-oriented focuses of the text.
The workbook is a disappointment, considering the quality of the
text.--R.J.S.

Gordon, S. Psychology for you (Rev. ed.). New York: Oxford Book Co.,
    1978. 512 pp. $5.40 paper.

This interesting and highly readable text appears to succeed in presenting a scientifically sound introduction to psychology in combination
with issues and topics of interest and relevance to young people of
today. Gordon has achieved his objective of producing a text that would
focus "on things that really interest and concern /students/. It would
go light on rats, pigeons, and reflexes; it would go heavy on the processes and problems of personality and interpersonal relations that are
the very stuff of contemporary living" (p. iii).

The format of the text is very attractive and appropriate. There is
visual indication of movement from topic to topic. The many photographs
are stimulating and current, and the illustrations are attractive and
understandable. The type face is very readable, pleasing, and different
from that used in most texts (the difference itself creates interest).

The reading level is of moderate difficulty, appropriate for high
school students who would choose to take a psychology course. Words that
describe Gordon's writing style in reference to the target population
are: interesting, creative, stimulating, lively. Gordon whets the appetite of the reader by treating topics lightly in terms of material; he
does not foster boredom with tedious detail. The book presumes no prior
knowedge of psychology but does presume the need of the reader to know
more about himself/herself.

The text has 26 chapters. It treats such topics as the psychology of
the individual, theories of human behavior, social problems, and social
change, concluding with "a personal statement from the author to the student" (p. 477). Other useful features are Things to Discuss, Things to
Do, Things to Read, and a list of Readings at the end of each chapter.

The author intended this text to be used in either a one-semester or
a two-semester course. The material opened up could be processed better
in a two-semester course although it could be handled in a one-semester
course.--L.M.

Grace, M. S., Nicholson, P. T., & Lipsitt, D. R. Your self: An
    introduction to psychology. New York: Hart Publishing Co., 1976.
    781 pp. $12.50 cloth; $7.95 paper.

Your Self is one of the more "relevant" high school psychology texts,
clearly written on a high school reading level and describing many situations that adolescents typically experience. The questions asked
throughout the chapters are excellent, building on information given in
the text, asking students to make comparisons, and often asking them to
gather additional information. Because they are frequently open-ended,
the questions also encourage class discussion of issues that are important to high school students.
    The book basically takes a psychoanalytic approach, emphasizing a
stage theory of development. In addition to describing childhood and
adolescence, the authors explore several stages of adulthood. They discuss major theorists--Freud, Erikson, Piaget, Kohlberg, Frankl, Skinner,
Rogers, and Maslow--and take pains to illustrate the validity of the
behaviorist and humanist approaches. They also explore motivation and
emotion, group dynamics, and the normal-abnormal continuum (which they
appropriately label as "a spectrum of grays").
    Although Your Self is a book most high school psychology students
would enjoy, it does have some limitations. Its descriptions of perception and learning are rather cursory, perception being discussed in terms
of persuasion and advertising. Also, it contains relatively few descriptions of the results of psychological research, and in that respect, it
is less scientific than some other texts.--J.J.P.
    See also Kasschau (1977b) and Turner (1976c).

Hall, E. Why we do what we do. Boston: Houghton Mifflin, 1973.
    184 pp. $6.95 cloth.

In a highly readable and interesting little book, Hall presents the
basic concepts and concerns of motivation and emotion, learning and
thinking, language, personality, and adjustment. In explaining these
areas of psychology, she uses examples similar to the experiences of the
reader. More important, she describes a number of well-known experiments
to illustrate her points; for instance, she explains the work of Milgram,
Miller, Sherif, and the Gardners in such an interesting manner that the
reader remembers the results of the experiment and their relationship to
the concept being illustrated.
    Not a text, this book is designed primarily for high school students
and adults who know little about psychology. As such it serves to introduce the reader to the field. Although necessarily somewhat superficial,
it nevertheless excites the reader's curiosity to investigate an area
further.--J.J.P.
    See Review of Hall (1974).

Harlow, H. F., McGaugh, J. L., & Thompson, R. F. <u>Psychology</u>. San
    Francisco: Albion Publishing Co., 1972. 481 pp. $10.75 cloth;
    $7.95 paper. IM, TF, SG.

Don't expect an encyclopedia; expect the authors not to disguise
their approaches, styles, and interests; savor but don't cherish the
facts; and cherish but don't sanctify the ideas. So warns the preface,
and the book more than confirms the expectations. Harlow writes on love
and cannot avoid talking about fear and anger and social behavior;
McGaugh reflects his interest in learning and memory, which leads to intelligence and thought and language; Thompson provides the necessary
neuroanatomy and neurophysiology and treats sensory processing, the
sleep-attention complex, and motivation. Chapters on heredity, personality and abnormal psychology, and development complete the contents.
    Several features of the book are impressive. Between no other pair
of covers can one find as complete a discussion of Harlow's findings and
their implications. The selection of the material included by McGaugh
and Thompson deserves the highest praise. The interest of all three
authors in the biology of behavior and the findings with primates provide
a common thread. And there is Harlow's style: His alliteration is
alluring and always about; he loves to turn a phrase as he turns to
phrases about love; and his puns are worth repeating. Some parents may
not find the double entendres as amusing as their offspring will, but
Harlow emphasizes for all that to understand the affectional system one
must integrate three subsystems: the mechanical, the secretory, and the
romantic.
    A word of caution is offered. Even with the book's extraordinary
interest, some college students would find it difficult. However, it
would be an invaluable addition to the library of the teacher.--J.K.B.
    See also Forgus (1972).

Harrison, A. A. <u>Psychology as a social science</u>. Monterey, Calif.:
    Brooks/Cole, 1972. 523 pp. $12.95 cloth. TF.

Harrison focuses on individual human behavior from a consistently
social-psychological perspective. He does not cover a full spectrum of
psychological topics; he restricts his attention to social behavior,
human development, and personality (including its assessment), omitting
physiological and sensory processes and treating the traditional subject
matter of learning only minimally.
    The book presumes no prior course work in psychology, it includes a
useful discussion of the nature of data and research method, and it is
scientifically responsible, stressing what Harrison calls "controlled
observation" as the source of evidence. Instead of the usual recitation
of historical figures and events, Harrison reviews the subfields of psychology and their relations with other social sciences. He regularly
introduces humanistic ideas and devotes a sizable part of one chapter to
explicit discussion of them. The book ends with a view of the social
responsibility of science as a way of relating psychology to social issues.

Harrison's writing is simple and clear, if a bit folksy at times.
The book is well organized and therefore quite readable. It is modestly
illustrated with photographs although many of them serve no better purpose than to break the monotony of the printed page. There are a good
index and a very extensive glossary of technical terms. For a course at
senior high levels that emphasizes social behavior and personality, Harrison's book can be recommended. However, it concerns itself with individual action and does little justice to concepts of society or culture.
It is a text in psychology and must not be used as if it were a comprehensive social science textbook.--R.G.H.
See also Kasschau (1973) and Review of Harrison (1973).

Harrower, M., & Gruber, H. E. <u>The psychologist at work</u>. Shrewsbury,
    N. J.: Key Education, 1972. 157 pp. $6.95 cloth. IM, SG,
    Table-Top Laboratory ($895.00).

In their relatively small and highly readable volume, Harrower and
Gruber have produced a remarkably fresh juxtaposition of the historical
solemnity and modern excitement of experimental psychology. Their major
objective is to portray for the intelligent layperson the major problems,
assumptions, and strategies of experimental psychologists as they struggle to elevate the discipline to the status of a respectable science.
The authors do an exquisite job of detailing the impact of the prescien-
tific metaphysical conventions of mechanism versus vitalism on contemporary thinking. They provide a very satisfying resolution of this old
chestnut that enables the reader to get on with the business at
hand--learning something of the facts of psychology and why they are important. For this contribution alone, the book would be an outstanding
choice for a serious encounter with psychology at the high school level.
Because most texts implicitly adopt one position or the other on this
issue, the issue itself is usually formally evaded but becomes, according
to many teachers, the basis for highly aroused, ill-informed, yet extensive classroom debate, effectively precluding any serious encounter with
the subject matter.
<u>The Psychologist at Work</u> is not intended to be, nor should it be mis-
taken for, a comprehensive summary of the current scene in experimental
psychology. Many readers will be astounded at the total omission of any
reference to operant psychology or the experimental analysis of behavior. Others, who might construe that oversight as a signal of virtue,
will search in vain for any treatment of the doings in contemporary social and humanistic psychology. Indeed, readers who received their
training since 1960 will be disappointed if they expect to find any support for their belief that their subspecialty is cornering the market on
truth. The reader who rejects this volume on such parochial grounds will
have missed the point and, perhaps deservedly so, will also miss a very
enlightening and entertaining encounter with the history and methods of
our science--an encounter that richly deserves to be shared with students.--H.S.P.

Hebb, D. O. <u>Textbook of psychology</u> (3rd ed.). Philadelphia: W. B.
    Saunders, 1972. 326 pp. $9.25 cloth. IM, TF, SG.

If you have students who like to read material that respects their
intelligence, who like to think without being told what to think, who are
satisfied more by finding the fruitful questions than by having too easy
answers, who depend more for their learning on their own resources and
initiative than on having it all laid out in detail, then Hebb's text may
well be the book for you. But be warned that the orientation is physio-
logical-developmental and that in the author's view an elementary text
should be scientific, not oriented toward personal adjustment (even if
the intended audience is taking a terminal introductory course). Also,
the text reflects Hebb's interests in and contributions to psychology.
Thus, the mechanisms of learning involve cell assemblies; the chapter on
learning and memory begins with "Memory: A Chemical Molecule?"; early
learning and sensory deprivation receive attention; statistics are introduced reluctantly; the chapter on motivation begins with arousal; and
both heredity and environment "are of 100 percent importance" (p. 162) in
determining intelligence.
    This third edition rearranges some of the material and incorporates
some of the findings of the six years since publication of its predecessor, including neural inhibition, Gardners' and Washoe's sign language,
and Chomsky. Each chapter has a summary, a brief study guide, and lists
of references on both special and general topics. There are also an
author index, a subject index, and a glossary.--J.K.B.
    See also Kasschau (1973).

Heimstra, N. W., & McDonald, A. L. <u>Psychology and contemporary</u>
    <u>problems</u>. Monterey, Calif.: Brooks/Cole, 1973. 395 pp. $6.95
    paper. TF.

This is not a book of readings but rather a collection of about 16
summaries of the research going on in psychology in relation to contemporary problems. It is a very good introduction to the methods of psychological investigation, and most of the topics should capture the interest
of high school or two-year college students--for example, problems in
environmental design, aggression and violence, and drugs and alcohol.
The book begins with an introduction describing the growing emphasis on
applied research, the difference between pure and applied research, and
the various new specializations that have arisen. It then reviews the
research going on to solve present-day human problems, at the same time
explaining the methodology required. Its style is fresh, immediate, and
conversational. It can easily be understood by persons with no prior
knowledge of psychology; it is almost jargonless, and all terms are
clearly explained. It is of moderate readability for the high school or
two-year college student. It would best be used as an important supplementary text, and the teacher would probably prefer to select parts of it
according to the interests of the students. Each topic is dealt with in
about 30-50 pages. The topics will probably be with us as problems for
some time to come. The authors point out that any selection of topics

must have some omissions, but it does seem strange that the whole bur-
geoning field of behavior modification has not been included, except for
passing references in the chapters on alcohol and overeating. However,
the book can certainly lead a class into investigating other subjects and
could even result in student-designed research--for example, a study of a
school or a neighborhood. If the book is not adopted as a supplementary
text, then it should at least be a resource on the bookshelf of every
psychology teacher.--M.M.
    See also Abma (1974).

Hilgard, E. R., Atkinson, R. C., & Atkinson, R. L. Introduction to
    psychology (6th ed.). New York: Harcourt Brace Jovanovich, 1975.
    658 pp. $14.50 cloth. IM, TF, SG, Mastery Instructor's Guide, Mas-
    tery Study Guide. (Now available in a 7th ed.)

    To reach the sixth edition, a text must be doing something right. In
the present case it is presenting an exciting, sophisticated, scholarly
treatment of psychology while giving extensive support to the harried
teacher.
    The text contains a year's worth of basic topics, but the chapters
are relatively independent so that virtually any order can be used to
suit the local situation. New in this edition, the first chapter presents five basic approaches to psychology: neurobiological, behavioral,
cognitive, psychoanalytic, and humanistic. These approaches reappear
throughout the text as appropriate--the authors do not slavishly include
each approach in each chapter. The authors claim that in their revision
they used comments by specialists on each topic, by students, and by instructors. This claim is readily believed, for the text is more readable
than the fifth edition, without sacrifice of the critical analysis of
experiments.
    The page layout complements the text. The left third of each page is
reserved for a set of well-integrated pictures, cartoons, and graphs.
White space for student notes is usually present. There are boxed critical discussions of contemporary topics.
    The test-item file, a new version of which is issued yearly, provides
in reproducible form a minimum of 20 solid multiple-choice questions per
chapter. The instructor's manual is a true guide that discusses basic
educational decisions, lists source materials, and provides for each
chapter (a) film suggestions, (b) lecture/demonstration suggestions, and
(c) short essay questions.
    The weakest part of the package is the study guide. For each chapter
it presents (a) the learning objectives, (b) a lengthy programmed unit to
be completed prior to reading the text, (c) a list of terms and concepts
for definition after reading the text, (d) a set of multiple-choice questions, and (e) suggested exercises or mini-studies. The preface does not
mention any validation study of the programmed units; from a brief analysis they seem to be somewhat flawed initial attempts at programming,
rather than a finished product. Also, although good in concept, the section on definition of terms needs page references to the text to encourage answer-checking.

Although clearly intended as an encyclopedic college text, the book could well be used with high school juniors and seniors who are college-bound. Less capable high school students will find it overwhelming.--C.P.

See also Melvin (1975), Murphy (1976), and Turner (1975f).

Isaacson, R. L., & Hutt, M. L. Psychology: The science of behavior (2nd ed.). New York: Harper & Row, 1971. 433 pp. $14.95 cloth. SG.

This second edition is written from a natural-science viewpoint and covers the pertinent literature up to 1970. The authors do an excellent job of surveying the field of experimental psychology. The book is as comprehensive as any general text on the market and presents all major theoretical viewpoints in experimental psychology. It starts with chapters on historical, genetic, and biological antecedents and proceeds to more complex behavior topics such as perception, learning, cognition, emotion, and motivation. Data, topics, and current theories are presented in a well-written and organized manner. Appendixes on the nature of theories and on the use of statistics are included to stimulate discussion and to use with the main text. The book deliberately omits chapters on social psychology, personality, abnormal psychology, and applied areas.

The book would be difficult at the first-year college level and extremely challenging for high school students. It could be used as a text for honor students in high school psychology or biology or as a text for a one-semester course in natural science for students who have had physics, chemistry, and biology. The teacher of high school psychology who wants a good solid current reference and an up-to-date bibliography in experimental psychology should consult this text.--P.W.

See also Van Krevelen (1973).

Kagan, J., & Havemann, E. Psychology: An introduction (3rd ed.). New York: Harcourt Brace Jovanovich, 1976. 597 pp. $13.50 cloth. IM, TF, SG.

This is a very readable and surprisingly short survey of psychology. Each of the 14 chapters, plus an appendix on statistics, is intended to be covered in one week. In addition to the expected topics of learning, memory, thinking, sensory processes, perception, genetics, emotion, motives, personality, individual differences, developmental psychology, and social psychology, there are such topics of current interest as extrasensory perception and altered states of consciousness. Most chapters begin with a description of the phenomenon under study, follow it with some experimental data, and conclude by providing a current theoretical explanation. The authors make no secret of their perception of contemporary psychology tending toward cognitive explanations. Each chapter has a good and detailed summary.

The breadth of coverage is great, but the author's desire to make this a semester text has led to a sketchy, although not necessarily

superficial, presentation. All numbered figures are closely tied to the
text and contribute to the reader's understanding, but unfortunately
there are some unnumbered figures that tend to distract.

  Although the book was designed as a college text, its high readability and the rapidity with which the topics are surveyed (thus practically
eliminating boredom) suggest serious consideration of it as a high school
text.--R.S.H.

  See also Covington (1977), Kasschau (1977b), and Turner (1976b).

Kalish, R. A. The psychology of human behavior (4th ed.). Monterey,
    Calif.: Brooks/Cole, 1977. 429 pp. $11.95 cloth; $3.95 paper. IM,
    TF, SG.

  This is an excellent text for a high school psychology course in the
social science curriculum. Kalish writes in an easy and interesting manner; his approach is humanistic; and he appears to cover all the topics
of interest to young people today. Although the biological bases of
behavior are not discussed in detail, the transient references in regard
to motivation and perception are clear, concise, and accurate.

  The 20 chapters are organized into five parts: an introduction covering (a) what is psychology and what are psychologists and (b) a preview
of motivation and personality; the basic principles of behavior, including perception, learning, cognition, and people in relation to their
physical environment; feelings and coping, including emotions and stress,
defense mechanisms, psychopathology, and the psychotherapies; developmental processes from birth to death, plus some group dynamics; and the
application of psychology to values, education, sex and marriage, and
career planning. Most of the photographs are meaningfully related to the
text and are supplemented by a number of clever, homemade cartoons.

  The instructor's manual largely consists of sets of objective and
subjective questions for each chapter, but there is also a final collection of 14 projects, one for each of the first 14 chapters, which are
classroom exercises of the kind published in APA's newsletter Periodically, now High Schol Psychology Teacher. The study guide provides for each
chapter an overview with missing words to fill in, some objective and
subjective questions for self-testing, and two "personal histories"
designed to encourage thought and discussion--what a management psychologist would call case studies.

  In summary, the book should not be used in courses that attempt to
present psychology as a science or to show its relationships with biology
and physiology. But for the typical high school class, with an emphasis
on self-development, adjustment to life, and various social problems, the
book should be hard to beat.--C.W.H.

  See also Popplestone (1978) and Turner (1977c).

Kendler, H. H. Basic psychology (3rd ed.). Menlo Park, Calif.: W. A.
    Benjamin, 1974. 798 pp. $14.95 cloth. IM, SG, Unit Workbook.
    Basic psychology: Brief version (3rd ed.). Menlo Park, Calif.:
    W. A. Benjamin, 1977. 483 pp. $10.95 paper. IM, TF, SG.

In Basic Psychology Kendler has written a very thorough no-nonsense
text in the classical tradition. Concerned with conveying psychology as
a hard science, he continually reiterates the themes of reliance on evidence, multi-causality of phenomena, objectivity, and knowledge of one's
information sources. He opposes the educational forces that he sees as
pandering to the "sensational and superficial," and in so doing, he attempts to clear up many commonsense misconceptions.

The author sees certain cognitive areas (perception, behavior modification, motivation, verbal behavior, and so forth) as major components of
basic and complex psychological processes and thus as fundamental to the
rest of the field. They receive considerably more attention than social
or abnormal psychology, for example, although there is a chapter devoted
to each of these areas. Findings from developmental psychology, however,
are integrated into the content of predominantly cognitive chapters.
Although such integration may be desirable, the teacher who wishes to
present developmental psychology as a separate topic will have some
gleaning to do.

By and large, the book is quite readable. The style is fluid and
occasionally even conversational. It is highly literate and draws from a
wide variety of resources, including history and literature as well as
psychology. The examples offered to illustrate the various concepts are
usually interesting and relevant to the student's own experience. One
also appreciates the occasional questions directed at the reader. The
vocabulary, though certainly not geared to the lowest common denominator
of a heterogeneous high school class, should be within the grasp of college-bound juniors and seniors, and it is for this group (as well as for
an introductory college class) that the text should be most appropriate.

Although the book does not presuppose a great deal of substantive
background, its tough-minded approach does assume an initially high level
of motivation. The author himself warns that students are "going to have
to expend a good deal of effort and thought" (p. ix) in use of the book.
Ideally that effort would span two semesters. However, teachers could
choose certain sections and eliminate others, depending on time con-
straints and class interests. Because of the author's bias, some sections (specifically Parts 2 and 3 on Basic Psychological Processes and
Complex Psychological Processes) would be harder to ignore than others.

Special features that the reader may find useful include: an introductory overview to each major section, a concise summary at the end of
each chapter, the use of bold-face type for new terms, an appendix dealing with introductory statistics, and a briefly annotated bibliography
for further reading. Of particular interest are the special sections
discussing popularized and socially relevant matters related to the substance of each chapter (extrasensory perception, use of mnemonics, homosexuality, etc.). A provocative full-page photograph occurs at the
beginning of each chapter; illustrations within the chapters tend to be
small, relatively infrequent, and unobtrusive.

See also Cone (1976) and Turner (1975c).

Kendler, H. H. Basic psychology (3rd ed.). Menlo Park, Calif.: W. A.
    Benjamin, 1974. 798 pp. $14.95 cloth. IM, SG, Unit Workbook.
    Basic psychology: Brief version (3rd ed.). Menlo Park, Calif.:
    W. A. Benjamin, 1977. 483 pp. $10.95 paper. IM, TF, SG.

In Basic Psychology Kendler has written a very thorough no-nonsense
text in the classical tradition. Concerned with conveying psychology as
a hard science, he continually reiterates the themes of reliance on evidence, multi-causality of phenomena, objectivity, and knowledge of one's
information sources. He opposes the educational forces that he sees as
pandering to the "sensational and superficial," and in so doing, he attempts to clear up many commonsense misconceptions.

The author sees certain cognitive areas (perception, behavior modification, motivation, verbal behavior, and so forth) as major components of
basic and complex psychological processes and thus as fundamental to the
rest of the field. They receive considerably more attention than social
or abnormal psychology, for example, although there is a chapter devoted
to each of these areas. Findings from developmental psychology, however,
are integrated into the content of predominantly cognitive chapters.
Although such integration may be desirable, the teacher who wishes to
present developmental psychology as a separate topic will have some
gleaning to do.

By and large, the book is quite readable. The style is fluid and
occasionally even conversational. It is highly literate and draws from a
wide variety of resources, including history and literature as well as
psychology. The examples offered to illustrate the various concepts are
usually interesting and relevant to the student's own experience. One
also appreciates the occasional questions directed at the reader. The
vocabulary, though certainly not geared to the lowest common denominator
of a heterogenous high school class, should be within the grasp of college-bound juniors and seniors, and it is for this group (as well as for
an introductory college class) that the text should be most appropriate.

Although the book does not presuppose a great deal of substantive
background, its tough-minded approach does assume an initially high level
of motivation. The author himself warns that students are "going to have
to expend a good deal of effort and thought" (p. ix) in use of the book.
Ideally that effort would span two semesters. However, teachers could
choose certain sections and eliminate others, depending on time con-
straints and class interests. Because of the author's bias, some sections (specifically Parts 2 and 3 on Basic Psychological Processes and
Complex Psychological Processes) would be harder to ignore than others.

Special features that the reader may find useful include: an introductory overview to each major section, a concise summary at the end of
each chapter, the use of bold-face type for new terms, and appendix dealing with introductory statistics, and a briefly annotated bibliography
for further reading. Of particular interest are the special sections
discussing popularized and socially relevant matters related to the substance of each chapter (extrasensory perception, use of mnemonics, homosexuality, etc.). A provocative full-page photograph occurs at the
beginning of each chapter; illustrations within the chapters tend to be
small, relatively infrequent, and unobtrusive.

See also Cone (1976) and Turner (1975c).

In the Brief Version, while holding constant to his philosophical
goals and general orientation, Kendler has pared down his text to approx-
imately two-thirds of its original length. He has accomplished the reduction by eliminating whole sections, such as the one on statistics, and
by trimming existing chapters in several ways--minimizing abstract theo-
rizing, limiting several topics to elementary processes, and reducing the
number of supportive studies discussed. He has nevertheless retained all
the special features as well as the basic flavor of the longer edition.

The study guide that accompanies the Brief Version is quite thorough
and would also be a useful supplement to the longer edition. A variety
of activities is presented, corresponding to each chapter. They vary in
difficulty from a programmed review, in which the student fills in blanks
in statements that summarize the major points in the text, to more
open-ended and demanding essay questions. Also included are a brief ori-
enting description of the material, a list of key terms and concepts, and
multiple-choice questions (with answers).

An instructor's manual is also provided for the Brief Version; it too
is suitable for use with the longer edition. It consists primarily of
examination questions of the true-false, multiple-choice, and essay variety.--E.B.

See also Popplestone (1978) and Turner (1977c).

Kimble, G. A., Garmezy, N., & Zigler, E. Principles of general psychology
     (4th ed.). New York: Ronald Press, 1974. 724 pp. $13.75 cloth.
     SG.

Teachers who have used any of the first three editions of this book
will find it hard to believe this is the latest edition in that succes-
sion. This book and the earlier editions have only three things in com-
mon--the title, the publisher, and two of the three authors. Following a
roughly developmental organization, the 21 chapters are arranged in seven
parts--"The Relevance of Psychology," "The Origins of Behavior," "The
Intellect and Its Development," "The Emergence of Personality," "Cognitive Psychology," "Special States and Disordered Behavior," and "Behavior
in Biological and Social Perspective." More consideration is given to
topics of general public interest than is true of most other recent
texts. This is at no sacrifice to the professional integrity of the
book. The three chapters on the intellect constitute probably the best
presentation of this topic in any introductory text. The language level
of the textual material might be a little tough for high school students. However, each chapter contains several half- to full-page boxes
that amplify material in the text and are written at a more easily read
level. Both students and teachers will appreciate the 32-page
double-column "Dictionary of Psychological Terms" in the back of the
book.--R.S.H.

See also Cone (1976), Parducci (1974), and Turner (1975b).

Klein, D., & Klein, M. E. Your self and others. Evanston, Ill.:
    McDougal, Littell, 1975. 206 pp. $5.16 paper. IM.

    This book is intended for use "in social studies courses, in some of
the more experimental courses in sociology and anthropology, and in psychology and sex education courses . . ." (p. 1, instructor's manual).
The chapters cover such issues as "Who Are You?" "What Makes You a 'Higher' Animal?" and "What Difference Does Being American Make?". The book
is not a psychology text and does not teach scientific method or methods
of critical thinking. It has no references and is outdated or inaccurate
on some psychological concepts (e.g., instincts, pp. 30-37) and research
(e.g., effects of teacher expectations, p. 136). The language is sexist,
and the attempt to be personal is often off base (e.g., "you, as a younger brother"). There is an implicit bias favoring learning explanations
for human behavior. The material on the school (pp. 84-85) sounds like
civics course content.
    On the other hand, teachers committed to teaching an "adjustment"
course may want to consider the book. It is a readable high-school-level
text, requiring no psychological sophistication, easily coverable in a
single semester. There is a real effort to help students understand the
human condition. The teacher's manual contains reading suggestions for
teachers and advanced students, as well as topics for discussion and
ideas for field trips, demonstrations, and assignments.--K.W.

Krech, D., Crutchfield, R. S., Livson, N., & Wilson, W. A., Jr. Elements
    of psychology (3rd ed.). New York: Alfred A. Knopf, 1974. 903 pp.
    $12.95 cloth. SG(2), Behavioral Objective Unit Workbook, Instruc-
    tor's Guide to Behavioral Objectives Unit Workbook.

Krech, D., Crutchfield, R. S., Livson, N., Krech, H., & Wilson, W. A.,
    Jr. Psychology: A basic course. New York: Alfred A. Knopf, 1976.
    563 pp. $12.95 cloth. IM, TF, SG.

    Why two packages from the same authors and publishers? They say that
they started out to produce a short version of Elements and it grew into
a different book. Although A Basic Course is shorter, whether the other
differences justify the second package is difficult to say. The content
coverage, in general, is about the same, with an orientation that may be
described as scientific and behavioral-physiological. The history and
methodology of psychology are given short shrift in both texts, together
with such "soft" topics as adjustment, childhood and adolescence, marriage and family life, and the applied fields of educational and industrial psychology. Both books have brief glossaries at the end of each
chapter, which are almost identical in their listings, and many of the
figures, pictures, and special topic boxes are the same. Each text concludes with a bibliography and a combined name-and-subject index. There
is some overlap between these two pairs, but in each case the Elements
version is considerably longer than its counterpart in the Basic Course.
    Elements looks more like a standard text. It begins with growth and
development and proceeds through the typical content categories of psychology to the individual in society. It is organized into nine parts of

three or four units (chapters) each. The order of the units is strange, with thinking, language, and intelligence coming before perception, learning, motivation, and emotion. The physiological bases of each psychological process are discussed in the chapter on that process, rather than as a separate subject. The statistical appendix is a substantial 25-page section on the fundamentals of psychological measurement. A combined glossary at the back of the text lists all the terms defined at the end of each chapter together with the appropriate page reference.

A Basic Course is organized into 19 chapters, from heredity and environment to the individual in society. Learning and memory come before thinking and language, but sensory experience and perception follow later. Biological foundations are inserted as Chapter 12, with the clarifying diagrams removed to an appendix, where they are called a "simu-lab"(?). Inconsistently a 23-page casebook of verbatim therapeutic sessions is placed at the end of the chapter on psychotherapies. There are more special boxes in this text, and the printing and color appear to be more lively than in Elements. There is no combined glossary at the end, and the statistical appendix is no more than a three-page dictionary of terms.

The student workbook for A Basic Course appears to be much more useful than that for Elements. The Basic Course workbook contains for each chapter (a) a set of objectives, (b) a programmed review for each objective, and (c) a set of multiple-choice questions identified by objectives; the Elements workbook has only open-ended study questions for each chapter. However, the Elements package includes an additional Student Guide and Review, which contains the missing programmed reviews and multiple-choice questions. Completing the Elements package is a Student Handbook, which consists of four pages of study hints and the missing combined glossary. The Basic Course package is completed by a separate paperback full of multiple-choice questions organized by objectives within chapters.--C.W.H.

See also Cone (1976), Gerow (1978b), Kasschau (1978), Millham (1974), and Turner (1975d).

Kuhn, D., Kingston, A., White, W., & Toomey, M. Human psychology: Development, learning, social interaction. New York: Harcourt Brace Jovanovich, 1975. 574 pp. $9.30 cloth. IM. Also available as three paperbacks titled Development, $3.60 paper; Learning, $3.60 paper; and Social interaction, $3.90 paper.

This text is for high school students with little or no background in psychology. The reader is introduced to three principal areas of psychology--human development, learning, and social interaction. The section on human development emphasizes the early years (birth to age 12). There is also a chapter on adolescence, but maturation and problems of the elderly are not discussed. The section on learning reviews such traditional areas as transfer, memory, forgetting, and extrinsic and intrinsic motivation. Investigations recommended for students in this section are appropriate and innovative. The chapters on social interaction examine sex-role differences, race, age, social norms (including a unit on mental health), and a variety of socially relevant concerns such as techniques of persuasion and pressure to conform.

With an introductory text the student whose knowledge of psychology is limited has to take a lot of faith. Although that is true of this book regarding its introductory and overview approach, a strong feature is its systematic and simple explanation of principles. Weaknesses fall into two categories. First, several significant areas of inquiry are not discussed (e.g., theories of personality). Second, not enough data from research studies are presented for interpretation. As a consequence, teachers may not find this text as attractive as some others.

The instructor's manual emphasizes a variety of activities designed to illustrate psychological principles. It contains a glossary and a list of films, including information on where to obtain them.--R.H.K.

See also Social Science Education Consortium (1977a).

Landauer, T. K. Psychology: A brief overview. New York: McGraw-Hill, 1972. 360 pp. $13.95 cloth. IM, SG.

This text is tightly written and is truly a brief overview of psychology. In 11 exceedingly well-written chapters Landauer ranges across the major fields of contemporary psychology. In the first few chapters he attempts to "grab" students' interest by introducing them to social psychology, personality, assessment, adjustment, and psychopathology. Only later does he introduce the chapters on physiological psychology, conditioning and learning, and psychological research.

The text makes minimal use of photographs. The few that are included are black and white.

The reading ability required to use this text with any degree of effectiveness appears to be quite high. Thus, the text would probably not be well received in a general high school psychology course although it might be usable in an honors section.

The companion study guide and workbook contains, for each chapter in the text, a review, demonstrations, problems, and a self-test.--D.G.E.

See also Kasschau (1973).

Lawson, R. B., Goldstein, S. G., & Musty, R. E. Principles and methods of psychology. New York: Oxford University Press, 1975. 528 pp. $12.00 paper. IM, Laboratory Manual and kit.

The text represents an attempt to present the fundamental principles and methods of psychology by exploring basic areas of psychology through controlled exposure to generalizable principles about each area. Chapters first present general concepts, both theoretical and empirical, then specific examples of applications of these concepts. The book is a highly ambitious undertaking, for it seeks to introduce the student to the entire range of current thinking about the nature of the discipline of psychology--no small task, especially given the book's emphasis on the meaning of data, experimental design, concepts of measurement, and hypothesis-testing. Empirical information is organized around six general areas: perception, information-processing, learning, motivation, social psychology, and individual differences. Research reviewed and synthesized is, for the most part, up-to-date. Coverage is clear, precise, and literate although frankly selective in choice of topics. These qualities make the book interesting to read and rewarding to study.

The authors' concerns with problems of measurement and their interest in visual psychophysics are reflected in a laboratory manual and set of experiments designed to augment the text. Unfortunately the laboratory kit does not appear to be able to reach its objective, which is to demonstrate important concepts to the student in a simple manner. The approach seems useful, but incomplete. For example, research on the influence of perception on sensory, cognitive, and motivational variables that affect learning is not well covered. Nevertheless, the text introduces psychological principles in a basic and useful way; it tries to make use of the margin of coherence and structure that exists in the field. Theory is related to practice, and research associated with topics covered in the book is reviewed fairly. It is disappointing that the laboratory kit fails to reach the level of competence and coherence that characterizes the text.--R.H.K.

See also Bell (1975), Schulz (1975), and Stanners (1976).

Lazarus, R. S. The riddle of man: An introduction to psychology.
    Englewood Cliffs, N. J.: Prentice-Hall, 1974. 628 pp. $11.95
    cloth. IM, BR, Modular Learning Program.

Lazarus' approach is multidisciplinary, to the extent that the subtitle might well have been An Introduction to Social Studies. Lazarus selected the material for this labor of love "to present psychology in the context of the great and classic /weighty, unresolved, poignant7 problems of mankind" (p. ix). Three of the four sections are distinguished accomplishments: "The Psychology of Aggression," "Prejudice," and "Adaptation Versus Alienation." However, the first section on "Environments of Man" suffers from inclusion of too much typical beginning-text material.

Learning is presented in an unusually broad context of four "main mechanisms": reward and punishment, imitation and identification, performance of role behaviors, and search for meaning and identity.

Lazarus sought "to challenge the reader without overwhelming him" (p. xi). For the good college student he has succeeded, but the level of writing is above all but the outstanding high school student. Stimulating examples, beautifully integrated into the textual flow, come from a multitude of sources: Arthurs Hoppe to Sophocles, Peanuts to Joyce to Shakespeare. The precise, concise section on utopian literary works was particularly enjoyable.

Although the book appears huge, and one can object to the small type in which the extensive and fascinating margin notes are printed, the text might well be used for an advanced introductory course. All potential text authors should study the brief, useful annotations provided for the suggested readings. The prologue should be read in detail before adoption.--C.P.

See also Lefton (1974), Popplestone (1975), and Turner (1974c).

Lefrancois, G. R. Of humans: Introductory psychology by Kongor.
    Monterey, Calif.: Brooks/Cole, 1974. 391 pp. $11.95 cloth. SG.

The author's aim in writing his text and the companion "experience" book was to provide an introduction to the discipline of psychology for the beginning college student. Emphasis is placed on useful knowledge

and practical applications. The text is written from the point of view
of "Kongor--a little blue individual from outer space" who is studying
human beings for the first time. The text consists of 25 reports from
Kongor's journal covering numerous traditional points on the psychological compass.

The author's intentions are honorable in that he seeks to develop a
refreshingly lively review of the field. His commonsense approach to
problems and his descriptions of research are supported by a clear style
remarkably free of jargon. Unfortunately the presentation often suffers
from a superficial analysis of complex problems exceeded only by a high
level of generality--for example, the treatment of psychoanalytic theories of personality. Information is provided in behavioral terms and
through Kongor's eyes, about the psychological characteristics of human
beings. Literature is presented and reviewed concerning biological
determinants of behavior, individual differences, physiological "behavior," human development, learning, social psychology, and the applications of psychology to applied fields, for example, teaching. The range
of specific areas defeats summary. Interesting student aids to reading
and note-taking are provided and are systematically linked to the companion workbook. In conclusion, Lefrancois has provided an engaging document, anthropologically oriented, which should help students question the
relevance and application of psychology to the human condition.--R.H.K.

Lewis, R. T., & Petersen, H. M. Human behavior: An introduction to
     psychology. New York: Ronald Press, 1974. 459 pp. $8.00 paper.
     SG.

This rather large paperback is intended for a one-semester or
one-quarter introductory course. The authors seem to agree that it is
more appropriate for the general student than for the psychology major.
It is organized into two main divisions: "Psychology as a Social Science" and "Psychology as a Biological Science." Within the divisions
each chapter relates psychology to some other scientific discipline or
applied area. Thus, in the first division psychology is related to philosophy, education, religion, sociology, anthropology, business, and the
government; in the second division it is related to biology, physiology,
biochemistry, and medicine. There is unequal coverage of the two major
areas, with 298 pages devoted to the first and 127 pages devoted to the
second.

The integration of psychology with many related areas is interesting
and emphasizes the "relevance" of the discipline, but it will probably
dismay or at least discommode the traditional teacher of the general-ex-
perimental approach. The discomfort will be heightened, of course, by
the relatively short shrift given to the biological aspects of psychology, quantitatively if not qualitatively.

The text is easy to read and well sprinkled with headings and subheadings. Each chapter ends with a summary of major ideas and suggested
readings. At the end of the book are references, a glossary, and an index. The student guide contains a short introduction, programmed
reviews, discovery activities (discussion questions), and self-tests
(multiple-choice items).

The book could be useful at the high school level as a supplementary
text in social science or behavioral science courses, and at the college
level in courses in the liberal arts, education, business, engineering,
etc.--C.W.H.

See also Sexton (1977) and Turner (1975b).

Liebert, R. M., & Neale, J. M. Psychology. New York: John Wiley,
    1977. 492 pp. $13.95 cloth. SG.

This text is worth consideration by high school psychology teachers.
It begins with a summary of the history of psychology. The subsequent 11
chapters discuss basic processes, such as perception, and current specialty areas, such as social psychology and abnormal behavior. Research
with human beings is emphasized.

Strong points of the text are its readability (it is lively and would
be only moderately difficult for high school students), clarity (difficult topics like Piaget's and Erikson's theories are very well presented)
and adaptability (a selection of chapters could be used, depending on the
length of the course). There is a glossary at the end of each chapter
and an excellent reference section in the back. Pictures and drawings
are carefully chosen to illustrate concepts. The microphotography, in
particular, is outstanding.

There are no study questions or student activities in the text itself, but each chapter ends with a summary and includes features called
Testing Your Understanding, and Psychology and the Problems of Society.
The latter feature discusses practical applications of psychological
principles--for example, the use of positive reinforcement with retarded
children.

Teachers should be aware of one negative point: The authors have
made a curious decision to emphasize human behavior to the point of ex-
cluding a cross-species perspective. This exclusion has a direct effect
on discussions of communication and identity, among other topics. Is it
tenable, now that so many of the barriers that separated humans from other animals have been removed, to present human behavior without that perspective? Can we not discuss Washoe's and Vicki's communication across
species and Gallup's studies in chimp self-awareness? Can we ignore the
fact that the paramecium can learn and other animals can manufacture
tools and hunt? These matters are not raised in this text.

The study guide will probably be of more help to the high school psychology teacher than it will be to the student. It provides as many good
questions and multiple-choice tests as one could want.--M.P.

See also Ericksen (1977), Popplestone (1978), and Turner (1977d).

Longman Group, Ltd. Psychology (10 booklets). York, England: Author,
    1976. Available in the United States from Social Studies School Ser-
    vice. $7.95 paper. IM.

Rather than presenting a standard one-volume text, the publisher of
this introduction adopted the alternative format of a series of 10 booklets, each 12-16 pages long and dealing with a different topic generally
covered in introductory psychology. Topics included are physiology, perception, thinking, learning, motivation and emotion, social psychology,

personality (two booklets), and an intriguing do-it-yourself survey unit on study habits and attitudes (two booklets). Each booklet begins with a study guide that is intended to serve as a road map to the sections ahead. This brief overview is interspersed with questions that serve to focus attention on key points. The remainder of each booklet consists of excerpts from a melange of recent introductory texts as well as appropriate selections from current periodicals and journals. In the limited space, an attempt has been made to emphasize material that is current, "relevant," and likely to be of interest to adolescents. The ratio of illustrative diagrams and photographs to written text is more than adequate.

The study guides are clearly written and quite readable in spite of occasional Anglicisms. However, the selections following the guides were written by a number of different authors, and there tends to be an inconsistency of style and level of difficulty. In addition, the print on several of the journal reprints is too small for comfortable reading.

Relatively little integration and coordination among the booklets is apparent; there is no index and the cross-referencing is meager.

Although students may be attracted by the novelty of the format, these booklets do not attain the breadth, depth, or sense of context achieved by most standard texts. As the authors state, the series is "intended to be no more than an introduction . . ."; they hope that "the interested student will go to the appropriate textbooks for more comprehensive information" (p. 1 of Personality 1). Perhaps the booklets would be more useful as a primer for a secondary school teacher who is teaching psychology for the first time and lacks extensive background in the discipline. They would at least introduce such a teacher to a variety of different authors' approaches. A bright and self-motivated student might use selected parts of this material for independent investigation. Because the booklets are physically as well as conceptually separable, any one could be used individually for a variety of purposes.

The teacher's guide that accompanies the series is brief, but it includes useful sections on other sources of information and materials.--E.B.

Lugo, J. O., & Hershey, G. L. Living psychology: Research in action (2nd ed.). New York: Macmillan, 1976. 580 pp. $6.95 cloth. IM, SG.

Many introductory psychology teachers will need to read only the goals of the authors to determine that this text is not for them: Understanding the principles and understanding the theories of psychology are listed third and fourth to "understanding yourself" and "understanding others." In the reviewer's opinion, the text is "relevant" in the worst sense of the term. Although more findings are included in this edition, the first edition's subtitle, An Experiential Approach, is far more appropriate than the current subtitle, particularly because research design is never discussed. How can one apply research if one cannot distinguish the sloppy from the well conducted?

The humanistic-oriented (Maslow, Rogers) text is divided into three major sections: "Understanding Yourself," "Understanding the Development of Human Behavior," and "The Dynamics of Human Behavior." Each of the 13 chapters is clearly focused for student learning: initial outline, suggestions for studying the chapter, introductory orientation (including Why Is It Important?), the main body of the chapter (including intermediate summaries), application to the student's life, and final summary. Except for length (580 pages versus 400) and the addition of a chapter on adulthood and aging, the text is highly similar to the first edition.

Minor difficulties with the text include: layout (e.g., cameo descriptions of eminent psychologists that are not clearly set off from the text); many pictures, few of which aid learning of the accompanying material; some careless statements or implications (for example, homosexuality--not homosexual acts--is illegal in many states; all learning is generalized; psychologists do research in mental illness, psychiatrists do not); and ambiguous use of the phrase "these writers" (it is not always clear who is intended, the psychologists just discussed or the text authors).

The reviewer believes that a major difficulty is the handling of the Freudian approach. The organization of the text makes an overview of the approach difficult, and the overall result may be an incomplete and inaccurate understanding. Defense mechanisms are discussed from a broad point of view, with the Freudian approach not distinguished; central topics such as toilet training and the Oedipus complex are not mentioned; the pressures of the external world and of the superego on the ego are not distinguished; and the diagrams of the house analogous to the ego and superego lead one to conclude that both are entirely conscious mechanisms. A contrasting of the Freudian and humanistic approaches would seem to be desirable in this style of text, but it simply is not done beyond the level of "humanism is best."

Further problems with the text are that it is unintelligibly compressed (in four pages: "intelligence, genetics, and learning," including Binet, Jensen, Doves' Chitling Test, and Guilford's structural model of intellect), simplistic (general grammatical level and definition of terms such as "potentialities"), and condescending (does a student really need to be told 12 times to preview the chapter?).

The student guide includes outlining exercises, multiple-choice and true-false questions, and small projects for each chapter. The teacher's manual includes little more than multiple-choice and true-false questions.--C.P.

See also Popplestone (1978) and Turner (1977a).

Malott, R. W., & Whaley, D. L. Psychology. New York: Harper & Row, 1976. (Originally published by Behaviordelia, Kalamazoo, Mich., and Harper's College Press, New York). 684 pp. $15.95 cloth. IM, TF, SG.

The 32 chapters of Psychology cover nearly every facet of modern psychology. Beneath the comic-book-like presentation, Malott and Whaley treat many key concepts with a depth and clarity that is not often found in introductory texts. The authors have also done an excellent job in showing the relationships among the many areas with which the book deals.

The task chosen by the authors to present the material is unfortun-
ate, however. They take the reader through a year of college at Big
State University through the eyes of several students. The group of students (all of whom seem to have formed much closer relationships with one
another than might be expected at the typical big state university) includes a variety of well-known stereotypes: the Jewish intellectual, the
angry black woman, the pretty high school cheerleader, the jock, etc.
The language used by the students in personal interactions, though probably typical of such interactions, may be offensive to some students or
teachers. Some of the descriptions of interactions are probably too explicit for use in the high school classroom, and the use of racial
epithets (even directed at one's self) is out of place in any classroom.
The reaction of a small (biased) sample of college students to whom
this reviewer showed the book was that the approach of the authors was
patronizing and somewhat demeaning. They all felt that they did not need
to be "told a story" in order to learn psychology. The book would probably not prove any more popular with high school students or teachers.--P.D.J.
See also Popplestone (1978).

McGaugh, J. L., Thompson, R. F., & Nelson, T. O. Psychology I: An
    experimental approach. San Francisco: Albion Publishing Co., 1977.
    438 pp. $12.95 cloth. SG.

This text presents a shocking pink exterior and a rather dull--ex-
clusively black and white--interior with minimal illustration. As proclaimed by the authors, the book is not encyclopedic. Chapters are not
quite standard: heredity, sleep and attention, intelligence (including
von Frisch's work on bee communication), and personality (tests and theories). Unfortunately the authors' goal of showing "how questions are
asked and how research provides clarification" (p. 3) is at best unevenly
achieved--floundering particularly because of the lack of a strong chapter on research design.
A number of generally obsolete ideas can be found--for example, a
focus on the ratio IQ and discussion of the Strong Vocational Interest
Blank rather than the Strong-Campbell Interest Inventory. There are also
numerous inaccuracies: for example, intellectualization given as a
Freudian defense mechanism; Little Albert being conditioned to fear a
white rabbit rather than a rat; "cumulative" omitted on the axis of cumulative response curves; and the three major varieties of behavior modification given as systematic desensitization, implosive therapy, and aversive conditioning. In some places the vocabulary expected of the student
is rather sophisticated--"seminal" experiment, "empathizing," "visceral"
symptoms, curve "parameter"--while elsewhere terms are carefully
defined--"predators" and "circadian."
Unfortunately, in the reviewer's opinion, there probably is a better
text for almost any type of class at the high school or college
level.--C.P.
See also Popplestone (1978) and Turner (1977c).

McKeachie, W. J., Doyle, C. L., & Moffett, M. M.   _Psychology_ (3rd ed.).
    Reading, Mass.: Addison-Wesley, 1976.   678 pp. $15.95 cloth.   IM,
    TF, SG, PSI package.

McKeachie, W. J., & Doyle, C. L.   _Psychology: The short course_.   Reading,
    Mass.: Addison-Wesley, 1972.   388 pp. $11.95 paper.   TF, SG, Course
    Evaluation Booklet.

Contrary to most encyclopedic texts, _Psychology_ presents an avowed
cognitive orientation centering around the organism's efforts to develop
an "internal model of the environment" (p. v).   The 18 chapters are organized into four sections: an opening chapter entitled "What is Psychology?"; three chapters on the cultural and biological "Background of
Behavior"; nine chapters on such standard topics as learning, memory, and
perception, labeled "The Determinants of Behavior"; and five chapters in
a section called "The Person," dealing with personality, abnormal psychology, and interpersonal topics.   An unusual but interesting chapter in
the section on determinants is "Action and Performance."
    This third edition represents considerable rewriting and updating of
the second edition.   The authors have made many efforts to enhance the
book's effectiveness as a teaching instrument--chapter outlines, chapter
summaries, suggested readings, occasional interesting "sidelights," both
chapter and full-text glossaries, and case histories and quoted material
printed in red.   These devices, along with the liberal use of subheadings
and the writing style of the authors, keep interest up.   The book clearly
is written for the first-year college student but should not bother the
better high school student.
    The very helpful instructor's manual contains a general discussion of
teaching as well as suggestions for lecture and discussion topics, films,
and demonstrations for each chapter of the text.--R.S.H.
    See also Kasschau (1977b) and Turner (1976b).
    Psychology: The Short Course is based on the second edition of _Psy-
chology_.   Rather than selecting certain chapters to make up _Psychology:
The Short Course_, the authors retained nearly every chapter but reduced
it to its essentials by careful editing.   Only the chapter on personality
measurement was omitted in its entirety.   The appendix on statistics is
also missing.   Teaching devices such as the glossary and the suggested
readings were retained in edited form.--M.J.
    See also Kasschau (1973).

Miller, G. A., & Buckhout, R.   _Psychology: The science of mental life_
    (2nd ed.).   New York: Harper & Row, 1973.   561 pp. $11.95 cloth.
    IM.

For high school teachers whose bookshelf is lined with standard introductory texts, _Psychology: The Science of Mental Life_ will be a refreshing change.   Most of the areas usually covered in an introductory
text are covered in this book, but they are organized in a different manner and with a different emphasis.   The book is actually a history of the
development of psychology--the evolution of different schools of thought
and the people responsible for them.   It is roughly chronological, beginning with Wundt and ending with the 20th-century humanists.   The people

and their theories are put into historical context to show the effects of
the current events of the time and the influences of the prevailing
trends in science, philosophy, and religion.

The reading level of the book is difficult--in content, vocabulary,
and level of sophistication. There are four appendixes, a glossary, and
the usual graphics and illustrations plus original sketches by Patrick
Korch to illustrate each chapter.

Although the book is probably too difficult to be used as a text in
an average high school course, it has a number of points to recommend it
as a reference book or source of supplemental readings. For a beginning
teacher or one who was not a psychology major, it provides an alternative
approach for a psychology course and gives a clear description of the
current status of the profession. It emphasizes the often-neglected fact
that psychology is a fallible science, one yet in its emerging stages,
and currently in a state of flux and internal conflict. The conclusion,
the biographical data (much more extensive than those found in most introductory texts), and the appendixes (the viewpoints of Skinner and
Rogers on the control of human behavior, A Career in Psychology--a booklet published by APA, Miller's APA presidential address--"Psychology as a
Means of Promoting Human Welfare," and an excellent introduction to statistics by F. L. Brown) are valuable supplemental materials. A final
point of recommendation is the book's high readability because of the
authors' enviable easy style and obvious competence.--B.M.N.

See also Rubinstein (1975) and Turner (1974a).

Morgan, C. T. A brief introduction to psychology (2nd ed.). New York:
McGraw-Hill, 1977. 499 pp. $8.95 paper. IM.

This "brief" text is similar in outline and content to the longer
text of Morgan and King. It is intended to be "an objective, science-oriented textbook which seeks to identify and explain the factors
that determine behavior" (p. 6). Chapters begin with sets of learning
objectives and cover traditional topics in scientific psychology.

Although the text proceeds in a well-integrated and concise fashion,
some perspectives are treated in a superficial or even misleading manner;
for example, students are told that the theories of Freud and Murray are
"state" theories that have failed to predict actual behavior and are being abandoned. Also, the nature of debates in the field of psychology is
neglected. Language development is treated as being a result of verbal
learning (which is a combination of imitation and operant conditioning),
and thinking is defined as the process of symbolic mediation. There is
no mention of the existence of competing points of view. Finally, although many secondary students might appreciate a unified approach to
"what we know," this text is probably a bit too dry and difficult to fulfill this function.

The instructor's manual provides overviews of chapters, sets of
teaching objectives, classroom exercises and demonstrations, and objective and essay questions. There is also a brief description of some
films.--K.W.

See also Popplestone (1978) and Turner (1977b).

Morris, C. G. Psychology: An introduction (2nd ed.). Englewood Cliffs,
    N. J.: Prentice-Hall, 1976. (Originally published by Appleton-Cen-
    tury-Crofts, New York.) 649 pp. $15.95 cloth. SG. (Now available
    in a 3rd ed.)

This second edition will be a strong contender for use in undergraduate, and perhaps also in high school, courses. Highly readable, it surveys the "essentials of psychology, from physiological facts and classical theories to current trends" (p. xi). It is both scholarly and practical. Unlike the usual introductory text, it stays close to research
data, is well documented, and consistently raises analytic questions. It
is comprehensive and it is current. About a third of the bibliographic
references were published in the 1970s.

Morris provides a concise, clear, balanced introduction to the field
of psychology. The chapters on the science of psychology and biological
bases of human behavior and development introduce the student to the complexity of the field and to continuing controversies concerning theory,
approaches to problems, and inquiry methods. The remainder of the book
provides an introduction to categories or fields of study (e.g., learning, memory, cognition, sensation, perception, motivation, personality,
therapies, etc.).

Psychological terms appear in bold type and are defined in the text.
There is an extensive glossary and bibliography at the end of the book.
Photographs and graphic illustrations are appropriate and interesting.
Each chapter is preceded by an outline and followed by a summary as well
as suggestions for further reading/study. In addition, the text contains
boxed inserts that review special topics (e.g., how to improve retention,
gestalt therapy, parents as therapists, and research on first-born children). The text is supplemented by a study guide/workbook that reviews
each chapter and provides a list of objectives, terms, and concepts, and
a series of self-tests for evaluation/review. Teachers who use the study
guide/workbook will need to develop their own review items and evaluation
procedures to supplement those provided.--R.H.K.

See also Kasschau (1977b) and Turner (1976b).

Moursund, J. Us people: A mini-max approach to human behavior.
    Monterey, Calif.: Brooks/Cole, 1972. 331 pp. $6.95 paper.

This is a well-written introductory text, suitable for a senior-level
high school psychology class. It contains a lot of material, much of it
reflecting recent research, yet it presents the material in an interesting and easily understood way. It should provide a good background to
students going on to take a college psychology course, as well as a
modest and relevant background in basic psychology to students not continuing their education.

The author has a rather strong behaviorist orientation and tends to
be somewhat critical of non-behaviorist psychology although non-behaviorist views are presented. The only topic one might wish had been included
is prejudice and racism. Not only is there no chapter devoted to the
problem, but there is not even any reference to it in the index. A major
criticism is that the book is blatantly sexist, particularly in the illustrations. Women are presented as sex objects or parents whereas men

are presented as competent and intelligent. This is not likely to encourage women to think of psychology as offering a potential career for
them.
The book has an index, discussion questions following each chapter,
and a bibliography at the end.--J.P.
See also Fincher (1973).

Mussen, P., Rosenzweig, M. R., Geiwitz, J., Aronson, E., Elkind, D.,
    Feshbach, S., Glickman, S. E., Murdock, B. B., Jr., Wertheimer, M., &
    Harvey, L. O., Jr. Psychology: An introduction (2nd ed.). Lexing-
    ton, Mass.: D. C. Heath, 1977. 780 pp. $14.95 cloth. IM, TF, SG.

This excellent introductory text is written for college use. It is
clearly and interestingly written and would be of moderate difficulty for
a high school student. The graphics are unusually eye-catching and helpful in explaining the text. To cover all the chapters would probably
take two semesters, but the authors have laid out the chapters so that a
one-semester course can be put together that emphasizes personality-so-
cial, or experimental-biological, or a general survey (p. vii). For an
introductory text this book has a great deal more social-personality-de-
velopmental psychology than many books of its kind. Each chapter was
written by a recognized psychologist in that area; continuity was ensured
by a careful overall editing. An extensive glossary, chapter summaries,
and key concepts are included as helps to students.
The instructor's manual includes for each chapter a useful (not too
short) summary with specific references, brief descriptions of class
demonstrations, and general-discussion or essay questions. (Objec-
tive-test questions or short-answer questions are not included.) Of special interest is an introductory discussion on course structure and grading that reflects and refers to current research on teaching.
In the study guide each chapter contains an abstract and general
questions to help focus the parallel text chapter before reading it, a
chapter review, and multiple-choice questions with explanations of the
answers. The study guide could also be used by teachers as a source of
test ideas and questions.--B.B.B.
See also Popplestone (1978) and Turner (1977c).

Notterman, J. M. Behavior: A systematic approach. Philadelphia:
    Philadelphia Book Co., 1970. (Originally published by Random House,
    New York.) 368 pp. $8.50 paper. BR, Laboratory Manual.

The book is in the operant tradition, and much of what is said in
that area is based on the book by the author and D. E. Mintz, Dynamics of
Response (New York: Wiley, 1965). There are only 84 references in the
bibliography. It is certainly not the usual survey text and seems weak
whenever the author gets away from what he knows best.--O.P.P.
See also Forgus (1972) and Leuba (1971).

Philip, F. The psychology primer. Del Mar, Calif.: Publisher's, Inc.,
     1975. 243 pp. $9.95 paper. (Now available in a 2nd ed.)

     The Psychology Primer is another in a long line of books that claim
to survey the field of psychology. It is chiefly distinguished by what
it does not do; it does not, as the preface states, "discuss all the fundamental principles of psychology."
     This is a book for popular consumption, a "basal" primer for the lay-
person interested in psychology. The photographs and figures are attractive, but they do not provide the reader with much information. Annotated references, called resource guides, are provided at the end of each
discussion section. However, a summary bibliography is not provided.
The language used is not always clear nor necessarily concise.
     The book attempts to provide a comprehensive introduction to the
field of psychology, an overview of the entire discipline, its vocabulary, its complexity, and some research of popular interest. The range
of topics is considerable and includes: heredity, learning, perception,
physiology of behavior, personality theories, abnormal psychology, and
social psychology. In this reviewer's judgment, the text seeks to cover
too much with too little. The result is fragmentation of factual information and fundamental psychological principles. Further, the book appears not to be oriented to the more scholarly student. For example, the
topic of hypnosis is dealt with as follows: "Hypnosis is not well understood and remains somewhat mysterious to the psychologist and everyone
else" (p. 125). The remainder of the text material concerning this topic
(only five more sentences) defines hallucination and states that psychologists have "not yet identified a 'hypnotizable' personality" (p.
126). The resource guide for this topic does not list any of the recent
publications by E. R. Hilgard or his associates. The most recent reference concerning hypnosis in the resource guide was published in 1972.
     The book does contain some practical information, for example, a
figure that classifies some major drugs by their street name, trade name,
source, medical use, usual dose, etc. On the whole, however, the text is
probably not useful and/or appropriate for introducing students to psychology. The coverage of topics is so limited and spread over so many
areas that many theoretical issues, a considerable amount of research,
and assumptions concerning the interpretive use of information are mini-
mized. In summary, this book appears to have been created for the general public and should, as a consequence, find popularity in that marketplace.--R.H.K.
     See also Turner (1975h).

Pronko, N. H. Panorama of psychology (2nd ed.). Monterey, Calif.:
     Brooks/Cole, 1973. 478 pp. $7.95 paper. TF.

     The recent plethora of new introductory texts has differed only lit-
tle from earlier plethoras. Each piece of work is proclaimed by author
and publisher to be all new and totally unique, grabbing or more gently
seducing students and giving them psychology as it really is. Pronko is
no exception to this apparent rule. He states, "In form and content. . .
this book is not at all conventional" (p. vii). And it isn't! First,

it is a friendly book, noticeably not doctrinaire or parochial in the sources from which it draws. Pronko not only has selected a variety of articles from a multitude of areas, but also has edited and rewritten all but a few. This was also the case in the first edition, which differs from this one only in the vintage of the works used. There is a total of 140 selections (most of them not exceeding two pages) in 12 major subject categories. By name, the subject categories are rather traditional--social psychology, personality, nervous system, etc. Within the categories, however, tradition does not hold sway. Included, for example, are short discussions of race and IQ, the "XYY syndrome," learning in plants, TV violence and aggression, and Milgram's obedience work. By Pronko's own admission, these and many more topics of great inherent interest cannot stand by themselves in introducing a student to the principles of psychology. Thus, Panorama should be used as a readings/reference source. It is not simply a readings book, though. Certainly if a teacher were beginning a library of resource material, Panorama would be very useful, regardless of its category.

In summary, the book is good. It presents a variety of psychological material in an interesting manner. However, the reading level is moderately difficult to difficult, despite the presence of a 24-page glossary. Post-secondary students would experience less of a problem in appreciating the material.--D.K.H.

See also Rubinstein (1975) and Turner (1974a).

Salzinger, K. Psychology: The science of behavior. New York: Springer Publishing Co., 1969. 306 pp. $8.95 cloth; $5.50 paper.

In his preface Salzinger notes his "indebtedness to B. F. Skinner" (p. vii). It is evident throughout the book. Salzinger develops operant conditioning in some detail and then uses it as his basis for discussing education, abnormal behavior, and social behavior. An unusual feature for a book with this orientation is the inclusion of chapters on ethology, physiological psychology, psychophysics, and developmental psychology. Salzinger has come as close as anyone to presenting the traditional survey course coverage from a reasonably consistent operant position. His accomplishment is sufficient justification for recommending the book.

On the negative side, there are relatively few illustrations, and the quality of the reproductions is not good. Salzinger's writing style tends toward little explanatory material to develop his points but quite adequate experimental material to support them.

All in all, it is a good book for a teacher to see how the operant position can be extended to a broad area of psychology, but it will probably not set well with the high school student.--R.S.H.

See also Rubinstein (1970).

Sandberg, J. H. Introduction to the behavioral sciences: An inquiry approach (2nd ed.). New York: Holt, Rinehart & Winston, 1975. 312 pp. $9.48 cloth. IM, Classroom Support Unit Multimedia Kit ($182.52).

This second edition is similar in content, design, and format to the earlier one. Like its predecessor, it attempts to introduce students to the scientific study of behavior by stressing the inquiry methodology that dominates the behavioral science disciplines. The 7 chapters and 54 readings are organized to minimize the memorization of factual data while focusing on active student involvement in the inquiry process. Specific instructions to students in the opening chapter (and to teachers in the accompanying guide) inform them as to their role in following the methodological procedures and in handling the readings and activities.

In this new edition the chapter on "Schizophrenia" has been replaced by one on "Women in American Society." However, the opening chapter's readings on "Water Witching" remain. Of importance to note, little emphasis is placed on personality and emotions--two popular topics with high school students. Indeed, much of the content found in traditionally organized texts is not included in this book.

Sandberg's text stresses the processing and interpretation of data relevant to understanding and predicting human behavior, rather than memorization of data. Lecture- and content-oriented teachers will at first feel awkward using this approach to studying (and teaching) the behavioral sciences. However, once the procedures and method are mastered, both teacher and students will appreciate the results. In addition, students will be capable of exploring areas of the behavioral sciences that may interest them more than the few included in this text.

Although the text is designed for a one-semester course, most teachers will complete it and its activities in 13-14 weeks. Ideally teacher and students alike will then go on to other areas of study, applying the inquiry processes advocated by Sandberg.

The expensive Classroom Support Unit includes silent and sound filmstrips, recordings, tests, dittoed handout masters, and an Individual and Group Activity component. Purchase and use of it are advertised as being optional, but most teachers will find it difficult to be without. Teachers who are not knowledgeable about or comfortable with the inquiry process will need the unit.--R.J.S.

See also Social Science Education Consortium (1977c).

Statt, D. A. Psychology: Making sense. New York: Harper & Row, 1977. 227 pp. $4.95 paper.

Statt's major goal in writing Psychology: Making Sense was to produce a concise yet informative and readable text that would not intimidate students by its breadth and complexity. In this aim he has succeeded, but the result is not as well integrated as he intended.

The material is organized around the central theme of using psychology to make sense of ourselves and our environment. The reader looking for the traditional headings generally associated with an introductory survey of psychology will find instead such topics as "Making Sense of What We Feel," "Dealing with Ourselves," and "Organizing Social Cues." Much of the standard curriculum (learning, perception, child development, etc.) is included (albeit somewhat cursorily); however, one must search through the innovative organization to locate familiar topics. There are quite a few inter-chapter cross-references, and some of the sections are better integrated than others. Within many of the chapters, however, the result sometimes resembles a patchwork quilt. For example, within a space of 11 short pages, we are introduced to the concepts of personality, norms and deviance, life-span development, and pluralistic ignorance. The transitions between intra-chapter subsections are frequently weak, and at times the integrating theme gets lost in the shuffle. Although Statt criticizes other, more voluminous texts for forcing readers to make their own links between sections, he himself often neglects such links within his chapters.

The writing style is light and conversational. However, the dearth of special features (standard fare in most introductory texts) may reduce the usefulness and enjoyability of this book for the beginner. For example, there are no summaries or suggested activities or photographs, and there is a minimal number of diagrams. Some of the more relevant and interesting studies are reported in little boxes set apart from the text, but it is not clear on what basis they differ from the studies reported as an integral part of the text. And although a relatively large number of seminal studies are included for a book this size, its abbreviated style precludes a consideration of some of the more important methodological and ethical issues those studies raise. In addition, in his desire to minimize the memorization of terminology, the author has not always indicated what the student ought to stress. Finally, some teachers may object to his generic use of third-person masculine pronouns (he, him, etc.).

The book would probably be most useful for a one-semester survey course or the psychological component of a social science umbrella course. Because of its brevity, it could be used in conjunction with independent readings for greater detail.--E.B.

See also Popplestone (1978) and Turner (1977c).

Tallent, N., & Spungin, C. I. Psychology: Understanding ourselves and others (2nd ed.). New York: American Book Co., 1977. 528 pp. $7.98 cloth. IM, Test and Activity Sheets.

As the title suggests, this text is oriented toward adjustment and abnormal psychology. Its orientation should prove interesting to high school students who enroll in psychology to find out about themselves and their relations to others. The authors' treatment of these topics is thorough and comprehensive. The text is suitable for a one-semester course focusing on mental health.

The strength of the book is also its main weakness. Little or no attention is paid to traditional areas of psychology such as perception, physiology, and social psychology. The treatment of learning is superficial and oriented toward practical applications. Consequently the text presents the student with a very unrepresentative picture of the discipline of psychology.

The readability of the text is within the range of the average high school student. Very little sophistication in psychology is needed to comprehend the content. The authors write in a clear style with many applications of content to real life. Unfortunately graphs and illustrations are presented in a drab brown tone that does little to enhance the attractiveness of the text.

The teacher's manual presents lists of films, recordings, and books that can be used to supplement the course. The booklet of tests and activities is made up of ditto masters that teachers may find useful. There is a 15-item objective test for each chapter. The activities are primarily busywork consisting of pencil-and-paper tasks such as crossword puzzles and anagrams.--S.C.

See also Social Science Education Consortium (1977c).

Vernon, J., & Suedfeld, P. (Eds.). Introduction to general psychology: A self-selection textbook (2nd ed.) (23 booklets). Dubuque, Iowa: Wm. C. Brown, 1966-73. $1.95 per booklet.

The day is past when psychology can be represented in texts as an assortment of topics from child development to abnormal behavior to psychophysics. The series reviewed here clearly supports this conclusion. In departing from the traditions of text publishing, Introduction to General Psychology: A Self-Selection Textbook strives to overcome the difficulties inherent in conventional coverage by "providing an authoritative but flexible textbook which allows a selection of topics in accordance with the content of a particular course and the demands of its students" (p. iii). Teachers are able to draw on 23 brief texts, each written by an authority in the field. The 23 booklets cover a wide range of topics (e.g., psychopharmacology, physiological aspects of memory, military psychology, personality, sleep and dreams, motivation, and statistics), and for the most part they cover the topics well. Each booklet introduces the student to theory and research appropriate to its topic. In general, the research literature associated with each topic is well represented, but descriptions of individual studies are brief and are often incorporated into the broader principle/topic under discussion. Overall, the selections have a strong scientific base. The writing is clear and moderately free from jargon, and the positions taken and arguments designed to support them are strong. In the short space available for this review it is impossible to provide a detailed analysis of each booklet. Thus, teachers should carefully review units for the purpose of selecting one or more that seem most appropriate to the needs of students. In conclusion, this series is solid and well done, up-to-date, and, with selective use by teachers, will no doubt continue to meet the needs of many teachers and students of psychology.--R.H.K.

See also Abma (1971).

Vernon, W. M. Introductory psychology: A personalized textbook (2nd ed.). Chicago: Rand McNally, 1976. 680 pp. $12.50 paper. IM.

Vernon gives us a markedly different form of text covering typical topics. Superficially it is a combined text-and-workbook. But the workbook is, in reality, 400 specific major concepts with questions designed to force the student to restudy text segments not adequately read. This is the text of choice for those interested in the Personalized System of Instruction/mastery learning; it is a strong contender for traditional courses in which the examinations are objective; instructors preferring to use short essay tests will appropriately reject the book.

Strengths of the text include superbly concise writing and cartoons that make genuine contributions to the understanding of the material (every one!). High school students who are not prepared for college work will find the text beyond them; others will master the material but find the reading much slower than their other books. This reviewer particularly liked the focus on levels of scientific work--description, prediction, control . . . --a theme that reappears numerous times.

Major weaknesses include the necessity of following the topic order in the text and an abominable page layout that focuses on the workbook rather than the text and makes the outlines at the beginning of each chapter difficult to comprehend. Also, the discussion of validity of intelligence tests would be clearer if emphasis were refocused on the notion of validity for a specific purpose rather than simply "validity."

Rand McNally will provide adequate copies of 40 multiple-choice tests for each chapter, thus avoiding local duplication expense. Although the tests are carefully keyed to the major concepts, questions are designed to measure only knowledge and comprehension (not the more complex levels of learning). Careful trial of the tests has provided data on both item difficulty and retention (based on a 10-month follow-up). Some teachers will find the tests too close to the check-up questions in the text; for them a set of 20 questions per chapter is provided in the instructor's guide.

Those seriously considering the text (and most teachers should be in this group) should obtain a copy of the text and guide and carefully examine at least one of the following topics: biological foundations, operant behavior, and psychopathology.--C.P.

Watson, D. Here's psychology. Lexington, Mass.: Ginn and Co., 1977. 422 pp. $8.75 cloth. IM, TF.

Here's Psychology is a high school text suitable for a one-term course in introductory psychology. The book is designed for all students of psychology, not simply those who plan to go to college. It treats psychology as a scientific discipline that has application to the students' own lives. The book is organized around traditional content areas of psychology with special chapters on sex roles, self-management, vocation, and marriage. The content of the text is exceptional in reflecting the latest developments in psychology. Some chapters could be deleted if necessary.

Several special features of the text aid learning and add interest. Each chapter begins with a statement of objectives and goals. Headings are frequently phrased as questions. Definitions are clearly marked in the text. There are frequent summaries of chapter segments. Special sections entitled Thinking Psychologically and Using Psychology encourage students to review important points and apply the points to problems or situations relevant to their own lives. There are general summaries at the end of each chapter.

The text is written in an interesting, semiformal style. Frequent concrete situations and descriptions of abstract concepts aid student learning. There are many visual illustrations. Use of the Fry readability formula revealed a reading level of ninth grade.

The instructor's manual contains suggestions for organizing material into lessons, lists of important terms, lists of references, numerous student learning activities, and a test-item file for each chapter.

Here's Psychology is an excellent text. It is up-to-date, clearly written, and interesting. It is especially suitable for the teacher who wishes to teach psychology as a scientific discipline that has application to problems in human adjustment.--S.E.

Weiner, B., Runquist, W., Runquist, P. A., Raven, B., Meyer, W. J., Leiman, A., Kutscher, C., Kleinmuntz, B., & Haber, R. Discovering psychology. Palo Alto, Calif.: Science Research Associates, 1977. 800 pp. $15.95 cloth. IM, TF, SG.

In Discovering Psychology Weiner and his colleagues have a rare achievement--a well-organized, clearly written, and understandable text. The prose is technical but not burdened with jargon. Psychological terms are carefully introduced and defined, then discussed in relation to theoretical concepts and the results of research. The text focuses on psychology as a discipline. This orientation is reflected in the comprehensive coverage of the field of psychology, ranging from neonatal influences to old age and from biological determinants of behavior to elementary statistics and the metric system. Areas of special interest to psychologists (e.g., learning, memory, personality disorders, psychophysics, etc.) are reviewed in detail. Information is organized in such a way that the reader is invited to ponder the significance and meaning of carefully presented and often conflicting experimental results. Each chapter concludes with a summary and a modest list of supplementary references. The many photographs complement the text, and the carefully crafted drawings are significant aids in explaining psychological phenomena that have been described in the text. Information deserving particular attention is highlighted by placement in colored boxes. A comprehensive bibliography and index are also provided.

Research and examples chosen to illustrate psychological phenomena are current. For example, the Patricia Hearst case is employed to illustrate the phenomenon of brainwashing. In the discussion of some areas of specialized knowledge, a more detailed presentation would have been preferable. For instance, a discussion of the theory of "identification with the aggressor" would have strengthened the discussion of the Hearst case. However, one cannot reasonably expect thorough coverage of all areas in an introductory text.

This book is not only appropriate for college-level students but merits consideration for adoption in high school psychology courses. Teachers adopting the text should probably supplement it with laboratory exercises and related materials/experiences.--R.H.K.

See also Gerow (1978a), Popplestone (1978), and Turner (1977d).

Wertheimer, M., Bjorkman, M., Lundberg, I., & Magnusson, D. Psychology: A brief introduction. Glenview, Ill.: Scott, Foresman, 1971. 236 pp. $9.95 cloth. IM, SG.

Of the few texts written expressly for secondary school use, Psychology: A Brief Introduction is easily the best this reviewer has seen. The authors have been quite successful in their attempt to present an overview of the fields of psychology without the use of an argot or technical language beyond the experience of the high school student. The text represents a departure from the traditional organization of intro- ductory psychology texts. The authors describe the human as an informa- tion-processing system and discuss the traditional areas of psycholo- gy--learning, perception, personality, etc.--within that framework. This conceptualization allows the authors to present psychology as an inte- grated science and should provide for a greater understanding by the stu- dent.

A good pedagogical device is the running glossary, by means of which the few technical terms used are defined in the margin of the page on which they appear. Curiously, however, suggested readings for each chap- ter do not appear until the end of the book, and although the difficulty level of the readings is variable, there is no indication of difficulty available to the student. Additionally a remarkable amount of material is covered within the book, but some topics are discussed only enough to whet the appetite of the more serious student; thus, teachers using this text in an advanced class might find it necessary to provide in-depth explanations of such topics.

The teacher's task is made easier by a resource book packed with in- formation. Included are course and chapter outlines, sample test ques- tions, annotated bibliographies of related materials, and extremely help- ful discussions of the principal issues raised in each chapter of the text. In addition, the study guide divides the 7 chapters into 10 sec- tions for study. The study-guide questions and exercises are well chos- en, but the organization of the guide is puzzling; in at least one in- stance the guide section deals with material presented at the first and last of a chapter, leaving intervening text material to the next section of the guide.

The text and accompanying materials seem appropriate for a one-semes- ter high school class.--P.D.J.

See also Forgus (1972), Norton (1973), and Social Science Education Consortium (1973).

Whaley, D. L., & Malott, R. W. Elementary principles of behavior (3rd ed.). Englewood Cliffs, N. J.: Prentice-Hall, 1971. (Originally published by Appleton-Century-Crofts, New York.) 454 pp. $10.95 paper. SG.

The book should really interest students. The style is informal and each chapter contains many excellent examples of the behavioral principle under study taken from real-life situations. In fact, this may well be the most "relevant" textbook in psychology as viewed from an operant per- spective. Most of the classical content of the typical eclectic intro- ductory course is omitted--an omission that may be for the best in the high school.

Important for the teacher is Chapter 22, which describes in detail the way in which the materials have been used at Western Michigan Univer- sity. Although few high school teachers are likely to confront 1,000 students simultaneously, extrapolation to the high school classroom should be relatively easy.

The book might require supplementation at the college level, but it could stand alone for a one-semester high school course. Because the text presents a specific bias, the teacher should examine it carefully before adoption rather than accept the reviewer's statement.[1]
See also Zeiler (1972).

Whittaker, J. O. Psychology of modern life. New York: Human Sciences Press, 1976. 436 pp. $9.95 cloth.

Designed to be used in an introductory, one-semester high school course, Psychology of Modern Life offers a general treatment of the discipline with particular emphasis on the concerns and needs of adolescents. Several sections are devoted to the teenager, social adjustment, dating, study techniques, career aspirations, etc. Thus, the text should be of interest to high school students.

The book tends toward a social psychological approach, with the last section devoted to current problems in American society. Whittaker often presents a topic within its sociological context, explaining the influence of the particular environment or culture on human behavior. This is important in helping students understand the variety of behavior and the impact of social norms on one's actions.

The author treats such topics as learning, perception, motivation, personality, and abnormality in a relatively general and superficial manner. Little time is spent on development, except for adolescence, and there is virtually no discussion of life after early adulthood. However, given the purpose of the text--an introduction to psychology--and its focus on the needs and concerns of adolescents, it should be a useful book for high school students, especially if supplemented by more in-depth material to meet student interests. Although it is not as precise nor as scientifically oriented as some texts, it will probably benefit the average student who wants to learn something about psychology without going too deeply into the subject.--J.J.P.

See also Epley (1976), Harris (1977), and Social Science Education Consortium (1978).

Wrightsman, L. S., & Sanford, F. H. Psychology: A scientific study of human behavior (4th ed.). Monterey, Calif.: Brooks/Cole, 1975. 656 pp. $14.95 cloth. IM, TF, SG, Auto-Tutorial Auto-Tape Series, Listening Guide to Accompany the Auto-Tutorial Tapes. (Now available in a 5th ed.).

Most large encyclopedic texts present an eclectic point of view that shifts from chapter to chapter. This text, however, in an effort to provide "a thorough and consistent integration" of the material, uses the concept of "assumptions about people" (p. v) as an organizing theme for each chapter. In addition, several other techniques have been employed

---

[1]The editors were unable to identify the writer of this review because the control card was lost and the original version of the review was put in storage several years ago.

to enhance the teachability of the book--chapter outlines at the beginning of each chapter (these outlines make up the Table of Contents), numbered summary statements and a list of a dozen basic concepts at the end of each chapter, informal summaries of research reports enclosed in boxes throughout the chapters, and a glossary of about 700 terms. As with the earlier editions, several of the chapters were initially written by other authors but edited into a consistent style.

This book is much better than the third edition. It is visually attractive, with a language level easily handled by the first-year college student. There is much interesting and quite up-to-date material included, but it is a very large book that would be difficult to cover in its entirety in one semester. This is probably the principal reason that makes it a questionable text for high school use.--R.S.H.

See also Murphy (1976) and Turner (1975g).

Zimbardo, P. G., & Ruch, F. L. Psychology and life (9th ed.). Glenview, Ill.: Scott, Foresman, 1975. 788 pp. $14.50 cloth. IM, TF, SG, BR, Unit Mastery System, Self-Instructional Program. (Now available in a 10th ed.).

The authors' aim in preparing this introductory package was threefold: to develop a college-level psychology course that rigorously explores the field while appealing to the students' experiences and interests; to enable students to succeed; and to assist teachers in preparing for and teaching the course. The text provides a means of achieving the first aim. It covers the basic topics in psychology thoroughly yet readably. The authors describe the research of various well-known psychologists as well as current and sometimes controversial findings. They also include differing explanations for behavior, leaving conclusions to the reader. For instance, while pointing out the limitations of behaviorism, they also indicate its usefulness. Throughout the book are "close-ups," diagrams, and illustrations that have a direct application to the reader's experiences. The authors have obviously tried to meet students "where they are" by including discussions on such topics as yoga, transcendental meditation, hypnosis, and sex roles. Sometimes this attempt to be "relevant" descends to a certain cuteness ("The House That Pavlov Built," "An All-Zimbo Text Festival"), but generally the authors succeed better than authors of more traditional texts in showing some direct applications of various psychological concepts. Because it is a college-level book, though, Psychology and Life would be useful only for brighter students or as a reference book in a high school psychology class.

The unit mastery system and the student workbook have been designed to help students succeed by improving their study skills. The unit mastery system helps students organize the textual material by having them answer a series of informational questions. Students read less than a chapter of the text, answer the questions, and take a quiz on the material covered when they feel they have mastered it. They move through the text at their own pace. The workbook provides an overview of each chapter, lists of key terms, a variety of self-tests, and research projects. The high school teacher would probably find the workbook more useful because of the different types of questions included and because of the research projects. However, the unit mastery system's plan could be applied effectively in the high school classroom.

The instructor's manual is most intriguing. It tries to help college teachers organize and prepare their course. A section is devoted to preparation steps that should be taken as much as three months before the first class. In addition, the authors discuss how to prepare a lecture and how to evaluate students, the teacher, and the course.

Zimbardo and Ruch have obviously devoted much thought to creating an interesting, useful, and success-oriented set of materials for an introductory college course. In high school the text would probably be most useful as a reference or supplemental book; the unit mastery system and workbook could be applied to fit the needs of the students.--J.J.P.

See also Campbell (1976), Cone (1976), and Turner (1975e).

46   PSYCHOLOGY TEACHER'S RESOURCE BOOK

References

Abma, J. S. The whole is greater than some of its parts. Contemporary Psychology, 1971, 16, 438-440. Review of Vernon & Suedfeld, 1966-73.

Abma, J. S. A little old, a little new. Contemporary Psychology, 1974, 19, 732-736. Reviews of Cox, 1973; Heimstra & McDonald, 1973.

Bell, H. H. Review of Lawson et al., 1975. Science Books and Films, 1975, 11, 119.

Campbell, D. E. Life with Psychology and life. Teaching of Psychology, 1976, 3, 191-192. Review of Zimbardo & Ruch, 1975.

Cone, A. L. Six luxury models. Contemporary Psychology, 1976, 21, 544-548. Reviews of Kendler, 1974; Kimble et al., 1974; Krech et al., 1974; Zimbardo & Ruch, 1975.

Covington, M. V. Short 'n' sweet. Teaching of Psychology, 1977, 4, 156-157. Review of Kagan & Havemann, 1976.

Cytrynbaum, S. Wanted: An experiential textbook. Contemporary Psychology, 1969, 14, 676-677. Review of Gallup, 1969.

Epley, S. W. Review of Whittaker, 1976. High School Behavioral Science, 1976, 4(1), 43-47.

Ericksen, S. C. The more things change. Teaching of Psychology, 1977, 4, 206-207. Review of Liebert & Neale, 1977.

Fincher, C. L. To mini-max is human . . . Contemporary Psychology, 1973, 18, 554. Review of Moursund, 1972.

Forgus, R. H. Something for everyone: Introductory texts. Contemporary Psychology, 1972, 17, 270-273. Reviews of Harlow et al., 1971; Notterman, 1970; Thompson & DeBold, 1971; Wertheimer et al., 1971.

Fretz, B. R. Looking at Looking at. Teaching of Psychology, 1977, 4, 96. Review of Geiwitz, 1976.

Fuchs, A. H. Principles' principals. Teaching of Psychology, 1977, 4, 97-98. Review of Bourne & Ekstrand, 1976.

Gerow, J. R. Group think. Teaching of Psychology, 1978, 5, 52. (a) Review of Weiner et al., 1977.

Gerow, J. R. Psychology is alive and well. Contemporary Psychology, 1978, 23, 400-403. (b) Reviews of CRM/Random House, 1977; Krech et al., 1976.

Harris, D. B. Review of Whittaker, 1976. Science Books and Films, 1977, 12, 188.

Kasschau, R. 17 inches of (mixed) pleasure. Contemporary Psychology, 1973, 18, 617-623. Reviews of Harrison, 1972; Hebb, 1972; Landauer, 1972; McKeachie & Doyle, 1972.

Kasschau, R. A. A professional's choice: Should we teach theory or practice? High School Behavioral Science, 1977, 4(2), 96-100. (a) Review of Engle & Snellgrove, 1974.

Kasschau, R. A. 22.1 centimeters of (mixed) pleasure: Psigns of the times. Contemporary Psychology, 1977, 22, 505-508. (b) Reviews of Grace et al., 1976; Kagan & Havemann, 1976; McKeachie et al., 1976; Morris, 1976.

Kasschau, R. A. Previews of CRM/Random House, 1977; Krech et al., 1976. Contemporary Psychology, 1978, 23, 101-102.

Langsam, G. Review of Geiwitz, 1976. High School Behavioral Science, 1977, 4(2), 92-96.

Lefton, L. A. A Riddle review. Teaching of Psychology, 1974, 1, 41. Review of Lazarus, 1974.

Leuba, C. Review of Notterman, 1970. Psychological Record, 1971, 21, 282.

Lowman, K. D. Directory of introductory psychology texts in print: 1979. Teaching of Psychology, 1979, 6, 49-54.

Meador, L. M. A product of experience. High School Behavioral Science, 1977, 4(2), 96-98. Review of Engle & Snellgrove, 1974.

Melvin, K. B. A solid citizen introductory psychology. Teaching of Psychology, 1975, 2, 92-93. Review of Hilgard et al., 1975.

Millham, J. It's Elements, my dear Watson. Teaching of Psychology, 1974, 1, 96-97. Review of Krech et al., 1974.

Murphy, L. E. Something for everyone. Contemporary Psychology, 1976, 21, 691-694. Reviews of Hilgard et al., 1975; Wrightsman & Sanford, 1975.

Norton, F. T. M. What is a nice book like you doing on a shelf like this? Teaching of Psychology Newsletter, March 1973, p. 15. Review of Wertheimer et al., 1971.

Parducci, A. Two views on Principles' principal parameters. Teaching of Psychology, 1974, 1, 95. Review of Kimble et al., 1974.

Popplestone, J. A. 12 pre-paradigmatic variations on a theme. Contemporary Psychology, 1975, 20, 711-717. Reviews of Bruno, 1974; Engle & Snellgrove, 1974; Lazarus, 1974.

Popplestone, J. A. Once more, dear friends. Contemporary Psychology, 1978, 23, 142-151. Reviews of Geiwitz, 1976; Kalish, 1977; Kendler, 1977; Liebert & Neale, 1977; Lugo & Hershey, 1976; Malott & Whaley, 1976; McGaugh et al., 1977; Morgan, 1977; Mussen et al., 1977; Statt, 1977; Weiner et al., 1977.

Review of Dallett, 1973. Science Books: A Quarterly Review, 1974, 9, 279.

Review of Hall, 1973. Science Books: A Quarterly Review, 1974, 10, 3.

Review of Harrison, 1972. Science Books: A Quarterly Review, 1973, 9, 5.

Rubinstein, J. Another member of the family. Contemporary Psychology, 1970, 15, 580. Review of Salzinger, 1969.

Rubinstein, J. Introductory potpourri. Contemporary Psychology, 1975, 20, 302-308. Reviews of Belcher, 1973; Dallett, 1973; Miller & Buckhout, 1973; Pronko, 1973.

Schulz, W. Preview of Lawson et al., 1975. Contemporary Psychology, 1975, 20, 914.

Sexton, V. S. Old and new: There's one for you. Contemporary Psychology, 1977, 22, 190-192. Reviews of Bourne & Ekstrand, 1976; Davidoff, 1976; Gardiner, 1974; Lewis & Petersen, 1974.

Social Science Education Consortium. Review of Wertheimer et al., 1971. Social Studies Curriculum Materials Data Book, Textbooks, October 15, 1973.

Social Science Education Consortium. Review of Kuhn et al., 1975. Social Studies Curriculum Materials Data Book, Textbooks, March 15, 1977. (a)

Social Science Education Consortium. Review of Sandberg, 1975. Social Studies Curriculum Materials Data Book, Project Materials, March 15, 1977. (b)

Social Science Education Consortium. Review of Tallent & Spungin, 1977. Social Studies Curriculum Materials Data Book, Textbooks, October 15, 1977. (c)

Social Science Education Consortium. Review of Whittaker, 1976. Social Studies Curriculum Materials Data Book, Textbooks, March 15, 1978.

Stanners, R. F. Experimental psychology, broadly interpreted. Contemporary Psychology, 1976, 21, 698-699. Review of Lawson et al., 1975.

Turner, R. H. Review of Fincher, 1972. Contemporary Psychology, 1973, 18, 347-348.

Turner, R. H. Previews of Belcher, 1973; Dallett, 1973; Miller & Buckhout, 1973; Pronko, 1973. Contemporary Psychology, 1974, 19, 142-144. (a)

Turner, R. H. Preview of Engle & Snellgrove, 1974. Contemporary Psychology, 1974, 19, 420. (b)

Turner, R. H. Preview of Lazarus, 1974. Contemporary Psychology, 1974, 19, 568-569. (c)

Turner, R. H. Preview of Bruno, 1974. Contemporary Psychology, 1975, 20, 74-76. (a)

Turner, R. H. Previews of Kimble et al., 1974; Lewis & Petersen, 1974. Contemporary Psychology, 1975, 20, 169-171. (b)

Turner, R. H. Preview of Kendler, 1974. Contemporary Psychology, 1975, 20, 261. (c)

Turner, R. H. Previews of Gardiner, 1974; Krech et al., 1974. Contemporary Psychology, 1975, 20, 435-436. (d)

Turner, R. H. Preview of Zimbardo & Ruch, 1975. Contemporary Psychology, 1975, 20, 533-534. (e)

Turner, R. H. Preview of Hilgard et al., 1975. Contemporary Psychology, 1975, 20, 755-757. (f)

Turner, R. H. Preview of Wrightsman & Sanford, 1975. Contemporary Psychology, 1975, 20, 834-837. (g)

Turner, R. H. Review of Philip, 1975. Contemporary Psychology, 1975, 20, 839. (h)

Turner, R. H. Previews of Bourne & Ekstrand, 1976; Davidoff, 1976. Contemporary Psychology, 1976, 21, 446. (a)

Turner, R. H. Previews of Kagan & Havemann, 1976; McKeachie et al., 1976; Morris, 1976. Contemporary Psychology, 1976, 21, 760-762. (b)

Turner, R. H. Preview of Grace et al., 1976. Contemporary Psychology, 1976, 21, 846. (c)

Turner, R. H. Preview of Lugo & Hershey, 1976. Contemporary Psychology, 1977, 22, 234-235. (a)

Turner, R. H. Preview of Morgan, 1977. Contemporary Psychology, 1977, 22, 630. (b)

Turner, R. H. Previews of Geiwitz, 1976; Kalish, 1977; Kendler, 1977; McGaugh et al., 1977; Mussen et al., 1977; Statt, 1977. Contemporary Psychology, 1977, 22, 725-727. (c)

Turner, R. H. Previews of Liebert & Neale, 1977; Weiner et al., 1977. Contemporary Psychology, 1977, 22, 785-787. (d)

Van Krevelen, A. Old wine in new bottles? Contemporary Psychology, 1973, 18, 173-176. Reviews of Edwards, 1972; Isaacson & Hutt, 1971.

Zeiler, M. D. Rigor or relevance? Contemporary Psychology, 1972, 17, 348-349. Review of Whaley & Malott, 1971.

Chapter 2

Reviews of Books of Readings

Books of readings are a potentially valuable source of information
and interest to both student and teacher. Thirty-three such books have
been reviewed for use in high school psychology. Most readings books in
specific areas of psychology have been omitted, and not all general books
of readings are reviewed here.

Below is an alphabetical listing of the books of readings. It is
followed by a tabular account of appraisals. Initials appearing at the
end of reviews are those of reviewers, whose full names are listed in the
Preface. The designation O.P.P., for Oberlin project participant, has
been used for all reviews done during the Oberlin project in summer 1970;
we are unable to identify individual authors of those reviews. The
references given at the end of some entries represent other reviews of
those entries. Addresses of publishers appear in Appendix A.

The reviewers were asked to provide information about the following
characteristics of each book, and to append their own comments (column 6
in the accompanying table):

1.   number of selections;
2.   reading level (appraised specifically for the high school stu-
     dent and ranked easy, moderate, or difficult);
3.   level of sophistication required (appraised specifically for the
     high school student and ranked low, medium, or high);
4.   interest value (to the high school student);
5.   unusual features (special characteristics, both good and poor,
     of the particular volume);
6.   comments (editorially selected from the reviews).

Books of Readings

Aronson, E. (Ed.). Voices of modern psychology: An introductory
    reader. Reading, Mass.: Addison-Wesley, 1969. 372 pp. $6.95 paper.
Atkinson, R. C. (Ed.). Contemporary psychology: Readings from Scien-
    tific American. San Francisco: W. H. Freeman, 1971. 484 pp.
    $12.00 cloth; $7.00 paper.
Atkinson, R. C. (Ed.). Psychology in progress: Readings from Scien-
    tific American. San Francisco: W. H. Freeman, 1975. 392 pp.
    $12.00 cloth; $6.25 paper.
Bishop, G. B., & Hill, W. F. (Eds.). Dimensions of psychology: In-
    troductory readings. Philadelphia: Lippincott, 1972. 475 pp.
    $5.95 paper.
Cohen, I. S. (Ed.). Perspectives on psychology: Introductory read-
    ings. New York: Praeger, 1975. 464 pp. $16.95 cloth.
Daniel, R. S. (Ed.). Contemporary readings in general psychology (2nd
    ed.). Boston: Houghton Mifflin, 1965. 417 pp. $6.95 paper.

Dulany, D. E., Jr., DeValois, R. L., Beardslee, D. C., & Winterbottom, M. R. (Eds.). Contributions to modern psychology: Selected readings in general psychology (2nd ed.). New York: Oxford University Press, 1963. 484 pp. $4.95 paper.

Dyal, J. A., Corning, W. C., & Willows, D. M. (Eds.). Readings in psychology: The search for alternatives (3rd ed.). New York: McGraw-Hill, 1975. 378 pp. $8.50 paper.

Eisner, T., & Wilson, E. O. (Eds.). Animal behavior: Readings from Scientific American. San Francisco: W. H. Freeman, 1975. 339 pp. $13.00 cloth; $7.95 paper.

Foss, B. M. (Ed.). New horizons in psychology. Baltimore: Penguin, 1966. 448 pp. $2.75 paper.

Gazzaniga, M. S., & Lovejoy, E. P. (Eds.). Good reading in psychology. Englewood Cliffs, N. J.: Prentice-Hall, 1971. 569 pp. $8.95 paper.

Gibbons, D. E., & Connelly, J. F. (Eds.). Selected readings in psychology. St. Louis, Mo.: C. V. Mosby, 1970. 273 pp. $5.95 paper.

Guthrie, R. V. (Ed.). Encounter: Issues of human concern. Menlo Park, Calif.: Cummings Publishing Co., 1970. 306 pp. $4.25 paper.

Harlow, H. F. (Ed.). Scientific American resource library: Readings in psychology (2 vols.). San Francisco: W. H. Freeman, 1969. Vol. 1, 427 pp.; Vol. 2, 401 pp. $24.00 cloth for the set.

Kagan, J., Haith, M. M., & Caldwell, C. (Eds.). Psychology: Adapted readings. New York: Harcourt Brace Jovanovich, 1971. 404 pp. $6.95 paper.

Karlins, M. (Ed.). Psychology and society: Readings for general psychology. New York: John Wiley, 1971. 514 pp. $14.00 cloth.

Katz, H. A., Greenberg, M. H., & Warrick, P. S. (Eds.). Introductory psychology through science fiction (2nd ed.). Chicago: Rand McNally, 1977. 550 pp. $9.00 paper.

King, R. A. (Ed.). Readings for an introduction to psychology (3rd ed.). New York: McGraw-Hill, 1971. 584 pp. $8.95 paper.

Maas, J. B. (Ed.). Readings in psychology today (3rd ed.). Del Mar, Calif.: CRM Books, 1974. 377 pp. $5.95 paper.

McCollom, I. N., & Badore, N. L. (Eds.). Exploring psychology: Introductory readings. New York: Thomas Y. Crowell, 1973. 456 pp. $8.25 paper.

McGuigan, F. J., & Woods, P. J. (Eds.). Contemporary studies in psychology. Englewood Cliffs, N. J.: Prentice-Hall, 1972. (Originally published by Appleton-Century-Crofts, New York.) 322 pp. $7.95 paper.

McKinney, F. (Ed.). Psychology in action: Basic readings (2nd ed.). New York: Macmillan, 1973. 499 pp. $7.25 paper.

Melvin, K. B., Brodsky, S. L., & Fowler, R. D., Jr. (Eds.). Psy fi one: An anthology of psychology in science fiction. New York: Random House, 1977. 299 pp. No price available.

Milgram, S. (Ed.). Psychology in today's world. Boston: Little, Brown, 1975. 387 pp. $6.95 paper.

Notterman, J. M. (Ed.). Readings in behavior. Philadelphia: Philadelphia Book Co., 1970. (Originally published by Random House, New York.) 386 pp. $5.95 paper.

Pronko, N. H. (Ed.). <u>Panorama of psychology</u> (2nd ed.). Monterey, Calif.: Brooks/Cole, 1973. 478 pp. $7.95 paper.

Sjule, G. (Ed.). <u>Contemporary psychology: A book of readings</u>. Encino, Calif.: Dickenson Publishing Co., 1970. 406 pp. $5.95 paper.

Stricker, G., & Merbaum, M. (Eds.). <u>Growth of personal awareness: A reader in psychology</u>. New York: Holt, Rinehart & Winston, 1973. 404 pp. $6.95 paper.

Ulrich, R., Stachnik, T., & Mabry, J. (Eds.). <u>Control of human behavior</u> (3 vols). Glenview, Ill.: Scott, Foresman. Vol. 1, 1966, 349 pp., $8.95 paper; Vol. 2, 1970, 378 pp., $8.95 paper; Vol. 3, 1974, 453 pp., $8.95 paper.

Wertheimer, M., & Rappoport, L. (Eds.). <u>Psychology and the problems of today</u>. Glenview, Ill.: Scott, Foresman, 1978. 439 pp. $7.95 paper.

Whittaker, J. O. (Ed.). <u>Recent discoveries in psychology: Readings for the introductory course</u>. Philadelphia: W. B. Saunders, 1972. 448 pp. $5.50 paper.

Wrench, D. F. (Ed.). <u>Readings in psychology: Foundations and applications</u>. New York: McGraw-Hill, 1971. 480 pp. $9.95 paper.

Zimbardo, P. G., & Maslach, C. (Eds.). <u>Psychology for our times: Readings</u> (2nd ed). Glenview, Ill.: Scott, Foresman, 1977. 424 pp. $6.95 paper.

TABLE 1

Reviewer Appraisals of Books of Readings

Books of readings	No. of selections	Reading level	Level of sophistication required	Interest value to high school students	Unusual features	Selected comments from reviews
Aronson, *Voices of modern psychology: An introductory reader.*	31	Difficult	High	Questionable	Is a collection of public addresses by eminent psychologists	Is oriented toward theory and data; would be a good resource book for the teacher—R. D.
Atkinson, *Contemporary psychology: Readings from* Scientific American.	55	Variable, generally moderate	High	High	Has outstanding illustrations	Might serve as the starting point for independent study projects on a wide variety of contemporary topics—J. K. B.
Atkinson, *Psychology in progress: Readings from* Scientific American. (See also Gillen, 1976.)	39	Moderate	Medium	High	Has a study guide	Presents information concerning "new discoveries in the quest for understanding of psychological processes that govern human behavior" on a continuum from basic to applied research—R. H. K.
Bishop & Hill, *Dimensions of psychology: Introductory readings.*	44	Difficult	High	Low to medium	Is strong on learning and has a heavy experimental emphasis	Section on social behavior and social problems would be of greatest interest to high school students—J. D.
Cohen, *Perspectives on pscyhology: Introductory readings.* (See also Weiss, 1975.)	35	Difficult	High	Limited to advanced students	Includes readings from nonpsychological literature that shed light on psychological issues; has cross-reference listing identifying articles that are topically related	Follows organization of many introductory texts—L. M.
Daniel, *Contemporary readings in general psychology* (2nd ed.). (See also Guthrie, 1968.)	68	Easy-difficult	Low-high	Parsimoniously stated findings; little effort to demonstrate relevance	Sources range from *Life* magazine to the *Bulletin of Atomic Scientists*	Contains mainly quite technical reports of empirical psychological research—O. P. P.

Table 1 (Continued)

Books of readings	No. of selections	Reading level	Level of sophistication required	Interest value to high school students	Unusual features	Selected comments from reviews
Dulany et al., *Contributions to modern psychology: Selected readings in general psychology* (2nd ed.).	49	Difficult	High	No	Contains mainly reports of empirical research	Is a good resource book for the high school teacher—O. P. P.
Dyal et al., *Readings in psychology: The search for alternatives* (3rd ed.). (See also Gillen, 1976.)	53	Moderate	Medium	Medium	Contains comments on the readings, and gets the reader actively to think about and work with the material	An unusual collection, exploring "relevant" topics—M. W.
Eisner & Wilson, *Animal behavior: Readings from Scientific American.*	34	Moderate	Medium	Medium-high	Has introductions to each section, which give theoretical background and discuss each article in the section	Last two sections are of greatest interest to psychologists—R. S. H.
Foss, *New horizons in psychology.*	21	Difficult	High	Interesting but dry	Emphasizes operant conditioning and physiological psychology	Contains no emphasis on applications of findings; places considerable reliance on the reader to evaluate controversies implicitly or explicitly raised by authors—O. P. P.
Gazzaniga & Lovejoy, *Good reading in psychology.* (See also Vogel, 1973.)	37	Difficult	High	Interesting but too sophisticated	Focuses on a small number of salient issues and areas in psychology	Is not recommended for use at the high school level—B. M. N.
Gibbons & Connelly, *Selected readings in psychology.* (See also Vogel, 1973.)	38	Moderate	Medium	Yes	Draws selections from popular books as well as journals	Is a most suitable collection for high school use—B. M. N.
Guthrie, *Encounter: Issues of human concern.*	27	Moderate	Medium	Yes; unusually appealing	Emphasizes mainly personality and adjustment	Should be of great interest to the 1970s high school student—O. P. P.

Table 1 (Continued)

Books of readings	No. of selections	Reading level	Level of sophistication required	Interest value to high school students	Unusual features	Selected comments from reviews
Harlow, Scientific American resource library: Readings in psychology (2 vols.). (See also Daniel, 1970.)	64, 51	Easy-moderate	Low-medium	Generally, yes	Written for the science-oriented layperson; liberally illustrated	Includes a good balance of relevant and abstract articles—R. A. K.
Kagan et al., Psychology: Adapted readings. (See also Vogel, 1973.)	35	Easy	Low-medium	Definitely	Is a mix of classics, relevant pieces, and "regular" psychology	Typical but commendable; does not distract the reader from its intended purpose of "bringing the material within the range of the beginning student's understanding"—P. O. M.
Karlins, Psychology and society: Readings for general psychology. (See also Vogel, 1973.)	33	Variable; moderate-difficult	Medium-high	High	Has a section titled "Psychology in the Service of Man," which is indicative of the book's focus	Has discussions and explanations preceding each section and each article—P. D. J.
Katz, Greenberg, & Warrick, Introductory psychology through science fiction (2nd ed.).	28	Moderate	Medium-high	Probably most attractive to college-oriented high school students	Uses science fiction to explore psychological concepts	Is organized into sections representing major concept areas in scientific psychology—for example, development, learning, personality; has introductions both to sections and to individual selections—K. W.
King, Readings for an introduction to psychology (3rd ed.). (See also Vogel, 1973.)	62	Easy-moderate	Low-medium	Yes	Includes information about careers in psychology	Gives applied areas unusually good treatment, with the exception of behavior modification—D. M. C.
Maas, Readings in psychology today (3rd ed.).	72	Moderate	Medium-high	Focus of most articles is not what one typically finds in high school psychology courses	Presents some of the best articles ever published in Psychology Today	Is appropriate for high school libraries but not as a text or basic reader; is too sophisticated for the high school student—R. J. S.

Table 1 (Continued)

Books of readings	No. of selections	Reading level	Level of sophistication required	Interest value to high school students	Unusual features	Selected comments from reviews
McCollom & Badore, *Exploring psychology: Introductory readings.* (See also Forgus, 1975.)	56	Easy	Low	High; scientifically sound and exciting to the student	Requires no previous knowledge of psychology for thorough enjoyment	Could almost serve as a text because of its well-written "bridges" and provocative discussion questions—M. M.
McGuigan & Woods, *Contemporary studies in psychology.* (See also Vogel, 1974.)	32	Easy-moderate	Low-medium	High	Aims to represent "psychology as it is" rather than "psychology as the uninitiated see it"; contains many articles rewritten by editors with authors' permission	Is successful in its aim, yet presents material easy enough for the "uninitiated"—B. M. N.
McKinney, *Psychology in action: Basic readings* (2nd ed.).	52	Moderate-difficult	Moderate	Medium-high	Combines empirical orientation with practical applications	Focuses on relevant social issues—M. W.
Melvin, Brodsky, & Fowler, *Psy fi one: An anthology of psychology in science fiction.*	20	Moderate	Medium-high	Probably most appealing to the more sophisticated science fiction readers and psychology students	Is an excellent anthology, with well-written introductions	Would not readily or easily teach the average or above-average high school student the difficult concepts reflected in the selections—R. J. S.
Milgram, *Psychology in today's world.* (See also Gillen, 1976.)	77	Easy	Low	High	Provides an excellent bridge between academic psychology and real-world problems; features a majority of articles written by professional journalists	Is restricted to topics of popular interest, giving some traditional areas short shift—P. D. J.
Notterman, *Readings in behavior.* (See also Vogel, 1973.)	30	Difficult	High	Limited to advanced classes in psychology or biology	Seasons some ponderous pieces with original reports of more spectacular recent achievements in empirical psychology	Is highly recommended but use is probably limited to accelerated classes in psychology or behavioral biology—H. S. P.

Table 1 (Continued)

Books of readings	No. of selections	Reading level	Level of sophistication required	Interest value to high school students	Unusual features	Selected comments from reviews
Pronko, *Panorama of psychology* (2nd ed.).	140	Moderate	Medium	Yes	Selections have been excerpted, condensed, and summarized, omitting many of the technical aspects that would bore the reader	Is frankly innovative, interesting, and well written; could almost be used as a text—D. K. H.
Sjule, *Contemporary psychology: A book of readings.*	42	Moderate	Low	Yes	Is weighted in favor of practical significance	Would be an excellent choice for high school use, but its datedness detracts from its contemporary intent—P. O. M.
Stricker & Merbaum, *Growth of personal awareness: A reader in psychology.* (See also Vogel, 1974.)	40	Easy	Low-medium	High	Contains selections written for the intelligent layperson, taken from newspapers and magazines of the popular press	Is an integrated package of interesting readings to supplement introductory courses—C. W. H.
Ulrich et al., *Control of human behavior* (3 vols.).	48, 50, 48	Easy, some difficult	Medium-high	Yes	Covers a diversity of areas, but basic theme is behavioral control	Although somewhat sophisticated, could be used in some high school classes—O. P. P./M. J.
Wertheimer & Rappoport, *Psychology and the problems of today.* (See also Kasschau, 1978.)	66	Difficult	High	Variable; some topics of high interest, others less stimulating to adolescents	Has thought-provoking photographs and quotations opening each section; has overviews preceding selections, introductions preceding sections, concluding essays following sections	Has timely, stimulating (in some cases, even exciting) selections from diverse sources; is concerned with the theoretical as well as the empirical; includes some highly controversial topics—E. B.
Whittaker, *Recent discoveries in psychology: Readings for the introductory course.* (See also Snellgrove, 1973.)	45	Moderate-difficult	Medium-high	Doubtful	Contains review-type articles that summarize data over a period of years; covers a range of topics	Does not live up to its title; few articles are stimulating—[a]

[a]Reviewer's name misplaced.

Table 1 (Continued)

Books of readings	No. of selections	Reading level	Level of sophistication required	Interest value to high school students	Unusual features	Selected comments from reviews
Wrench, *Readings in psychology: Foundations and applications.* (See also Vogel, 1973.)	34	Variable; easy-difficult	Variable; low-high	Medium	Aims to enhance students' "ability to evaluate psychological research evidence" by presenting reports of studies *in toto*	Has some odd omissions, some puzzling inclusions; has enough valuable articles to be a source book for the high school teacher but is more appropriate for use in college—M. M.
Zimbardo & Maslach, *Psychology for our times: Readings* (2nd ed.). (See also Popplestone, 1978.)	54	Moderate-difficult; appropriate for 12th grade	Medium	Medium-high	Has an eclectic and somewhat interdisciplinary flavor and a large proportion of distinctly contemporary selections; has overviews preceding sections, "thought-provoking questions, issues, or intellectual challenges" following sections.	Represents a real effort to guide the student and reinforce significant learning—J. M. C.

References

Daniel, R. S. Readings for the tuned in and the turned on. Contemporary Psychology, 1970, 15, 559-560. Review of Harlow, 1969.

Forgus, R. H. Esoteric introductions to psychology. Contemporary Psychology, 1975, 20, 636-639. Review of McCollom & Badore, 1973.

Gillen, B. Readings: "Pop" or "semi-pro"? Contemporary Psychology, 1976, 21, 409-411. Reviews of Atkinson, 1975; Dyal et al., 1975; Milgram, 1975.

Guthrie, P. Psychology: Present, past-present, and perplex. Contemporary Psychology, 1968, 13, 284-285. Review of Daniel, 1965.

Kasschau, R. A. Review of Wertheimer & Rappoport, 1978. Contemporary Psychology, 1978, 23, 374.

Popplestone, J. A. Once more, dear friends. Contemporary Psychology, 1978, 23, 142-151. Review of Zimbardo & Maslach, 1977.

Snellgrove, L. A mixed bag. Contemporary Psychology, 1973, 18, 652-654. Review of Whittaker, 1972.

Vogel, J. L. Potluck psychology: Books of readings. Contemporary Psychology, 1973, 18, 318-322. Reviews of Gazzaniga & Lovejoy, 1971; Gibbons & Connelly, 1970; Kagan et al., 1971; Karlins, 1971; King, 1971; Notterman, 1970; Wrench, 1971.

Vogel, J. L. Nine more: Books of readings. Contemporary Psychology, 1974, 19, 601-604. Reviews of McGuigan & Woods, 1972; Stricker & Merbaum, 1973.

Weiss, E. Review of Cohen, 1975. Science Books and Films, 1975, 11, 118.

Chapter 3

Reviews of Laboratory Manuals

This chapter contains reviews of laboratory manuals potentially useful to the beginning student of psychology. The manuals are classified below by various features that may be of interest. Initials appearing at the end of reviews are those of reviewers, whose full names are listed in the Preface. The designation O.P.P., for Oberlin project participant, has been used for all reviews done during the Oberlin project in summer 1970; we are unable to identify individual authors of those reviews. Addresses of publishers appear in Appendix A.

1. Animal behavior: Animal Welfare Institute; Hainsworth; McConnell; Orlans; Price & Stokes.
2. Animal suppliers listed: Flory & Sherman; Michael; Notterman; Orlans.
3. Brief summaries of classical published research: McConnell.
4. Expensive apparatus required: Flory & Sherman (detailed instructions for building it are given); McConnell; Michael; Notterman; Ost et al. (about one half require expensive apparatus).
5. Extensive statistics required and statistical tables given: Jung & Bailey; Notterman.
6. Human behavior (with most apparatus provided or easy to construct): Bunker et al.; Chandler; Fernald; Hergenhahn; Jung & Bailey; Ost et al.; Ray.
7. Innovative treatments of human behavior: Chandler; Homme & Klaus; Jung & Bailey; Ost et al.
8. Manuals designed to accompany particular textbooks: Ballachey; Michael; Notterman.
9. Material on preparing laboratory reports: Chandler; Hergenhahn; Jung & Bailey.
10. Operant approach: Christiano; Flory & Sherman; Hergenhahn; Homme & Klaus; Michael; Notterman; Ost et al.; Reese.
11. Statement on humane care and treatment of animals: Animal Welfare Institute; Hergenhahn; Orlans; Reese.
12. Statement on ethical principles in research with humans: Animal Welfare Institute; Hergenhahn; Jung & Bailey; Orlans.

Chapter 11 contains APA's Guidelines for the Use of Animals in School Science Behavior Projects and Guidelines for the Use of Human Participants in Research or Demonstrations Conducted by High School Students, with which every high school psychology teacher using demonstrations, experiments, or laboratory exercises should be thoroughly familiar.

Animal Welfare Institute. Humane biology projects (3rd ed.). Washington, D. C.: Author, 1977. 57 pp. Single copy free to teachers.
Although the book is designed to aid in the teaching of high school biology, about 15-20 of the 129 projects are also suitable for the high school psychology student or class. Examples of such projects are Eye Dominance, Depth Perception, Reaction Time, and Animal Senses. Several projects involve the

observation of animal behavior, which could be applied to the field of psychology by emphasizing the skills necessary for accurate observations as well as the errors made by different individuals observing the same phenomena.

Where animals are used in projects, considerable emphasis is placed on their proper care and treatment. A statement on the ethical care and treatment of animals is included at the beginning, and a statement on the ethical use of humans in experiments appears in the section titled "You as the Subject of Study." The reading level is easy for the average high school student. All materials needed for the projects related to psychology are easily obtained or constructed in a school shop.--L.S./M.J.

Ballachey, E. L. Study guide with brief research projects for Individual in society (D. Krech, R. S. Crutchfield, & E. L. Ballachey. New York: McGraw-Hill, 1962). New York: McGraw-Hill, 1963. 242 pp. $5.95 paper.

Although designed mainly for projects to be conducted outside the classroom by individual students, the suggested experiments can be adapted for high school classroom use. Experiments might also be assigned to individual students for extra credit. Extensive and time-consuming data collection and analysis are necessary for most experiments, but problems can be avoided by assigning the job of analysis to student committees. Specifically for social psychology, the manual includes experiments on communication, language, group behavior, and attitude formation and change.--O.P.P.

Bunker, B. B., Pearlson, H. B., & Schulz, J. W. A student's guide to conducting social science research. New York: Human Sciences Press, 1975. 120 pp. $3.95 paper.

One's first reaction to this book might be negative, but one should then be reminded of the title and read the concluding note To the Teacher. The book is not a self-sufficient text, nor is it meant to be. It is a student's guide, meant to be used closely with the teacher.

There are three sections. Part 1, Research Guide, making up the first half of the book, gives an accurate but very sketchy (e.g., "hypotheses" are simply and totally defined as "specific predictions") overview of the total research process--from identifying a problem through analyzing data to planning further research. Part 2 examines two published experiments, one concerning dating and the other concerning student power in school programs, in terms of the steps outlined in Part 1. Part 3 consists of class projects to give students some experience with surveys, field observations, controlled experiments, and formulation and testing of hypotheses.

An active and knowledgeable teacher is essential to this book. The language level seems appropriate for the high school student. References, which usually are really suggestions for further study, appear at the end of each subsection within Parts 1 and 2. They would be more valuable if annotated; if one is not familiar with them, one might not know which to use for further information on a particular point. Figure 9 on page 95 may confuse some people because the wrong numerator was used in the example.--R.S.H.

Chandler, K. A. Laboratory experiences for introductory psychology. Chicago: Aldine-Atherton, 1969. 97 pp. $3.45 paper.

The manual and an accompanying instructor's edition provide students with 11 experiments in such areas of psychology as perception, motor learning,

aptitudes, and thinking. The manual is readable for students at the senior
high school level. Subjects and apparatus needed for experiments are easily
obtained, sources of equipment are given for several experiments, and references are provided for each experiment. The manual includes an introductory
section on writing lab reports, complete with an example. There are places
for recording data, questions are asked of students (with limited space for
answers), and the pages are tear-outs.

In the case of certain experiments, more expository detail would be helpful. For example, in Experiment 4 a stopwatch is used to time verbal
responses of subjects, but no specific instructions are given for timing subjects' responses. It is difficult to time a verbal response accurately with
only a stopwatch, and this shortcoming should be pointed out in the instructor's edition. In Experiment 6 the author states that the order of presenting
different lists of words ". . . may well contribute to differences obtained
. . ." (p. 54), but he does not explain, nor ask students to explain, why.
Consequently the teachers who use this manual (as well as most others) may
wish to provide supplementary guidance in critical interpretation of procedures and results.--L.S.

Christiano, J. M. Experiments in operant conditioning: A self-instructional
     text. Bayport, N. Y.: Life Science Associates, 1974. 61 pp. $3.95
     paper.
There are a number of adequate short texts and lab manuals on the basic
principles of operant conditioning already on the market. Christiano has
written a really good combination of the two. He assumes that neither teacher
nor student has had experience in training rodents. As he indicates in the
introduction, this book contains everything one needs to know to raise and
condition a rat or mouse.

The first five units are devoted to basic terminology and such relevant
topics as how to set up and maintain a small rodent colony, how to collect and
record data, how to handle rodents, and how to deprive the subjects safely.
Units 6-12 cover the basic operant conditioning procedures of dipper and magazine training, shaping bar-pressing, extinction and spontaneous recovery,
schedules of reinforcement, creative training, stimulus discrimination, and
chaining. These units, like those on handling and deprivation, contain all
necessary data sheets and graphs, with clear examples of how observations are
to be recorded on them. Units 13 and 14 present brief but excellent discussions of professional applications of operant conditioning and the relevance
of these procedures for human behavior in general.

Throughout the manual Christiano writes clearly. Technical jargon is kept
to a minimum, and the reading level is appropriate for most high school
juniors and seniors.

Because of its self-instructional format, the book lends itself well to
use in independent study, as well as serving as a lab manual to supplement a
course in psychology or biology. The length of the course and the level of
sophistication of the students can determine whether all 14 units are assigned
or whether only the most basic exercises are undertaken.

All in all, Christiano's book deserves a four-star rating. Although it
will be particularly useful to the inexperienced high school or two-year college teacher with a very limited budget, it will serve well any teacher who is
seeking a clear introduction to basic experiments in operant conditioning.--D.M.C.

Fernald, L. D., Jr. Experiments and studies in general psychology.
   Boston: Houghton Mifflin, 1965. 200 pp. $5.95 paper.
   These 21 units of material, designed to supplement general psychology
texts and readings, might well serve as the text and lab manual of a one-semester high school course or as the core material for a two-semester high
school course. Included are units on such areas as behavior disorders and
sociometric methods as well as standard areas such as learning and psychophysics. The author states that the book was designed "specifically for those
general psychology courses for which laboratory apparatus, space, and hours
are unavailable" (p. ix). The material is clearly presented, with questions
that should provoke class discussions leading to transfer of material to
real-life situations. As a whole, the book would serve to introduce the high
school student to a wide range of psychological topics with an emphasis on
human behavior. In the hands of a sensitive teacher the book could serve as a
starting point for an exciting, "relevant" course. An instructor's manual
with adequate discussion questions is provided and is essential to the understanding of the author's objective. The questions allow the student a broad
range of responses that demand discussion to provide feedback and direction.--O.P.P.

Flory, R. K., & Sherman, J. G. Student laboratory experiments in operant conditioning. Roanoke, Va.: Scholars' Press, 1974. 97 pp. $4.00 paper.
   The nine experiments, just under two hours each, are healthy offspring of
the operant learning laboratories at Columbia University in the 1950s. A
brief introduction, a concise explanation of procedure, data forms, and questions are provided for each study.
   The manual includes superbly detailed instructions and blueprints for construction of a rat chamber, pellet dispenser, and control box. Also provided
are lists of apparatus, caging, and animal suppliers. Two reference works on
rat illness are noted.
   The manual is of uniformly high quality but of rather limited use, even
for those seeking an exclusively operant manual. Maintaining rats at 80% of
free-feeding weight would be difficult in a high school situation although 24-
or 48-hour deprivation could be substituted. More serious restrictions are
the minimal integration with learning principles and minimal information to
lead a curious student to related work. The burden thereby placed on both
teacher and text is probably overwhelming for most high school and university
settings; energetic, creative instructors with small classes may find the manual ideal.
   Most high schools (and colleges with large laboratories) will still find
the manual by Ellen Reese (Experiments in Operant Behavior) preferable when
combined with apparatus constructed by the plans in Scientific American, November 1975, pages 128-134.--C.P.

Hainsworth, M. D. Experiments in animal behavior. Boston: Houghton Mifflin,
   1967. 206 pp. $6.48 paper.
   Experiments in Animal Behavior is a superb little volume that merits serious consideration for a somewhat specialized function at the secondary level:
an in-depth supplement to the animal behavior component of the Biological Sciences Curriculum Study curriculum. The approach of the book is frankly exper-
imental-ethological, and the suggested experiments are ingeniously designed to
yield clear descriptive data on the behavior of a variety of lower organisms,

including protozoa, hydra, worms, insects, and amphibians. Teachers of secondary-level psychology courses are not likely to select this book because its subject matter overlaps little with the content of contemporary psychological pedagogy. This bias will prevent students from being exposed to an unusually clear and elegant exposition of scientific thought. Hainsworth leads the student to draw the obvious conclusions from data that would appear unambiguous, then gently suggests sources of contamination and alternate explanations. For accelerated secondary students, this material is as exciting and educationally sound as any available today in the psychological marketplace. Regardless of the level of one's educational charges, however, Experiments in Animal Behavior should be read and enjoyed by every serious teacher of the natural science of behavior.--H.S.P.

Hergenhahn, B. R. A self-directing introduction to psychological experimentation (2nd ed.). Monterey, Calif.: Brooks/Cole, 1974. 441 pp. $11.95 paper.

The 38 studies are organized into three chapters: 19 experiments in human behavior that require no technical apparatus (7 are new to this edition); 10 human experiments requiring standard laboratory apparatus; and 9 operant/Skinnerian rat studies. The 19 studies in the first chapter meet well Hergenhahn's avowed intention to present experiments that are of current interest to professionals as well as to students. The 19 studies in the second and third chapters are rather typical student projects although a couple have new twists. The apparatus is either not essential (e.g., one could use index cards instead of a memory drum), or it is easily built in a high school shop (e.g., a mirror-tracing device or a rat-conditioning chamber).

Each study includes (in admirably precise, concise style) a brief introduction, a complete explanation of method, data-analysis instructions, discussion questions (some standard, some provocative), extensive references, and--when appropriate--materials and data sheets.

The manual includes a chapter on report-writing (unfortunately based on the now obsolete 1967 APA Publication Manual): content, typing instructions, and a typed sample. The data-analysis chapter provides computation formulas, worked examples, and tables for three descriptive and seven inferential statistics. Some teacher background in statistics is assumed, but the statistics can be ignored throughout with only slight injury to the student's terminal proficiency. Ethics of research are considered for both human and animal subjects.

This creatively different, designed-for-college manual may suit those teachers who (a) have a background in experimentation (terms are introduced with the briefest of definitions; research design is implicitly treated), (b) teach superior high school students (the manual is pitched at a sophisticated reading level--approximately above-average first-year college students), (c) have a college library available, and (d) focus on human behavior. The manual is also recommended for a gifted student seeking initial ideas for science fair projects.--C.P.

Homme, L., & Klaus, D. J. Laboratory studies in the analysis of behavior: A
    manual of operant conditioning procedures for students in behavioral psy-
    chology (2nd ed.). Palo Alto, Calif.: Westinghouse Learning Press,
    1961. 102 pp. $4.75 paper.
    Although neobehavioristic in orientation, the manual can be used in an
introductory course. The first of three parts of the manual is devoted to a
series of 10 studies that demonstrate such classical phenomena as shaping,
extinction, secondary reinforcement, and chaining. Although the authors state
that each exercise takes about two hours to complete, many require more time.
Part 2 deals with the operant conditioning of human subjects and nicely takes
care of the question so often raised by students concerning whether or not
rats are people! Part 3 succinctly discusses experimental design and data
analysis in a low-level fashion that should not yield trembling responses from
anyone ordinarily encountering difficulties in these matters. The reviewer,
having used the manual as both student and teacher, feels it would be entirely
appropriate for most high school courses in psychology. Equipment needs are
minimal, and the apparatus construction required is described in
detail.--O.P.P.

Jung, J., & Bailey, J. H. Contemporary psychology experiments: Adaptations
    for laboratory (2nd ed.). New York: John Wiley, 1976. 212 pp. $6.95
    paper.
    In most respects the preface and to-the-instructor sections adequately
describe this laboratory manual: It is aimed at the college undergraduate,
its contents are true experiments rather than demonstrations, and no equipment
is needed. Although excellent for the more sophisticated college class, the
manual is probably impossibly advanced for the high school setting because it
requires that students have access to an extensive journal collection and that
data be collected outside of class. The 18 studies (11 of which were retained
from the 1966 edition) are moderately detailed variations on a published
study, each with an extension suggested in broad terms, for a total of 36 projects. There are a brief section on ethical issues and a four-page summary of
APA report format. Topics include experimenter bias, verbal conditioning and
instructional set, risk-taking, and invasion of personal space. One aim of
the authors was to demonstrate that not all experiments "arrive at definitive
and easily reproducible results" (p. vii). The authors have succeeded in
achieving this aim, and the result is a manual of high student interest and
realism, and one that places heavy demands on the teacher.
    The studies can be analyzed satisfactorily with simple techniques: graph,
percentage, mean (unfortunately termed "average"). The suggestions for inferential statistics are often dated; for example, multiple t-tests are used for
comparisons after ANOVA, rather than Tukey or Scheffe, and Siegel's 1956 Nonparametric Statistics for the Behavioral Sciences is cited rather than Mostel-
ler and Rourke's 1973 Sturdy Statistics. Also, the writing style is occasionally strained ("grows with increasing acceleration," p. 2) and prone to over-
statement. Nevertheless, this is the only published manual that the reviewer
would consider using for a college class without extensive modification.--C.P.

McConnell, J. V. (Ed.). <u>A manual of psychological experimentation on plana-
   rians</u> (2nd ed.). Ann Arbor, Mich.: Journal of Biological Psychology,
   1967. 128 pp. $3.50 paper.
   The manual contains eight sections on about everything needed for simple
and somewhat complex experiments on planarians. A ninth section contains 50-
plus pages of annotated bibliography that covers a wide variety of experimental data on planarians. For high school teachers or students who contemplate
experimenting with planarians, this is <u>the</u> source of information.
   Although the manual is written specifically for high school students,
those who wish to use it should have a basic understanding of classical conditioning procedures and terminology. Knowledge of operant techniques and terminology would also be of help. In addition, there should be some knowledge
of elementary chemistry terms, procedures for mixing solutions in correct pro-
portions, and some equipment (forming glass tubes) commonly found in a chemistry lab. If the more complicated grafting techniques are used, students will
also need a dissecting microscope.
   The manual contains many helpful suggestions on avoiding the pitfalls of
experimenting with planarians. The experiments would be most suitable for
more advanced high school psychology students.--L.S.

Michael, J. <u>Laboratory studies in operant behavior</u>. New York: McGraw-Hill,
   1963. 101 pp. $7.50 cloth.
   The manual was designed for a first-year-level college course in conjunction with the <u>Analysis of Behavior</u> by J. G. Holland and B. F. Skinner (New
York: McGraw-Hill, 1961). Michael imagines each student with an operant station, and the exercises are designed to be conducted for two hours a day, five
days a week for two weeks. The book is tied so closely to commercially constructed equipment that many of the detailed procedural instructions would
otherwise be inappropriate. The high school instructor might find the book
useful as a source of demonstrations. Also, the introduction closes with a
partial list of suppliers of equipment, rats, rat housing, food, and timers.--O.P.P.

Notterman, J. M. <u>Laboratory manual for experiments in behavior</u>. Philadelphia: Philadelphia Book Co., 1970. (Originally published by Random
   House, New York.) 119 pp. $2.95 paper.
   Notterman's manual is really designed for beginning courses in experimental psychology at the college level. It offers descriptions, instructions, and
recording materials for 10 experiments that range from psychophysical methods
through classical and operant conditioning to conflict and personality-test-
ing. Unfortunately a well-equipped behavior laboratory is a necessary pre-
requisite for nearly all of the studies, and this requirement may exceed the
resources of most high schools and junior colleges. However, if adequate
facilities are available, the manual would provide an excellent range of experiences in experimental measurement and manipulation of behavioral variables.
   All of the experiments are designed to yield data that can be analyzed
with relatively simple nonparametric techniques, which are themselves
described in the manual. Thus, under the guidance of a well-trained biology
or psychology teacher, the accelerated high school student who uses this manual could become a prime candidate for a summer research scholarship in virtually any behavioral laboratory.--H.S.P.

Orlans, F. B. <u>Animal care from protozoa to small mammals</u>. Menlo Park, Calif.:
    Addison-Wesley, 1977. 374 pp. $10.95 paper.
    Individual chapters on groups of animals (e.g., hydras, worms, insects,
fish, amphibians, reptiles, gerbils, and hamsters) discuss proper caging,
handling, diet, common diseases, suppliers, and post-study disposal. Many
comments helpful to choosing a species are included, along with some research
topic suggestions and references to laboratory manuals both biological and
psychological.
    One surprising omission is a chapter on birds. Although most birds are
not suitable under typical elementary or secondary school conditions, mention
of that fact would seem appropriate, along with some material on pigeons that
would be suitable. Similarly the chapter on experiments with humans seems
rather strange without at least some comment about the inappropriateness of
experiments with other primates at this level of education.
    Although much of the material is exemplary (e.g., the discussion of the
ecological risk of releasing an animal after an experiment and the giving of
temperatures in both Celsius and Fahrenheit), there are occasional lapses in
at least two of the nine chapters that this reviewer closely examined. (The
reviewer is inadequately familiar with the organisms dealt with in seven of
the chapters to offer a detailed evaluation of the technical discussion but
did read those chapters for clarity.) For instance, the statements that two
male rats/mice over the age of six weeks cannot share the same cage (p. 268)
and that rats cannot tolerate wire-mesh cage floors for over eight weeks (p.
262) and that wearing gloves while handling rats "will result in savage animals" (p. 268) are all untrue. The author also fails in several places adequately to distinguish between ritual fighting of small mammals to maintain a
hierarchy and actual fighting.
    In the reviewer's opinion, the most distressing feature of the book is the
rather blind acceptance of the standards of the Humane Society of the United
States for elementary and secondary schools. The standards miss the mark in
two regards: They are unduly strict, on occasion, for vertebrate work, and
they are quite casual about reckless disregard for lower organisms. The idea
seems to be that animals are worth protecting to the degree that they superficially resemble humans. The reviewer would suggest instead the weighing of
the pedagogical benefit (including the ability of the student to comprehend,
the ability of the teacher to supervise, and the physical facilities available) against the value of the organisms to be temporarily or permanently in-
jured, all in a very serious context of "regard for all life." Thus, work
quite in violation of the Humane Society's standards might be appropriate at
the Bronx High School of Science, and numerous studies casually suggested in
the text would be inappropriate at most elementary schools (e.g., extreme pH
media for euglena, squashing stentors, preparing fresh juice of brine shrimp,
and snipping off snail tentacles).
    Overall, the reviewer would recommend the book with reservations, primar-
ily reservations concerning the ethical attitude toward educational projects.--C.P.

Ost, J. W. P., Allison, J., Vance, W. B., & Restle, F. <u>A laboratory introduc-
    tion to psychology</u>. New York: Adademic Press, 1969. 214 pp. $7.00
    paper.
    The experiments with rats and the five experiments on human sensory pro-
cesses require equipment not ordinarily available to high school teachers.

The eight experiments in human learning and performance can be used separately and do not require expensive and complicated apparatus. All eight of these experiments are interesting and, with the possible exception of the two game experiments, are easy to perform. Adequate data sheets are included. In all cases, however, the teacher would need to know more about the topic and about the treatment of data and their implications than is given in the manual itself.--O.P.P.

Price, E. O., & Stokes, A. W. Animal behavior in laboratory and field (2nd ed.). San Francisco: W. H. Freeman, 1975. 130 pp. $7.00 paper.
    Animal Behavior in Laboratory and Field is an exceptional laboratory manual! Following the brief introductory chapters (in which general methods of observing and recording animal behavior are described) are two sections--the first on laboratory studies and the second on field studies--that deal with perhaps the broadest range of species in any laboratory manual currently available. More than 20 species are represented.
    Only a very few of the experiments require the use of species that would be troublesome to house in most secondary schools. The bulk of the experiments are to be carried out on species that require only minimal animal-care facilities--for example, blowfly, garter snake, earthworm, flour beetle, cricket, and cichlid fish.
    The experimental methods are clearly and interestingly described and include suggestions for proper data collection, care of the experimental animals, construction of apparatus, etc. Most of the experiments require very simple apparatus that could be constructed in any high school shop or made up from components found in a high school chemistry or biology laboratory.
    A great many of the studies use invertebrates. Of those that require the use of vertebrates, only one calls for surgery (the implantation of testosterone beneath the skin). Several of the recommended "additional studies" do require minor surgery or injections, but these could be left out of the curriculum in those schools in which the teacher lacks training in the technique. Students are likely to find most interesting the opportunity for field observation of five species (including homo sapiens) in their natural environment.
    Few of the experiments require a high level of expertise on the part of the student or teacher. Any secondary school psychology program that includes a unit on animal behavior would profit from the use of Animal Behavior in Laboratory and Field.--P.D.J.

Ray, W. S. Simple experiments in psychology: A laboratory manual. New York: Human Sciences Press, 1973. 120 pp. $4.95 paper.
    This laboratory manual contains nine well-thought-out experiments and exercises that are appropriate for basic high school psychology courses. The experiments represent a variety of areas in psychology. The primary goals of the author are to make the student aware of the need for control and standardized experimental conditions and to evaluate both the reliability of selected information and sources of information. The author's effort will be appreciated by any high school teacher whose students relate to lab periods as playtime or feel that the behavior of "one friend who lives down the street" is a sufficient sample to generalize to the entire world.

In addition to including an instructor's manual and a separate Student's Introduction, Ray gives other indications of appreciating the needs of high school students and teachers. All instructions are clearly written in language that beginning psychology students can understand. A Self-Test is given after each procedure section to ensure that all experimenters or "task administrators" know exactly what is to be done. There are summaries of procedures for quick reference by students. Discussion sections relate the specific hypothesis and purpose of each exercise to the real world.

All apparatus can be easily constructed by students at very minimal cost. The text is drilled for loose-leaf binders and is not bound; thus, the experiments can be reorganized to fit individual curriculums and can be handed out to students at appropriate times. No special knowledge or facility with statistics is required. Teachers need only be able to calculate means and percentages.--J.M.C.

Reese, E. P. Experiments in operant behavior. New York: Irvington Publishers, 1964. (Originally published by Appleton-Century-Crofts, New York.) 209 pp. $8.95 paper.

The manual is more than just an expanded pigeon-using version of the Homme and Klaus manual. It is carefully--almost too carefully--planned for use not only in a one-semester two-hour twice-weekly lab meeting but also for shorter (trimester) periods. It answers the frequent criticism that the student is given no information concerning care, handling, and biological nature of the subject. Further, lists of equipment (both necessary and optional) and suppliers, and directions for homemade apparatus, are supplied. In addition, the manual contains an explication of the rationale for operant-conditioning experimentation, as well as the APA statement "Guiding Principles for the Humane Care and Use of Animals." Given that a high school curriculum in psychology or biology includes two two-hour-per-week laboratories, this manual would be an appropriate choice for the high school course in psychology. It could also serve as a source for demonstrations conducted by the teacher.--O.P.P.

Chapter 4

Psychological Periodicals for the High School

The selection of periodicals that follows was made from those published by APA, those offered members of APA at special rates, and a few
selected for special reasons. Using criteria of cost and suitability for
the high school audience, we have noted several for attention (*) but
have offered brief descriptions for all. The periodicals are first
listed alphabetically, then all except Psychological Abstracts are categorized by type.
    Given space and budget limitations, careful selection is essential.
Examination of a publication may be desirable before ordering. A copy
may be available in a local college or public library, or a publisher may
be willing to supply a sample for examination purposes.
    No attempt was made to survey more popular sources. Some of these
sources are quite good and interesting; others may be used as bad examples. For a listing of additional journals and more detailed descriptions, see A. Markle and R. C. Rinn, Author's Guide to Journals in Psychology, Psychiatry, and Social Work (New York: Haworth Press, 1977) or
M. Tompkins and N. Shirley, Serials in Psychology and Allied Fields (2nd
ed.) (Troy, N. Y.: Whitston Publishing Co., 1976).
    For $7.50 a high school psychology teacher can become an affiliate of
the APA. High School Teacher Affiliates receive the APA's monthly newspaper, the Monitor, and are eligible for subscriptions to APA journals at
member rates, which are substantially less than regular rates.

Periodicals by Category

Journals of Original Empirical Research Reports

Adolescence
American Journal of Orthopsychiatry
American Journal of Psychology
Animal Learning and Behavior
Child Development
Developmental Psychology
Educational and Psychological Measurement
Genetic Psychology Monographs
Journal of Abnormal Psychology
Journal of Applied Behavior Analysis
Journal of Applied Psychology
Journal of Biological Psychology/The Worm Runner's Digest
Journal of Comparative and Physiological Psychology
Journal of Consulting and Clinical Psychology
Journal of Counseling Psychology
Journal of Educational Psychology
Journal of Experimental Child Psychology
Journal of Experimental Psychology: Animal Behavior
   Processes
Journal of Experimental Psychology: General
Journal of Experimental Psychology: Human Learning and
   Memory
Journal of Experimental Psychology: Human Perception and
   Performance
Journal of Experimental Social Psychology
Journal of General Psychology
Journal of Genetic Psychology
Journal of Personality
Journal of Personality and Social Psychology
Journal of Psychology
Journal of Research in Personality
Journal of Social Psychology
Journal of the Experimental Analysis of Behavior
Memory and Cognition
Merrill-Palmer Quarterly
Perception and Psychophysics
Perceptual and Motor Skills
Physiological Psychology
Psychological Record
Psychological Reports
Science
Teaching of Psychology

Journals of Application and Interpretation

Adolescence
American Journal of Orthopsychiatry

American Psychologist
Behavior Research Methods and Instrumentation
Child Development
Developmental Psychology
Educational and Psychological Measurement
Journal of Abnormal Psychology
Journal of Applied Behavior Analysis
Journal of Applied Psychology
Journal of Consulting and Clinical Psychology
Journal of Counseling Psychology
Journal of Educational Psychology
Journal of Experimental Child Psychology
Journal of Psychology
Journal of Research in Personality
Journal of Social Issues
Journal of the Experimental Analysis of Behavior
Merrill-Palmer Quarterly
Personnel and Guidance Journal
Professional Psychology
Psychological Reports
Psychology in the Schools
Teaching of Psychology

Journals of Theories and Literature Reviews

American Journal of Orthopsychiatry
American Psychologist
American Scientist
Child Development
Contemporary Psychology
Journal of General Psychology
Journal of the Experimental Analysis of Behavior
Personnel and Guidance Journal
Psychological Bulletin
Psychological Record
Psychological Reports
Psychological Review
Scientific American

Journals and Magazines with General and/or Popular Appeal

American Psychologist
American Scientist
Current Lifestudies
Human Behavior
Journal of Biological Psychology/The Worm Runner's Digest
Journal of Social Issues
Psychology Today
Science
Scientific American

TABLE 2

Descriptions of Psychological Periodicals

Journal name and address for subscription orders	Issues per year	Cost per year (in dollars)†			Reading level	Typical article length (in pages)	Description
		Library	Individual	Student			
Adolescence Libra Publishers, Inc., 391 Willets Rd., Roslyn Heights, Long Island, NY 11577	4	$20.00	$16.00	$16.00	Medium	8–20	Covers a somewhat wider range of topics than the title suggests
American Journal of Orthopsychiatry American Orthopsychiatric Association, Publications Sales Office, 49 Sheridan Ave., Albany, NY 12210	4	$16.00	$16.00	$10.00	Medium	5–15	Concern is with maintenance of normal human behavior and treatment of behavior disorders
American Journal of Psychology University of Illinois Press, Urbana, IL 61801	4	$15.00	$15.00	$15.00	Medium-high	6–12	Reports of original research in general-experimental psychology and short notes, discussions, and book reviews
American Psychologist American Psychological Association, 1200 Seventeenth St., N.W., Washington, DC 20036	12	$18.00	$18.00 ($5.00 for APA members)	$18.00 ($5.00 for student affiliates of APA)	Medium-high	1–6	The official publication of the APA containing archival documents, comments, convention calendars, and regular articles on current issues or broad aspects of psychology
American Scientist Sigma Xi, The Scientific Research Society, 345 Whitney Ave., New Haven, CT 06511	6	$15.00	$15.00	$15.00	Medium-high	4–12	Articles, book reviews, and letters representing all sciences; averages about one article on psychology per issue
Animal Learning and Behavior The Psychonomic Society, 1108 West 34th St., Austin, TX 78705	4	$20.00	$10.00	$ 6.25	Medium-high	4–6	Reports of research in the broad categories of animal learning, motivation, emotion, and comparative animal behavior

*Recommended for the high school audience on the basis of cost and suitability.
†Prices are subject to change and should be verified before ordering.

Table 2 (Continued)

Journal name and address for subscription orders	Issues per year	Cost per year (in dollars)†			Reading level	Typical article length (in pages)	Description
		Library	Individual	Student			
Behavior Research Methods and Instrumentation The Psychonomic Society, 1108 West 34th St., Austin, TX 78705	6	$25.00	$12.50	$ 8.00	Medium-high	3–7	Papers on methods, designs, instrumentation, techniques, and computer technology for behavioral research; product information; notes
Child Development University of Chicago Press, 5801 Ellis Ave., Chicago, IL 60637	4	$40.00	$40.00	$40.00	Medium-high	10–20	Empirical reports and theoretical papers relating to basic issues in development
Contemporary Psychology American Psychological Association, 1200 Seventeenth St., N.W., Washington, DC 20036	12	$25.00	$25.00 ($10.00 for APA members)	$25.00 ($10.00 for student affiliates of APA)	Medium	1–2	Critical reviews of books, films, tapes, and other media, representing a cross section of psychological literature
Current Lifestudies Curriculum Innovations, Inc., 501 Lake Forest Ave., Highwood, IL 60040	9	$ 3.50 (minimum of 15 subscriptions to one address)	$ 3.50 (minimum of 15 subscriptions to one address)	$ 3.50 (minimum of 15 subscriptions to one address)	Low	3–8	A magazine for high school students; accompanied by a teacher's edition; articles on human development and psychology; Human Sexuality Supplement available for $ .95 additional per student
Developmental Psychology American Psychological Association, 1200 Seventeenth St., N.W., Washington, DC 20036	6	$30.00	$30.00 ($12.00 for APA members)	$30.00 ($12.00 for student affiliates of APA)	Medium-high	1–8	Chronological age as well as sex, socioeconomic status, and effects of physical-growth variables are all considered developmental variables for the entire age span and for retardate and cross-species comparisons

*Recommended for the high school audience on the basis of cost and suitability.
†Prices are subject to change and should be verified before ordering.

Table 2 (Continued)

Journal name and address for subscription orders	Issues per year	Cost per year (in dollars)†			Reading level	Typical article length (in pages)	Description
		Library	Individual	Student			
Educational and Psychological Measurement P.O. Box 6807, College Station, Durham, NC 27708	4	$25.00	$25.00	$25.00	Medium-high	8-16	Discussions of problems in measurement of individual differences, reports on research and development, and discussion of the use of tests and testing programs for various purposes
Genetic Psychology Monographs Journal Press, P.O. Box 543, 2 Commercial St., Provincetown, MA 02657	4	$30.00	$30.00	$30.00 (special teacher and student rate of $75.00 for subscription to all five Journal Press journals)	Medium	20-50	Developmental, comparative, and clinical psychology; each number contains one or more complete researches
*High School Psychology Teacher (formerly Periodically) American Psychological Association, Clearinghouse on Precollege Psychology, 1200 Seventeenth St., N.W., Washington, DC 20036	5	Free	Free	Free	Low	Not applicable	Brief information items on resources for teaching psychology at the secondary school level; briefings on instructional topics; demonstrations; reviews of instructional materials
*Human Behavior Subscription Department, P.O. Box 2810, Boulder, CO 80302	12	$14.00	$14.00	$14.00	Low-medium	3-7	Articles on social science topics, interviews with social scientists, and news about current research

*Recommended for the high school audience on the basis of cost and suitability.
†Prices are subject to change and should be verified before ordering.

Table 2 (Continued)

Journal name and address for subscription orders	Issues per year	Cost per year (in dollars)†			Reading level	Typical article length (in pages)	Description
		Library	Individual	Student			
Journal of Abnormal Psychology American Psychological Association, 1200 Seventeenth St., N.W., Washington, DC 20036	6	$28.00	$28.00 ($14.00 for APA members)	$28.00 ($14.00 for student affiliates of APA)	Medium-high	6–10	Basic research and theory in the broad field of abnormal behavior, its determinants, and its correlates
Journal of Applied Behavior Analysis Department of Human Development, University of Kansas, Lawrence, KS 66045	4	$18.00	$10.00	$ 6.00 (four-year limit)	Medium-high	6–10	Applications of operant conditioning principles to problem behavior and teaching techniques
Journal of Applied Psychology American Psychological Association, 1200 Seventeenth St., N.W., Washington, DC 20036	6	$30.00	$30.00 ($16.00 for APA members)	$30.00 ($16.00 for student affiliates of APA)	Medium-high	6–10	Primarily original investigations of applications of psychology in business and industry
Journal of Biological Psychology/The Worm Runner's Digest P.O. Box 7590, Ann Arbor, MI 48107	2	$ 5.00	$ 5.00 ($4.00 for APA members)	$ 4.00	Low-medium	1–6	Papers and book reviews in biological psychology and humorous articles and cartoons
Journal of Comparative and Physiological Psychology American Psychological Association, 1200 Seventeenth St., N.W., Washington, DC 20036	6	$45.00	$45.00 ($20.00 for APA members)	$45.00 ($20.00 for student affiliates of APA)	High	6–10	Research reports on physiological mechanisms of behavior or biological mechanisms of species-typical behavior
Journal of Consulting and Clinical Psychology American Psychological Association, 1200 Seventeenth St., N.W., Washington, DC 20036	6	$32.00	$32.00 ($18.00 for APA members)	$32.00 ($18.00 for student affiliates of APA)	Medium-high	4–8	Research in clinical psychology, psychological diagnosis, psychotherapy, and personal psychopathology

†Prices are subject to change and should be verified before ordering.

Table 2 (Continued)

Journal name and address for subscription orders	Issues per year	Cost per year (in dollars)†			Reading level	Typical article length (in pages)	Description
		Library	Individual	Student			
Journal of Counseling Psychology American Psychological Association, 1200 Seventeenth St. N.W., Washington, DC 20036	6	$20.00	$20.00 ($8.00 for APA members)	$20.00 ($8.00 for student affiliates of APA)	Medium-high	3–8	Research on counseling theory and practice
Journal of Educational Psychology American Psychological Association, 1200 Seventeenth St. N.W., Washington, DC 20036	6	$30.00	$30.00 ($15.00 for APA members)	$30.00 ($15.00 for student affiliates of APA)	Medium-high	6–10	Original investigations and theoretical papers dealing with problems of learning and teaching and with the psychological development, relationships, and adjustment of the individual
Journal of Experimental Child Psychology Academic Press, Inc., 111 Fifth Ave., New York, NY 10003	6	$88.00	$44.00	$44.00	Medium-high	6–12	Papers in which the behavior and development of children are clearly related to their determining variables
Journal of Experimental Psychology: Animal Behavior Processes American Psychological Association, 1200 Seventeenth St., N.W., Washington, DC 20036	4	$14.00	$14.00 ($7.00 for APA members)	$14.00 ($7.00 for student affiliates of APA)	High	14	Experimental studies of the basic mechanisms of perception, learning, motivation, and performance, especially in infrahuman animals
Journal of Experimental Psychology: General American Psychological Association, 1200 Seventeenth St., N.W., Washington, DC 20036	4	$14.00	$14.00 ($8.00 for APA members)	$14.00 ($8.00 for student affiliates of APA)	High	16	Integrative reports in any area of experimental psychology

†Prices are subject to change and should be verified before ordering.

Table 2 (Continued)

Journal name and address for subscription orders	Issues per year	Cost per year (in dollars)†			Reading level	Typical article length (in pages)	Description
		Library	Individual	Student			
Journal of Experimental Psychology: Human Learning and Memory American Psychological Association, 1200 Seventeenth St., N.W., Washington, DC 20036	6	$24.00	$24.00 ($14.00 for APA members)	$24.00 ($14.00 for student affiliates of APA)	High	11	Experimental studies on fundamental acquisition, retention, and transfer processes in human behavior
Journal of Experimental Psychology: Human Perception and Performance American Psychological Association, 1200 Seventeenth St., N.W., Washington, DC 20036	4	$20.00	$20.00 ($10.00 for APA members)	$20.00 ($10.00 for student affiliates of APA)	High	11	Experimental studies of information-processing operations and their relation to experience and performance
Journal of Experimental Social Psychology Academic Press, Inc., 111 Fifth Ave., New York, NY 10003	6	$49.00	$24.50	$24.50	Medium-high	6–12	Current research in various areas of social psychology
Journal of General Psychology Journal Press, P.O. Box 543, 2 Commercial St., Provincetown, MA 02657	4	$30.00	$30.00	$30.00 (special teacher and student rate of $75.00 for subscription to all five Journal Press journals)	Medium	4–16	Experimental, physiological, and theoretical psychology with briefly reported replications, refinements, and comments

†Prices are subject to change and should be verified before ordering.

Table 2 (Continued)

Journal name and address for subscription orders	Issues per year	Cost per year (in dollars)†			Reading level	Typical article length (in pages)	Description
		Library	Individual	Student			
Journal of Genetic Psychology Journal Press, P.O. Box 543, 2 Commercial St., Provincetown, MA 02657	4	$30.00	$30.00	$30.00 (special teacher and student rate of $75.00 for subscription to all five Journal Press journals)	Medium	6–10	Developmental, comparative, and clinical psychology with briefly reported replications and refinements and occasional book reviews
Journal of Personality Duke University Press, P.O. Box 6697, College Station, Durham, NC 27708	4	$18.00	$18.00 ($12.00 for APA members)	$18.00 ($12.00 for student affiliates of APA)	High	10–15	Scientific investigations in the field of personality; current stress is on experimental studies of behavior dynamics and character structure, personality-related consistencies in cognitive processes, and development of personality in its cultural context
Journal of Personality and Social Psychology American Psychological Association, 1200 Seventeenth St., N.W., Washington, DC 20036	12	$60.00	$60.00 ($20.00 for APA members)	$60.00 ($20.00 for student affiliates of APA)	Medium-high	4–12	Original reports of research, methodology, and theory in personality and social psychology; criticism; literature reviews
Journal of Psychology Journal Press, P.O. Box 543, 2 Commercial St., Provincetown, MA 02657	6	$45.00	$45.00	$45.00 (special teacher and student rate of $75.00	Medium	4–16	Broad subject coverage

†Prices are subject to change and should be verified before ordering.

Table 2 (Continued)

Journal name and address for subscription orders	Issues per year	Cost per year (in dollars)†			Reading level	Typical article length (in pages)	Description
		Library	Individual	Student			
Journal of Research in Personality, Academic Press, Inc., 111 Fifth Ave., New York, NY 10003	4	$45.00	$22.50	$22.50 (for subscription to all five Journal Press Journals)	Medium-high	6–12	Experimental studies in the field of personality, with treatment of general, physiological, motivational, learning, perceptual, cognitive, and social processes
Journal of Social Issues, Society for the Psychological Study of Social Issues, Publication Office, P.O. Box 1248, Ann Arbor, MI 48106	4	$20.00	$14.00	$ 9.00	Low-medium	4–20	Issues typically organized around a single theme or topic, seeking to bring theory and practice into focus on human problems of the group
Journal of Social Psychology, Journal Press, P.O. Box 543, 2 Commercial St., Provincetown, MA 02657	6	$45.00	$45.00	$45.00 (special teacher and student rate of $75.00 for subscription to all five Journal Press journals)	Medium	6–10	Studies of persons in group settings and of culture and personality; special attention to cross-cultural articles and notes and to briefly reported replications and refinements
Journal of the Experimental Analysis of Behavior, Kay Dinsmoor, Department of Psychology, Indiana University, Bloomington, IN 47401	6	$30.00	$10.00	$ 5.00	Medium-high	1–16	Primarily reports of experiments relevant to the behavior of individual organisms; operant conditioning

†Prices are subject to change and should be verified before ordering.

Table 2 (Continued)

Journal name and address for subscription orders	Issues per year	Cost per year (in dollars)†			Reading level	Typical article length (in pages)	Description
		Library	Individual	Student			
Memory and Cognition The Psychonomic Society, 1108 West 34th St., Austin, TX 78705	6	$37.00	$18.50	$12.00	Medium-high	4–8	Reports of research in human memory and learning, conceptual processes, psycholinguistics, problem-solving, thinking, decision-making, and skilled performance
Merrill-Palmer Quarterly Merrill-Palmer Institute, 71 E. Ferry Ave., Detroit, MI 48202	4	$14.00	$14.00	$14.00	Medium	4–12	Papers representing the various disciplines bearing on human development, personality, and social relations
Perception & Psychophysics The Psychonomic Society, 1108 West 34th St., Austin, TX 78705	12	$60.00	$30.00	$20.00	High	3–7	Experimental investigations of sensory processes, perception, and psychophysics
Perceptual and Motor Skills P.O. Box 9229, Missoula, MT 59807	6	$91.40	$45.70 (for members of APA or equivalent professional organization)	$45.70 (for student affiliates of APA or equivalent professional organization)	Medium	4–12	Experimental, methodological, and theoretical articles dealing with perception or motor skills
Personnel and Guidance Journal American Personnel and Guidance Association, 1607 New Hampshire Ave., N.W., Washington, DC 20009	10	$20.00	$20.00	$20.00	Medium	4–8	Articles directed to the common interests of counselors and personnel workers at all educational levels and dealing with professional and scientific issues, critical integrations of published research, and descriptions of new techniques

†Prices are subject to change and should be verified before ordering.

Table 2 (Continued)

Journal name and address for subscription orders	Issues per year	Cost per year (in dollars)†			Reading level	Typical article length (in pages)	Description
		Library	Individual	Student			
Physiological Psychology The Psychonomic Society, 1108 West 34th St., Austin, TX 78705	4	$25.00	$12.50	$ 8.00	High	4–6	Reports of studies in which physiological manipulations and/or measures are employed as independent or dependent variables
Professional Psychology American Psychological Association, 1200 Seventeenth St., N.W., Washington, DC 20036	6	$18.00	$18.00 ($12.00 for APA members)	$18.00 ($12.00 for student affiliates of APA)	Low-medium	4–6	Articles on the applications of psychology and the education and training of professional psychologists
Psychological Abstracts American Psychological Association, 1200 Seventeenth St., N.W., Washington, DC 20036	12	$260.00	$260.00 ($45.00 for APA members)	$260.00 ($45.00 for student affiliates of APA)	Medium	One paragraph	Nonevaluative summaries of the world's literature on psychology and related subjects
Psychological Bulletin American Psychological Association, 1200 Seventeenth St., N.W., Washington, DC 20036	6	$35.00	$35.00 ($15.00 for APA members)	$35.00 ($15.00 for student affiliates of APA)	High	6–12	Evaluative reviews and interpretations of substantive and methodological issues in the psychological research literature
Psychological Record Kenyon College, Gambier, OH 43022	4	$10.00	$ 6.00	$ 6.00	Medium-high	6–12	Theoretical and experimental articles, comments on current developments in psychology, and book reviews
Psychological Reports P.O. Box 9229, Missoula, MT 59807	6	$91.40	$45.70 (for members of APA or equivalent professional organization)	$45.70 (for student affiliates of APA or equivalent professional organization)	Medium	4–10	Experimental, theoretical, and speculative articles, special reviews, and comments

†Prices are subject to change and should be verified before ordering.

Table 2 (Continued)

Journal name and address for subscription orders	Issues per year	Cost per year (in dollars)†			Reading level	Typical article length (in pages)	Description
		Library	Individual	Student			
Psychological Review American Psychological Association, 1200 Seventeenth St., N.W., Washington, DC 20036	6	$20.00	$20.00 ($8.00 for APA members)	$20.00 ($8.00 for student affiliates of APA)	High	10–20	Articles that make theoretical contributions to any area of scientific psychology
Psychology in the Schools Clinical Psychology Publishing Co., Inc., 4 Conant Square, Brandon, VT 05733	4	$25.00	$15.00 (for APA members)	$10.00	Medium	6–12	Research, opinion, and practice in the field of school psychology
Psychology Today P.O. Box 2990, Boulder, CO 80302	12	$12.00	$12.00	$12.00	Low-medium	2–6	Popular and serious articles, experimental reports, and analyses covering a wide variety of topics; book reviews
Science American Association for the Advancement of Science, 1515 Massachusetts Ave., N.W., Washington, DC 20005	52	$60.00	$28.00 (includes AAAS membership)	$18.00 (includes AAAS membership)	Medium-high	1–8	Articles and brief technical reports representing all sciences; book reviews; science news; letters; editorials
Scientific American 415 Madison Ave., New York, NY 10007	12	$18.00	$18.00	$18.00	Medium	8–12	Articles, book reviews, letters, and other short notes representing all sciences
Society Magazine (formerly *Transaction*) transaction, inc., Rutgers—The State University, New Brunswick, NJ 08903	6	$18.00	$15.00 (single issue free to teachers who order 10 or more of that issue for classroom use)	$10.00	Low-medium	1–10	Articles, comments, and book reviews in the social sciences, representing not only our own but other cultures

*Recommended for the high school audience on the basis of cost and suitability.
†Prices are subject to change and should be verified before ordering.

Table 2 (Continued)

Journal name and address for subscription orders	Issues per year	Cost per year (in dollars)†			Reading level	Typical article length (in pages)	Description
		Library	Individual	Student			
Teaching of Psychology Robert S. Daniel, Editor, Department of Psychology, McAlester Hall, University of Missouri, Columbia, MO 65201	4	$10.00	$ 4.00	$ 4.00	Low-medium	3–4	Articles and other materials on the teaching of psychology, chiefly at the college level; book and media reviews

*Recommended for the high school audience on the basis of cost and suitability.
†Prices are subject to change and should be verified before ordering.

Society Magazine

Journals, Magazines, and Newsletters Concerned with Teaching

    American Psychologist
    Contemporary Psychology
    Current Lifestudies
    High School Psychology Teacher
    Journal of Educational Psychology
    Journal of Experimental Psychology: Human Learning and
       Memory
    Psychology in the Schools
    Teaching of Psychology

Chapter 5

Supplementary Readings:
Biographies, Novels, Case Studies, and Other Books
Written at a High-Interest Level

Ivan N. McCollom

In addition to the regular textbook and technical references, students may wish to have access to books of a slightly different nature. These are books that will be read not because they are required but because they are interesting reading. They should, of course, be sound psychology as well. The list that follows is an attempt to identify such books for the first course in psychology, particularly at the high school level. Such a list must be fairly long. There needs to be ample room for choice, for what will interest one student will not interest another.

This list is not designed to be placed in the student's hands "as is." The instructor will need to select those titles that relate to the course content. Also, there will be some books of which some instructors will not approve, for various reasons. And each instructor will no doubt have favorites that are not included here.

Particular caution should be exercised in relation to novels. Novelists have a freedom not given to psychologists; they can have their characters behave as they choose. Psychologists are limited to statements of behavioral relationships that have been found to be valid. But there are some novelists who are good psychologists. Some novels present valid portraits of human behavior. Students will need special help in learning to distinguish between plausible and implausible portraits.

The list for the second edition of the Resource Book was compiled by Glen R. Thomas of Mary Washington College. In this revision I have added a number of titles and deleted some that did not meet my own criteria. However, because no one can have read all of the books from which a selection might be made, there are titles remaining because I do not know them and am relying on the judgment of the compiler of the previous list. The instructor has the final responsibility for judging the adequacy of a book as a contribution to the course being taught. The final judges of the interest level will always be the students. Their judgments will vary, dependent on many factors.

General

Adcock, C. J. Fundamentals of psychology. Baltimore: Penguin, 1964. $2.95 paper. A textbook, but highly readable and sufficiently brief to make it a good overview at the beginning of a first course in psychology or a review at the end.

Cantril, H., & Bumstead, C. H. Reflections on the human venture. New York: New York University Press, 1960. $12.00 cloth. Quotations from a wide range of literature woven into a book that provides a depth of understanding of psychology.

Hall, C. H. A primer of Freudian psychology. New York: New American
    Library, 1973. $1.25 paper. An introduction to the ideas of a pio-
    neer psychologist whose name has become a household word.

Wilson, J. R. (Ed.). The mind. Morristown, N. J.: Silver Burdett,
    1969. $10.20 cloth. (Originally published by Time-Life Books,
    1964.) A beautifully illustrated book providing an overall view of
    the field of psychology; a good introduction or a good review.

Methods of Measurement and Experimentation

Agnew, N. M., & Pyke, S. W. The science game: An introduction to
    research in the behavioral sciences (2nd ed.). Englewood Cliffs,
    N. J.: Prentice-Hall, 1978. $7.95 paper. An explanation of the
    methods, procedures, and tools used by behavioral scientists.

Anderson, B. F. The psychology experiment: An introduction to the
    scientific method (2nd ed.). Monterey, Calif.: Brooks/Cole, 1971.
    $4.95 paper. A helpful book for students interested in performing a
    psychological experiment.

Dustin, D. How psychologists do research: The example of anxiety.
    Englewood Cliffs, N. J.: Prentice-Hall, 1969. Out of print. An
    explanation, by example, of the necessary steps in performing good
    psychological research.

Gardner, M. Fads and fallacies in the name of science (2nd ed.).
    New York: Dover, 1957. $3.50 paper. A discussion of ideas that
    pretend to be valid but do not meet the tests of science.

Huff, D., & Geis, I. How to lie with statistics. New York: W. W.
    Norton, 1954. $5.95 cloth; $1.95 paper. An entertaining and useful
    account of how the innocent reader is often misled by the misuse of
    statistics and graphs.

Porteus, S. D. A psychologist of sorts: The autobiography and publi-
    cations of the inventor of the Porteus Maze Tests. Palo Alto,
    Calif.: Pacific Books, 1969. $7.50 cloth. A life story that takes
    the reader through a variety of experiences, including the creation
    of a test of intelligence that the author used with people of diverse
    origins, such as Australian aborigines and African Bushmen.

Sarbin, T., & Coe, W. The student psychologist's handbook. New York:
    Harper & Row, 1969. Out of print. A handbook containing definitions
    of the various fields of psychology, sources of psychological infor-
    mation, and a model for research papers.

Sharp, E. The IQ cult. New York: Coward, McCann & Geoghegan, 1972.
    Out of print. A good discussion of the history of mental testing and
    some of the weaknesses of tests now in use. A few of the author's
    assumptions and statements need to be questioned, however.

Sensation, Perception, and the Nervous System

Bartley, S. H. Perception in everyday life. New York: Harper & Row, 1972. $6.95 paper. A human-interest discussion of perception, "the true connector between man and nature," as it relates to us all.

Gregory, R. L. Eye and brain: The psychology of seeing (2nd ed.). New York: McGraw-Hill, 1973. $4.95 cloth; $3.95 paper. A fascinating, well-illustrated, and lucidly written introduction to the psychology of visual perception.

Nathan, P. The nervous system. Philadelphia: J. B. Lippincott, 1969. Out of print. An interestingly written book about the relationship between the nervous system and behavior.

Rudolph, M., & Mueller, C. G. Light and vision. Morristown, N. J.: Silver Burdett, 1966. (Originally published by Time-Life Books.) $10.20 cloth. A well-illustrated introduction to the nature of light and the function of the eye in the sense of vision.

Warshovsky, F., & Stevens, S. S. Sound and hearing (Rev. ed.). Morristown, N. J.: Silver Burdett, 1969. (Originally published by Time-Life Books, 1967.) No price available. A readable and beautifully illustrated explanation of how we hear.

Child Development

Bettelheim, B. Children of the dream. New York: Macmillan, 1969. $7.95 cloth. (Avon Books, $1.95 paper.) A study of children in an Israeli kibbutz.

Bronfenbrenner, U. The two worlds of childhood. New York: Russell Sage Foundation, 1970. $7.95 cloth. (Simon & Schuster, $2.95 paper.) A comparative study of American and Russian methods of childrearing.

Chukovsky, K. From two to five (Rev. ed. Translated and edited by Miriam Morton). Berkeley, Calif.: University of California Press, 1963. $2.95 paper. A delightfully written book by the most loved author of books for children in the Soviet Union, about how children learn to understand, speak, read, and write their native language, whatever it may be.

Coles, R. Uprooted children: The early lives of migrant farm workers. Pittsburgh, Pa.: University of Pittsburgh Press, 1970. $6.95 cloth. A well-documented study of fear and oppression.

de Bono, E. The dog exercising machine. New York: Simon & Schuster, 1970. $3.95 paper. A collection of drawings by children, intended to show how children's minds work and to help the reader better understand the nature of creativity.

Fraiberg, S. The magic years. New York: Charles Scribner's, 1968.
$7.95 cloth; $2.95 paper. A description of emotional development in
childhood.

Ginott, H. G. Between parent and child. New York: Macmillan, 1965.
$6.95 cloth. (Avon Books, $2.25 paper.) A book written to make life
between parent and child less irritating and more rewarding.

O'Gorman, N. The storefront. New York: Harper & Row, 1970. Out of
print. A description of the world of children in a Manhattan ghetto.

Smith, L. E. Killers of the dream (Rev. ed.). New York: W. W. Norton,
1961. $12.95 cloth; $3.95 paper. An autobiographical account of a
childhood spent in a home and community with double standards.

Adolescence

Anderson, S. Tar: A midwest childhood. Cleveland, Ohio: Press of Case
Western Reserve University, 1969. Out of print. A novel about a
young boy striving to adjust to a world of duplicity, disappointment,
and self-doubt.

Baldwin, J. Go tell it on the mountain. New York: Dial Press, 1953.
$6.95 cloth. (Dell, $1.50 paper.) A largely autobiographical novel
about a young black's experience in Harlem and his subsequent work as
a minister.

Frank, A. Anne Frank: The diary of a young girl (Rev. ed). Garden City,
N. Y.: Doubleday, 1967. $7.95 cloth. (Pocket Books, $1.75 paper.)
A record of the intimate feelings of a brilliant girl in hiding from
the Nazis.

Ginott, H. G. Between parent and teenager. New York: Macmillan, 1969.
$6.95 cloth. (Avon Books, $2.25 paper.) A book that should help
parents better understand their adolescent offspring and, perhaps,
help adolescents better understand their parents.

Goethals, G. W., & Klos, D. C. (Eds.). Experiencing youth: First-person
accounts (2nd ed.). Boston: Little, Brown, 1976. $7.95 paper.
Accounts by college-age youths of their problems with parents, sexuality, and drugs.

Hesse, H. Siddhartha. New York: New Directions, 1951. $7.50 cloth;
$1.75 paper. The story of a young Indian boy who is searching for
himself.

Konopka, G. The adolescent girl in conflict. Englewood Cliffs, N. J.:
Prentice-Hall, 1966. $2.95 paper. An examination of delinquency in
girls.

Kovar, L. C. _Faces of the adolescent girl_. Englewood Cliffs, N. J.: Prentice-Hall, 1968. Out of print. An attempt to explain the various stresses faced by girls during adolescence.

Lockwood, D. _I, the aboriginal_. Adelaide, Australia: Rigby, Ltd., 1962. No price available. The enchanting and instructive life story of an Australian aborigine; a book not readily available in this country but worth the trouble of locating (through a library or bookstore).

McCullers, C. _Member of the wedding_. Boston: Houghton Mifflin, 1946. $7.95 cloth. (New Directions, $1.75 paper.) A novel about an adolescent girl's efforts to understand the nature of love and the adult world.

Mitchell, E. B., & Allen, T. D. _Miracle hill: The story of a Navajo boy_. Norman, Okla.: University of Oklahoma Press, 1967. $6.95 cloth. The true story of a Navajo boy and the inner conflicts involved in his attempts to adjust to both his tribal ways and the ways of the white man.

Parks, G. _The learning tree_. New York: Harper & Row, 1963. $9.95 cloth. (Fawcett World Library, $1.75 paper.) The fictionalized autobiography of an adolescent black, now a renowned photographer, growing up in a small Kansas town.

Steffens, L. _A boy on horseback_. New York: Harcourt Brace Jovanovich, 1935. $5.50 cloth; $3.75 paper. (Also published as Vol. 1 of _The autobiography of Lincoln Steffens_. New York: Harcourt Brace Jovanovich, 1931.) A well-told story of a boy growing up in California a century ago.

Exceptional Children

Axline, V. M. _Dibs: In search of self_. Boston: Houghton Mifflin, 1964. $6.95 cloth. (Ballantine Books, $1.75 paper.) A book about a five-year-old emotionally disturbed child, significant to much older young people who are trying to find their places in the world.

Baruch, D. W. _One little boy_. New York: Dell, 1964. $2.75 paper. An account of what a psychologist learned about a severely disturbed eight-year-old and his parents, and the child's remarkable recovery.

Bettelheim, B. _The empty fortress_. New York: Free Press, 1967. $10.95 cloth; $4.95 paper. Three case studies of autistic children, a section on "wolf" children, and a discussion of the literature on infantile autism.

Bettelheim, B. _Paul and Mary: Two case histories of truants from life_. Garden City, N. Y.: Doubleday, 1961. $1.95 paper. Case studies of the rehabilitation of emotionally disturbed children.

Brown, C. Down all the days. New York: Stein & Day, 1970. Out of print. A remarkable story of an Irish boy with a very severe physical handicap.

Buck, P. S. The child who never grew. New York: John Day, 1950. $2.95 cloth. A famous writer's personal account of her own mentally retarded child.

Gibson, W. The miracle worker. New York: Alfred A. Knopf, 1957. $7.95 cloth. (Bantam, $1.50 paper.) An account of the use of discipline in teaching Helen Keller.

McCurdy, H. G. (Ed.). Barbara: The unconscious autobiography of a child genius. Chapel Hill, N. C.: University of North Carolina Press, 1966. Out of print. The story of Barbara, a child who never went to school but wrote her first long story at the age of five and by nine had written a book that was later published.

Nichols, P. Joe Egg. New York: Grove Press, 1968. $2.95 paper. A depiction of adjustments within a family to a mentally retarded child.

Wilson, L. This stranger, my son: A mother's story. New York: G. P. Putnam's, 1968. $6.95 cloth. An account of a retarded child.

Teaching and Learning

Ashton-Warner, S. Teacher. New York: Simon & Schuster, 1963. $8.95 cloth; $2.45 paper. A New Zealand teacher telling of her innovative methods of teaching Maori children.

Burgess, A. A clockwork orange. New York: W. W. Norton, 1963. $1.95 paper. A novel about conditioning in the real world.

Holt, J. How children fail. New York: Dell, 1972. $1.50 paper. A discussion of why children are failing to learn much that we hope to teach them.

Holt, J. How children learn. New York: Dell, 1972. $2.45 paper. Portraits of children, particularly preschoolers, as they learn to use language and ideas.

Kinkade, K. A Walden Two experiment. New York: William Morrow, 1972. $7.95 cloth; $3.25 paper. An account of an attempt to try out the ideas of reinforcement discussed in Skinner's novel, Walden Two.

Kozol, J. Death at an early age: The destruction of the hearts and minds of Negro children in the Boston public schools. Boston: Houghton Mifflin, 1967. $7.95 cloth. (Bantam, $1.95 paper.) An account of the author's experience teaching black children in a Boston school.

Leonard, G. B. Education and ecstasy. New York: Dell, 1969. $2.75
   paper. A critical look at schools--what they are doing and what they
   might be doing.

Neill, A. S. "Neill! Neill! Orange peel!" New York: Hart Publishing
   Co., 1972. Out of print. Probably the best source of information
   about Neill's radical approach to childrearing; a description of the
   school (Summerhill) that Neill directed for more than 50 years.

Neill, A. S. Summerhill: A radical approach to child rearing. New
   York: Hart Publishing Co., 1960. $10.00 cloth; $4.95 paper. A very
   popular book explaining Neill's basic concept of freedom in education.

Northway, M. L. Laughter in the front hall. Toronto: Longmans Canada,
   1966. $2.65 cloth. A little book of enjoyable essays on teaching
   children how to live.

Popenoe, J. Inside Summerhill. New York: Hart Publishing Co., 1970.
   Out of print. A 16-year-old American boy describes in words and photographs his four years as a student in A. S. Neill's famed Summerhill School in England.

Skinner, B. F. Walden Two revisited. New York: Macmillan, 1976.
   (Originally published, 1948.) $7.95 cloth; $2.50 paper. A novel of
   a modern utopia based on operant conditioning, written in a way that
   leaves very few readers neutral about Skinner.

Voeks, V. On becoming an educated person (3rd ed.). Philadelphia: W. B.
   Saunders, 1970. $4.25 paper. A book with very great appeal to most
   students because it helps them do better the things they feel they
   should do.

Women on Words and Images. Dick and Jane as victims: Sex stereotyping
   in children's readers (2nd ed.). Princeton, N. J.: Author, 1975.
   $2.00 paper. Examples of the ways in which the books that children
   are given to read in school develop sex stereotypes.

Motivation and Emotion

Blatz, W. E. Human security: Some reflections. Toronto: University of
   Toronto Press, 1966. $2.50 paper. A book that provokes readers to
   think and helps them discover how to face problems.

Brown, J. A. Techniques of persuasion: From propaganda to brainwashing.
   Baltimore: Penguin, 1963. $2.95 paper. A discussion of how opin-
   ions and behavior patterns are established and changed.

Cantril, H. The invasion from Mars: A study in the psychology of panic.
   Princeton, N. J.: Princeton University Press, 1940. Out of print.
   A psychologist's analysis of the spread of panic in the New York area
   following a radio play that was apparently a bit too realistic.

Cullum, A. <u>The geranium on the window sill just died but teacher you went right on</u>. New York: Harlan Quist, 1971. $5.95 paper. A most unusual little book that reveals much about the feelings of school children.

de Saint Exupery, A. <u>The little prince</u>. New York: Harcourt Brace Jovanovich, 1943. $5.95 cloth; $1.50 paper. A delightful little fantasy about a very simple social structure that has much to teach us about the interaction of motives in the extremely complex societies of real life.

Eibl-Eibesfeldt, I. <u>Love and hate</u>. New York: Schocken Books, 1974. $4.50 paper. A discussion of the inherited factors and the social controls that develop various behavior patterns.

Fromm, E. <u>The art of loving</u>. New York: Harper & Row, 1956. $8.95 cloth; $1.50 paper. An attempt to help readers learn how to love by developing their total personality, including humility, courage, faith, and discipline.

Grier, W. H., & Cobbs, P. M. <u>Black rage</u>. New York: Basic Books, 1968. $7.95 cloth. (Bantam, $1.95 paper.) A psychological study of the effects of racism on American blacks, revealing many of their emotional conflicts.

Hersey, J. R. <u>Hiroshima</u>. New York: Alfred A. Knopf, 1946. $5.95 cloth. (Bantam, $1.50 paper.) An account of the reactions of survivors of the Hiroshima atomic bomb, illustrating human behavior under severe emotional stress.

Karlin, W., Paquet, B. T., & Rottman, L. (Eds.). <u>Free fire zone: Short stories by Vietman veterans</u>. New York: McGraw-Hill, 1973. $2.95 paper. Stories in rough language, but not as rough as the experiences of the young Americans who lived them.

Toffler, A. <u>The culture consumers</u>. New York: Random House, 1972. $10.00 cloth. An explanation of who the culture consumers are and why they respond to cultural events.

Turnbull, C. M. <u>The mountain people</u>. New York: Simon & Schuster, 1972. $8.95 cloth; $2.95 paper. A description of an African tribe whose social goals, under conditions of extreme deprivation, were replaced entirely by selfish goals. The complete disintegration of personality that followed warns of the possible consequences of the breakdown of our social structures.

Zimbardo, P. G. <u>Shyness: What it is, what to do about it</u>. Reading, Mass.: Addison-Wesley, 1977. $9.95 cloth; $5.95 paper. A discussion of what causes shyness, its consequences, and how it can be overcome.

Social Behavior

Argyle, M. The psychology of interpersonal behavior. Baltimore: Penguin, 1967. $2.95 paper. An introductory explanation of the dynamics that control human interactions.

Berne, E. Games people play. New York: Grove Press, 1964. $6.50 cloth; $1.95 paper. A discussion of social strategies, pointing out the game-playing nature of many human behaviors.

Frankl, V. Man's search for meaning (Rev. ed.). Boston: Beacon Press, 1963. $7.95 cloth. (Pocket Books, $1.75 paper.) A description of a psychiatrist's experiences in a World War II German prison camp and his conclusions about the need for meaning in life.

Fromm, E. Escape from freedom. New York: Irvington Publishers, 1941. $17.00 cloth. (Avon Books, $2.25 paper.) A study of the human conflict between freedom and the desire for dependency and passivity.

Fromm, E. Man for himself. New York: Holt, Rinehart & Winston, 1947. $7.00 cloth. (Fawcett World Library, $1.50 paper.) An examination of human and technological values in conflict.

Fromm, E. The sane society. New York: Holt, Rinehart & Winston, 1955. $5.95 paper. (Fawcett World Library, $1.75 paper.) An argument that majority values may be destructive. (Twenty million Frenchmen can be wrong.)

Golding, W. Lord of the flies. New York: Coward, McCann & Geoghegan, 1954. $7.95 cloth. (G. P. Putnam's, $1.75 paper.) A novel about a group of boys stranded on a remote island and the conflicts that arose among them in their competition for leadership.

Huxley, A. Brave new world and Brave new world revisited. New York: Harper & Row, 1932, 1958. $3.75 paper. A novel that was one of the first attempts to look at the social implications of behavior-control procedures; and a reprise.

Koestler, A. Darkness at noon. New York: Macmillan, 1941. (Bantam, $1.75 paper.) A novel depicting life in a prison and changes in thought patterns during a revolution.

Malcolm X & Haley, A. Autobiography of Malcolm X. New York: Grove Press, 1966. (Ballantine Books, $1.95 paper.) An account of the changes in values induced by society in the life of a black American.

Orwell, G. Animal farm. New York: Harcourt Brace Jovanovich, 1954. (New American Library, $1.25 paper.) A powerful satire exloring the implications of various political systems, the evils of totalitarianism, and the origins of prejudice.

Orwell, G. 1984. New York: Harcourt Brace Jovanovich, 1949. (New
   American Library, $1.50 paper.) A novel describing how behavior is
   molded in a totalitarian society.

Riesman, D., Glazer, N., & Denney, R. The lonely crowd: A study of the
   changing American character (Abridged ed.). New Haven, Conn.: Yale
   University Press, 1950. $18.50 cloth; $4.45 paper. A sociologically
   oriented classic that introduced the concept of the "inner-directed"
   person.

Schlesinger, A., Jr. Violence in the sixties. New York: New American
   Library, 1968. Out of print. A historian's brief look at the meaning of American violence in the span of one decade.

Smith, M. B., Bruner, J., & White, R. Opinions and personality. New
   York: John Wiley, 1956. Out of print. A study that attempts to
   show the relationships that exist between an individual's personality
   structure and the opinions he or she holds.

Abnormal Behavior and Treatment

Capote, T. In cold blood. New York: Random House, 1966. $8.95 cloth.
   (New American Library, $1.95 paper.) A gripping true story giving an
   in-depth account of two psychopaths.

Grant, V. This is mental illness: How it feels and what it means.
   Out of print. Boston: Beacon Press, 1963. Case studies.

Green, H. I never promised you a rose garden. New York: Holt, Rinehart
   & Winston, 1964. $6.95 cloth. (New American Library, $1.75 paper.)
   A firsthand report, written as a novel, of the struggles of a schizo-
   phrenic girl in a mental hospital and of the help she received from a
   psychiatrist.

Kaplan, B. (Ed.). Inner world of mental illness: First-person accounts
   of what it was like. New York: Harper & Row, 1964. $10.95 paper.
   Accounts, many by famous people, of their own emotional disturbances.

Kesey, K. One flew over the cuckoo's nest. New York: Viking Press,
   1962. $7.95 cloth. (New American Library, $1.75 paper.) A novel
   about patients in a state mental hospital; actually a discussion of
   the nature of the social establishment as a whole, not to be read as
   a realistic description of a modern mental hospital.

Levin, M. Compulsion. New York: New American Library, 1968. Out of
   print. A novel about the Leopold-Loeb murder case, one of the first
   in which psychological test data were used as part of the defense.

Parker, B. A mingled yarn: Chronicle of a troubled family. New Haven,
   Conn.: Yale University Press, 1972. $12.50 cloth. An account of
   the emotional deterioration of the various members of a family; a
   true story that reads like a novel.

Plath, S. *The bell jar*. New York: Harper & Row, 1971. $10.95 cloth.
(Bantam, $1.95 paper.) A novel, almost certainly autobiographical,
about an intellectually brilliant young woman who goes through a nervous breakdown and an attempt at suicide.

Rubin, T. I. *Jordi/Lisa and David*. New York: Ballantine Books, 1968.
$1.50 paper. Two stories about adolescent patients in a sanitarium
working their way out of severe emotional disturbances.

St. Cyr, M. *The story of Pat*. Paramus, N. J.: Paulist/Newman Press,
1972. Out of print. A description of the problems of the brain-dam-
aged child.

Schreiber, F. R. *Sybil*. New York: Warner Books, 1974. $2.25 paper.
The story of a young woman with multiple personalities.

Watts, A. W. *Psychotherapy East and West*. New York: Random House,
1975. $1.95 paper. A discussion of religious differences between
Eastern and Western society and their influence on psychotherapy.

Sleeping and Dreaming

Dement, W. C. *Some must watch while some must sleep*. Stanford, Calif.:
W. H. Freeman, 1976. $4.95 paper. A very readable, often humorous,
scientifically sound review of research on sleeping and dreaming.

Luce, G., & Segal, J. *Sleep*. New York: Coward, McCann & Geoghegan,
1966. $7.95 cloth. A detailed and authentic yet popular book.

Seuss, Dr. *Dr. Seuss's sleep book*. New York: Random House, 1962.
$3.95 cloth. A discussion of sleep--with illustrations--by the
famous comic illustrator and writer of children's books.

Webb, W. B. *Sleep: The gentle tyrant*. New York: Prentice-Hall, 1975.
$8.95 cloth; $3.95 paper. A good introduction to the study of sleep,
with illustrations and some text material borrowed from Dr. Seuss's
book.

Animal Behavior

Breland, K., & Breland, M. *Animal behavior*. New York: Macmillan, 1966.
Out of print. A description by a husband-and-wife team of psychologists of how they taught chickens to play baseball and pigs to sweep
the floor. They teach the reader much more about the behavior of
animals.

Burtt, H. E. *The psychology of birds*. New York: Macmillan, 1967. $5.95
cloth. A book that should interest even the most casual observer of
birds, written by a retired psychology professor who took up bird-
watching as a hobby.

Dethier, V. G. To know a fly. San Francisco: Holden-Day, 1962. $3.75
  paper. An introduction to methods of experimental psychology that
  makes learning a fun process and makes research sound very exciting.

Goetsch, W. The ants. Ann Arbor, Mich.: University of Michigan Press,
  1957. $2.95 paper. An explanation of the complicated social struc-
  ture of the ants.

Hayes, C. The ape in our house. New York: Harper & Row, 1951. Out of
  print. The story of an infant chimpanzee taken into a home and
  reared as if it were a human child.

Kellogg, W. N., & Kellogg, L. A. The ape and the child. New York:
  McGraw-Hill, 1933. Out of print. A classic study comparing a chimpanzee and a child reared in the same home.

Lilly, J. C. The mind of the dolphin. New York: Avon Books, undated.
  $.95 paper. A discussion of the dolphin--next to humans, the most
  intelligent of all animals.

Lorenz, K. King Solomon's ring. New York: Thomas Y. Crowell, 1952.
  $6.95 cloth. (Apollo Editions, $1.95 paper.) Fascinating literature, a source of much knowledge of animal behavior, and an opportunity to become better acquainted with a unique personality, the author.

Maeterlinck, M. The life of the bee. New York: Dodd, Mead, 1912.
  Out of print. A classic study of the behavior of bees.

Premack, A. J. Why chimps can read. New York: Harper & Row, 1976.
  $8.95 cloth; $2.95 paper. A review of various studies of the development of language in chimpanzees.

Riopelle, A. J. (Ed.). Animal problem solving. Baltimore: Penguin,
  undated. Out of print. Various examples of how animals approach
  problem-solving.

Southwick, C. Primate social behavior. New York: Van Nostrand Reinhold,
  1963. Out of print. A study of the social bonds among groups of
  monkeys, baboons, and gorillas.

Tinbergen, N. Animal behavior. New York: Time-Life, 1965. $7.95 cloth.
  A very readable book, by one of the world's best ethologists, that is
  enhanced by many well-chosen illustrations.

van Lawick-Goodall, J. In the shadow of man. Boston: Houghton Mifflin,
  1971. $10.00 cloth. (Dell, $3.45 paper.) A study of chimpanzees in
  the wild, describing the growth and development of chimps and also
  presenting remarkable parallels with human development, revealing
  some new perspectives on childrearing.

Williams, M. Horse psychology. New York: British Book Center, 1976.
    $8.50 paper. (J. A. Allen, $7.00 paper.) Much information about
    horses and about behavior in general, including the behavior of
    humans, from a woman who is both a psychologist and a lover of horses.

Special Applications of Psychology

Allport, G. W. The individual and his religion (Rev. ed.). New
    York: Macmillan, 1967. $1.95 paper. An old book, and a bit dated,
    but students who have an interest in religion continue to find it
    relevant.

Chapanis, A. Man-machine engineering. Monterey, Calif.: Brooks/Cole,
    1965. $4.50 paper. A book that should have particular appeal to
    students interested in careers in industrial design and engineering.

Maslow, A. H. Eupsychian management. Homewood, Ill.: Richard D. Irwin,
    1965. $6.95 paper. A very informal report by one of the country's
    most outstanding psychologists, who was employed by a manufacturing
    firm and given complete freedom to investigate what he wished and
    comment on what he found.

Oakley, A. Sex, gender, and society. New York: Harper & Row, 1972.
    $2.95 paper. A discussion of the origins of sex differences and the
    extent to which they are biological (male and female) or cultural
    (masculine and feminine).

Terkel, S. Working. New York: Pantheon Books, 1972. $10.00 cloth.
    (Avon Books, $2.25 paper.) An account of what people say about what
    they do on their jobs and how they feel about it.

Chapter 6

Audiovisual Materials

James B. Maas and Carol M. Howe

There are literally hundreds of audiovisual materials with some
potential for use in high school psychology courses. Space limitations
preclude presenting information regarding each one. Therefore, it was
decided to list relatively comprehensive sources, to provide some commen-
tary on selected film, videotape, slide, and audiotape series, and to
note, by topic, specific films with which the editors have some familiar-
ity or that are recommended for viewing by textbook authors. Readers
desiring a comprehensive listing of audiovisuals in psychology should
consult Index to Psychology: Multimedia, third edition (Los Angeles,
Calif.: National Information Center for Educational Media, 1977).

Addresses of all sources mentioned appear at the end of this chapter.

Film Catalogs

The following list includes university film libraries and film companies that have sizable holdings in psychology; each publishes a catalog
of its holdings, usually offering the listed items for rent. The list
also includes film catalogs published by agencies that are not themselves
distributors. The frequent film user would be well advised to obtain
several of the catalogs and thus become informed about the multitude of
films available for instructional use and the various sources of them.
Addresses for the libraries and companies are listed at the end of this
chapter.

Because some films are exceedingly popular, it is a good idea to sub-
mit requests for rental dates several months in advance.

There are undoubtedly university film libraries, film companies, and
film catalogs in addition to those listed below. Two considerations
guided the choices for listing here: geographic balance and information
obtainable about size of holdings.

Agency for Instructional Television.

Anti-Defamation League of B'nai B'rith. This agency distributes films,
    filmstrips, and publications about prejudice, ethnic and minority
    groups, and the disadvantaged.

Aspect IV Educational Films.

Boston University, Krasker Memorial Film Library.

California, University of (Berkeley), Extension Media Center.

Carousel Films.

CRM/McGraw-Hill Films.

Document Associates.

Film Programmer's Guide to 16mm Rentals, prepared by Kathleen Weaver and
   published in 1975 by Reel Research. This book lists practically
   every film made by Hollywood and foreign producers. It includes a
   film's general and specific topics, where the film can be acquired,
   and the rental prices of the film. It is one of the most helpful and
   complete film guides on the market.

Films by and/or About Women, published in 1972 by Women's History
   Research Center.

Florida State University, Film Library.

Guidance Associates.

Human Relations Media.

Illinois, University of, Visual Aids Service. Separate catalogs are
   available for psychology and guidance and for social science.

Indiana University, Audio-Visual Center. Indiana University has an
   especially large collection. All National Educational Television
   (NET) films appear to be available, including the Focus on Behavior
   series and a special series of 15 films on exceptional children.

International Film Bureau.

Kent State University, Audio Visual Services. The Kent State University
   collection appears to be one of the most complete in the country. Of
   particular interest is the special issue-oriented catalog.

Maine, University of, Instructional Systems Center, Film Rental Library.

Michigan, University of, Audio-Visual Education Center.

Minnesota, University of, Audio-Visual Library Services.

National Audiovisual Center.

National Film and Video Center.

National Film Board of Canada.

New York University, Film Library. New York University has especially
   large and useful holdings for behavioral science purposes, including
   the Vassar series and the Character Formation in Different Cultures
   films.

Pennsylvania State University, Audio-Visual Department. Pennsylvania
   State University publishes the Psychological Cinema Register, an almost exhaustive listing of available, relevant films.

A Selective Guide to Materials for Mental Health and Family Life
   Education (3rd ed.), published in 1976 by the Mental Health Materials
   Center.

Sunburst Communications.

Time-Life Multimedia. Time-Life Multimedia is the US distributor for the
   British Broadcasting Corporation. It has titles from the NOVA public
   television series, the American Film Institute and its Center for
   Advanced Film Study, independent international productions, and
   others.

Film Series and Special Collections

   The abbreviations at the end of entries in the following list refer
to distributors of the series described in the entries. At the end of
the chapter, full names and addresses of the distributors are given.

   The Actualization Group. This seven-film series shows actual psychological group therapy. The viewer is able to observe and study progress of the group through the seven-part therapy session. PFI and PSU.

   Albert Ellis: Rational Emotive Psychotherapy. Albert Ellis, founder
of rational emotive therapy, explains and demonstrates his approach in
five films:
Rational Emotive Psychotherapy, Rational Emotive Psychotherapy Applied to
Groups, A Demonstration with an Elementary School Age Child, A Demonstration with a Young Divorced Woman, and A Demonstration with a Woman Fear-
ful of Expressing Emotion. APGA.

   Alcohol education. In 1975 the U. S. Department of Health, Education, and Welfare released two film series to help young people make
responsible decisions concerning the use of alcoholic beverages. The
first set is called Jackson Junior High (four 15-minute films). The
second set is entitled Dial A-L-C-O-H-O-L (four 30-minute programs).
Both sets are available in videotape or 16mm format. NAC.

   America's Crises. The series is a set of 17 films produced by National Educational Television in 1964-65. Titles include Cities and the
Poor (Parts 1 and 2), Cities: Crime in the Streets, Cities: The Rise of
New Towns, The Community, Emotional Dilemma, The Hard Way, The Individual, Marked for Failure, Old Age--Out of Sight, Out of Mind, Old Age--The

Wasted Years, Parents, Religious Revolution and the Void, Semester of Discontent, Teacher Gap, Trouble in the Family, Troubled Cities, and Young Americans. The series is becoming outdated rapidly. IU, KSU, and UMinn.

Animal Behavior. Five films produced by the National Geographic Society investigate animal learning and its relationship to animal behavior. Titles are: Do Animals Reason?, The Function of Beauty in Nature, Invertebrates: Conditioning or Learning?, Konrad Lorenz: Science of Animal Behavior, and The Tool Users. CM.

Behavior in Business. This series shows how the science of human behavior stimulates an organization's productivity and efficiency. The seven films are: Business, Behaviorism and the Bottom Line, Communication: The Nonverbal Agenda, Group Dynamics: "Groupthink," Leadership: Style or Circumstance?, Productivity and the Self-Fulfilling Prophecy, Transactional Analysis, and Women in Management: Threat or Opportunity?. BU, UC, CRM/MHF, UI, and KSU.

Behavior Theory in Practice. The series is a set of four films that not only present basic concepts of conditioning, both classical and operant, but also illustrate the usefulness of the principles in a wide variety of settings. Titles include Respondent and Operant Behavior (the first in the set); Shaping Various Operants, Various Species (including work on programmed learning with humans); Generalization, Discrimination, and Motivation (with some material on intracranial self-stimulation); and Sequences of Behavior (including a demonstration of the training of seeing-eye dogs). Produced in 1966, the series is widely used and highly regarded at the college level. UI, IU, KSU, UMich, PSU, and PH.

Carl Rogers on Marriage. In these five films Carl Rogers shares his views on the relationship between men and women. Film titles are Persons as Partners, An Interview with Hal and Jane, An Interview with Bob and Carol, An Interview with Nancy and John, and An Interview with Jane and Jerry. APGA.

Character Formation in Different Cultures. This classic set of films relating to cultural differences and their effects was prepared in the early 1950s at least in part under the direction of both Margaret Mead and Gregory Bateson. Titles include A Balinese Family, Bathing Babies in Three Cultures, Childhood Rivalry in Bali and New Guinea, First Days in the Life of a New Guinea Baby, Karba's First Years, and Trance and Dance in Bali. UC, UI, and NYU.

Childhood: The Enchanted Years. This two-film series attempts to prove that infants are born with a highly individualized temperament and innate abilities to develop certain distinctly human skills. IU, KSU, UMich, UMinn, and PFI.

Concepts in Transactional Analysis. The five films in the series are Stroke Seeking Behavior: Therapeutic Traps and Pitfalls, Patsy, Mary, Charlotte, and Bruce. The names are those of participants in group therapy sessions, who present different problems to illustrate concepts of transactional analysis. APGA.

Conflict and Awareness. Subjects in this 13-film series include suicide, homosexuality, parent-child relationships, parental divorce, job interviewing, group conformity and rejection, self-identity/sex roles, and others. CRM/MHF and KSU.

A Conversation with Carl Rogers. In these two films Carl Rogers comments on psychotherapy, the phenomenological approach to human beings, and education. PFI.

Cornell Candid Camera Collection. Over 200 sequences from yesteryear's Candid Camera television series have been selected by J. B. Maas and other psychologists at Cornell University for educational use. A catalog of titles, with annotations, is available free from Du Art Film Labs. Films are for purchase only and range from $10 to $70. For a description of the nature of the collection, see J. B. Maas and K. M. Toivanen, "Candid Camera and the Behavioral Sciences," Audio-Visual Communication Review, 1969, 17, 307-314. DAFL.

Dating and Marriage/A Series. These three films cover teenagers' questions about dating and contain a discussion of marriage. How Close Can You Get?, One or Many?, and What Do Girls Want from Boys? are the titles. CHF, UI, and KSU.

Development of the Child. The series, which was produced in consultation with Jerome Kagan and Howard Gardner, comprises three films: Cognition, Infancy, and Language. HARM, UI, IU, KSU, UMinn, and PSU.

Drug education. Sources of information on drug education films are the Addiction Research Foundation, Pyramid, and the Wisconsin Clearinghouse on Alcohol and Other Drug Information. ARF, P, and WC.

Even Love's Not Enough: Children with Handicaps. This set of four sound and color filmstrips is designed to inform adults how to aid the handicapped child in reaching his or her full potential. PMF.

Experimental Psychology. Classic Experiments in Behavioral Neuropsychology, The Split Brain and Conscious Experience, and Research in Animal Behavior are the three films in this series. HARM.

The Family/A Series. This series of five films opens up urgent issues of adolescence. Titles are Can a Parent Be Human?, I Owe You Nothing!, Ivan and His Father, Mom, Why Won't You Listen?, and Wait Until Your Father Gets Home! BU, CHF, UI, and KSU.

Filming the Wellsprings of the Spirit. This is a good collection of films on meditation, holistic health, biofeedback, Alan Watts, Hinduism, mysticism, Ram Dass, and similar subjects. HFF.

Focus on Behavior. Produced in 1963 with the cooperation of the American Psychological Association, this set of 10 films has been widely acclaimed. The films vary somewhat in quality and in the speed with which they are becoming outdated. Titles include Brain and Behavior, Chemistry of Behavior, Computers and Human Behavior, Conscience of a Child, Learning About Learning, The Need to Achieve, No Two Alike, Of Men and Machines, Social Animal, and A World to Perceive. BU, UC, UI, IU, KSU, UMich, UMinn, and PSU.

Frederick Perls and Gestalt Therapy. This two-part film is the most recent and most comprehensive audiovisual work on the theories of Frederick Perls. The first film presents the essence of gestalt therapy; the second part goes into technique and practice. PFI.

Frontiers of Psychological Inquiry. This is a widely acclaimed series of experiential color films by J. B. Maas designed to demonstrate psychological phenomena and stimulate students to pursue psychological issues on their own. The films serve as thought-provoking supplements to lectures and are accompanied by teacher's guides for holding intensive discussions. The specific titles are The Maze, an award-winning documentary on the life and works of an artist who was hospitalized for a time with schizophrenia; Sleep and Dreaming in Humans, showing the procedures used for recording all-night sleep and dreaming behavior (with W. Dement); The Sleeping Brain, demonstrating techniques for ascertaining the structures and functions of sleep and dreaming mechanisms (with M. Jouvet); and 2-Dimensional Motion Perception and 3-Dimensional Motion Perception, illustrating cues for perception of motion (with G. Johansson). HM and PSU.

Great Scientists Speak Again. This series of six 16mm color films features impersonation-lectures by Professor Richard Eakin. The scientists portrayed are Louis Pasteur, William Harvey, Charles Darwin, Gregor Mendel, William Beaumont, and Hans Spemann. UC.

Harcourt Brace Jovanovich series. The six films in the series provide an in-depth study of major topics in psychology. Titles are Child's Play: Window on Development, Divided Brain and Consciousness, Human Memory, The Psychology of Eating, Schizophrenia, and When Will People Help? The Social Psychology of Bystander Intervention. HBJ.

Harlow films. The series comprises two very well-done films relating to Harry Harlow's work with mothering procedures and their effects on the behavior of chimpanzees. Titles are Mother Love and The Nature and Development of Affection. KSU and PSU.

Individual Psychology. In these two films Rudolph Dreikurs examines
the background and basic concepts of individual psychology. Individual
Psychology in Counseling and Education (in two parts) and A Demonstration
With A Parent, A Teacher, and A Child (in two parts) are the titles.
APGA.

Inside Out. Thirty 15-minute programs are designed to help 8- to
10-year-olds deal with physical, emotional, and educational problems.
AIT and KSU.

Maslow and Self-Actualization. In this two-film series Abraham Maslow, whose theories made much of the concept of self-actualization, discusses aspects of self-actualization and recent research and theory relating to those aspects. Part 1 is concerned with honesty and awareness,
Part 2 with freedom and trust. UMich, PSU, and PFI.

Mental Health Association films. The Mental Health Media Center distributes about 30 films that were either produced or approved by the Mental Health Association. A few titles are: Depression: A Study in Abnormal Behavior, The Fragile Mind, Journey, and Only Human. MHMC.

National Broadcasting Company films. The National Broadcasting Company has produced a number of films of relevance focusing on contemporary
problems of society. Some currently available titles include A Chance to
Learn (issues and possible solutions for central-city schools), In the
Name of Law (violence and the breakdown of law and order), A Little
Younger/A Little Older (the generation gap, drugs, and the problems of
affluence), Oh, Woodstock! (the festival viewed both by young participants and by adults, including two psychologists), and The Orange and the
Green (prejudice and culture conflict in Northern Ireland). FI.

Notable Contributors to the Psychology of Personality. The series is
a set of 17 films consisting of interviews conducted by Richard I. Evans
with notable psychologists. Subjects are Gordon Allport, Raymond Cat-
tell, Erik Erikson, Hans Eysenck, Erich Fromm, Ernest Hilgard, Carl Jung,
R. D. Laing, Konrad Lorenz, Arthur Miller, Gardner Murphy, Henry Murray,
Jean Piaget and Barbel Inhelder, J. B. Rhine, Carl Rogers, Nevitt Sanford, and B. F. Skinner. The films would probably not be of much interest to average high school students but might appeal to those in a higher
level course. MAC and PSU.

Ordinal Scales of Infant Psychological Development. The series was
prepared by Ina C. Uzgiris and J. McVicker Hunt in 1966 to illustrate
behavioral phenomena of early sensory-motor development as described by
Piaget. There are six films in the series, including Development of
Means, Development of Schemata, Imitation, Object Permanence, Object Relations in Space, and Operational Causality. They may not be appropriate
for a general introductory high school course. UC and UI.

Otto. This series of five films deals with abnormal behavior. Four perspectives are involved: psychoanalytic, behavioral, phenomenological, and social. The films are available in 16mm and video cassette. IU.

Project Head Start films. Project Head Start in the Office of Child Development, Department of Health, Education, and Welfare, has produced 35 films relating to cultural deprivation and its effects, and illustrating training procedures. MTPS.

Psychic phenomena. Three films record the latest scientific psychic phenomena: To Solve the ESP Mystery: Extra-Sensory Perception Is No Dream, To Discover A New Psychic Force--P.K.: Even Healing May Be Possible with Psychokinesis, and The Occult: X Factor or Fraud?. The films present both scientifically and sensibly the points of view of practitioners. DA and NYU.

Psychology Today. The series consists of eight films: Abnormal Behavior, Aspects of Behavior, Development, Information Processing, Learning, Personality, The Sensory World, and Social Psychology. The Learning film is truly outstanding. BU, CRM/MHF, UI, and KSU.

Rollo May and Human Encounter. Part 1 of this series is entitled Self-Self Encounter and Self-Other Encounter. Part 2 is entitled Manipulation and Human Encounter--Exploitation of Sex. PSU.

The Science of Life. This filmstrip series focuses on the social implications of biology. BF.

Self-Incorporated. Fifteen 15-minute programs, with a teacher's guide, are designed to help 11- to 13-year-olds cope with emotional, physical, and social problems that confront them. AIT and KSU.

Sense Perception. Prepared in 1960 by the Moody Institute of Science, the two original films (The Wonder of the Senses and The Limitation of the Senses) have also been made available as a third condensed and combined version. The films focus on the role of learning in sensation and perception. BU, UI, IU, and KSU.

Sex education. At least one company makes a point of indicating in its catalog that it handles sex education films (as well as others): Perennial Education, Inc. PE.

Sex, Feelings, and Values. The six short open-ended films in the series are Sex Mis-Education, Early Homosexual Experiences, Parents' Voices, Sex Morals, Sex Fears, and Sex Games. DF.

Social problems. These two new films are An Ounce of Prevention by Harvard Productions, on the serious problem of alcoholism in our society, and Violent Youth: The Unmet Challenge by Altana Films, on juvenile crime. HARM.

Social psychology. Six films on social psychology are titled Taking Care of Business, Max Out, Nonverbal Communication, Human Aggression, Invitation to Social Psychology, and Conformity and Independence. HARM.

Studies of Normal Personality Development. This is a very well-known and highly regarded set of films made over a period of years at the Child Development Laboratory School at Vassar College. Some have to do with the use of play techniques in studying child personality (Balloons: Aggression and Destruction Games, Finger Painting, etc.); others deal with the behavior of essentially normal children at various age levels (Abby's First Two Years: A Backward Look, This Is Robert, When Should Grownups Help?, etc.). All have a focus on childhood behavior. UC and NYU.

Target Five. This two-part film series features Virginia Satir. Part 1 deals with the manipulative response form as demonstrated in family therapy. Part 2 describes and demonstrates three necessary aspects of an actualizing relationship: hearing and listening, understanding, and mutual meaning. PFI.

The Teenage Years. Especially directed to young teens, the films in the series are titled The Amazing Cosmic Awareness of Duffy Moon, Blind Sunday, The Bridge of Adam Rush, Follow the North Star, Hewitt's Just Different, The Horrible Honchos, Me and Dad's New Wife, Mighty Moose and the Quarterback Kid, My Mom's Having a Baby, P. J. and the President's Son, Rookie of the Year, and Sara's Summer of the Swans. They are available as 16mm films or video cassettes. TLM.

Three Approaches to Group Therapy. This three-part series is a sequel to the "Gloria" films (see the next entry). Part 1 shows Everett L. Shostrom's theories of Actualizing Therapy. Part 2 demonstrates the technique of Rational Emotive Therapy, developed by Albert Ellis. Part 3 deals with Decision Therapy, developed by Harold Greenwald. PFI.

Three Approaches to Psychotherapy. The three films cover client-centered therapy, demonstrated by Carl Rogers, gestalt therapy demonstrated by Frederick Perls, and rational emotive therapy, demonstrated by Albert Ellis. BU, KSU, UMich, UMinn, NYU, and PFI.

Transactional Analysis. Emily Ruppert demonstrates the principles of transactional analysis in the following films: A Demonstration with Elaine, A Demonstration with Art, and A Demonstration with Pat. APGA.

Understanding Early Childhood: Ages 1 Through 6. These four sets of five filmstrips each deal with child development and behavior. PMF.

United States government films. Catalogs of films available from the federal government may be obtained from the National Audiovisual Center and the National Medical Audiovisual Center. NAC and NMAC.

Youth Under the Influence. A new series of 13 films centers on personal problems of youth that affect our entire society. Sample titles
are: Alcoholism: I Was Goin' To School Drunk, Cancer: The Wayward
Cell, Depression and Suicide: You Can Turn Bad Feelings into Good Ones,
Hard Drugs: It's Not the Going Up That Hurts, It's the Coming Down, Homosexuality and Lesbianism: Gay or Straight--Is There a Choice?, and
Smoking: Games Smokers Play. All of the films interview individuals
involved in the particular problem. UC, DA, and NYU.

Television Courses

Available courses on introductory psychology are:

Introduction to Psychology. Twenty-four 30-minute lessons. Teacher:
    Paul L. Brown. Text: E. R. Hilgard, R. C. Atkinson, and R. L. At-
    kinson, Introduction to Psychology (5th ed. New York: Harcourt
    Brace Jovanovich, 1971). (Available from Paul L. Brown, Department
    of Psychology, State University College, New Paltz, NY 12562.)

Introductory Psychology. Twenty-one 17- to 30-minute lessons.
    Teachers: Frank Costin, Don Dulany, William Greenough, and David
    Lieberman. Text: none. (Available from C. J. McIntyre, Office of
    Instructional Resources, University of Illinois, 205 South Goodwin,
    Urbana, IL 61801.)

Introductory Psychology. Fifty-eight 30-minute lessons. Teacher:
    Richard A. Kasschau. Text: none. (Available from Richard A. Kass-
    chau, Department of Psychology, University of Houston, Houston, TX
    77004.) Also available from the same source (independent of but cor-
    related with the introductory course): Issues in Modern Psychology:
    Interviews with Contemporary Scholars (nine interviews).

Man and His Motives (Psychology II). Fifteen 30-minute lessons.
    Teacher: Kenneth J. Gergen. Text: none. AIT.

Principles of Behavior (Psychology I). Fifteen 30-minute lessons.
    Teacher: Bernard W. Harleston. Text: none. AIT.

Television courses on psychology-related subjects are available from
the Agency for Instructional Television.

Slides and Overhead Transparencies

There are many slide and overhead transparency sets useful in illustrating psychological apparatus, major concepts and paradigms, psychological tests, physiological systems, perceptual phenomena, and results of
classic experiments. These slides and transparencies, often coupled with
the teacher's own visual aids, increase student understanding, shorten

the time needed to clarify concepts, and provide for greater student participation through demonstrations and visual experiments. Semidarkness
is not required when teachers use overhead projectors, rear-screen projection methods, or the Kodak Ektalite Daylight Projection Screen.

The most comprehensive set of 35-millimeter slides (300, in color) is
the Slide Group for General Psychology (J. B. Maas), covering all areas
of the introductory course. The slide set includes an instructor's guide
and student study guide. It is available from McGraw-Hill Book Co. A
second set, including 200 additional color slides, is also available.

Several excellent slide or transparency sets, somewhat narrower in
scope than the Slide Group for General Psychology, are:

Anatomical Transparencies for Neurobiology. R. King, M. Glickstein,
    and E. LaBossiere, 1972, 72 transparencies. MHB.

General Psychology, Parts 1-5. Research Media, 36 transparencies, color;
    Part 1--Statistics, Part 2--Perception, Part 3--Physiology, Part
    4--Heredity, and Part 5--Learning.

Introduction to Psychology: A View of Behavior, Parts 1-11 (Rev. ed.)
    (slide-tape program with administration manual, instructor's guide,
    student workbook, and tests). Paul L. Brown, 1977; Part 1--Psychology
    as a Science, Part 2--Classical Conditioning, Part 3--Operant Condi-
    tioning, Part 4--Human Learning, Part 5--Physiological Psychology,
    Part 6--Motivation, Part 7--Feeling and Emotion, Part 8--Sensation
    and Perception, Part 9--Child Development and Intelligence, Part
    10--Social Influences on Behavior, and Part 11--Development of Per-
    sonality. RM.

Perception and Problem Solving, Parts 1-5. Research Media, 51
    transparencies, color; Part 1--Visual Perception, Part 2--Mir-
    ror-Tracing Kit, Part 3--Problem Solving, Part 4--Stereo and Binocu-
    lar Perception, and Part 5--Experiments in Perception.

Slide Set for Introductory Psychology. W. B. Saunders, 1977, 151 slides.

Transparencies for General Psychology. H. Slucki, 1968, 64
    transparencies (36 color). SF.

Slide or transparency sets on a range of very specific topics are
available from the following sources:

Lansford Publishing Co.

Life Science Associates.

Zimbardo, P. G. Stanford Prison Experiment (a 50-minute slide-cassette
    presentation, with script; available from P. G. Zimbardo, P. O. Box
    4395, Stanford, CA 94305).

Audio Catalogs and Programs

From their catalogs, most of the audiovisual centers seem to be much more visual than audio. Most, however, indicate the availability of at least some audio material. In addition, the following sources have been located:

American Academy of Psychotherapists, Tape Library.

American Association for the Advancement of Science.

Audio Colloquies. The colloquies are interviews with eminent behavioral and social scientists. HARM, 1977.

Audio-Forum.

Audiotapes on the Health and Behavioral Sciences, distributed by the University of California (Berkeley), Extension Media Center.

BMA Audio Cassette Programs.

Center for the Study of Democratic Institutions. The Center's holdings include over 600 tapes, many dealing with the topics of race and culture.

Florida, University of, College of Education, Institute for Development of Human Resources.

Instructional Dynamics, Inc. This group publishes a series of cassette tapes that can be called "Mental Health Seminars" (e.g., Personal Adjustment by Carl Rogers).

Lansford Publishing Co.

Listening Library, Inc.

Michigan, University of, Audio-Visual Education Center. The University publishes a separate catalog for its audio tape recordings.

National Center for Audio Tapes.

National School Public Relations Association.

Pacifica Tape Library.

Psychology Today cassettes. Ziff-Davis Publishing Co. offers over 100 audio cassettes covering a wide range of topics in psychology and mental health.

Psychotherapy Tape Review.

Sound Seminars in Psychology. Over 300 cassettes make up this
   collection, distributed by Jeffrey Norton Publishers. Most feature
   very well-known psychologists, who speak on a wide variety of subjects.

Topical Listing of Films and Filmstrips

Entries in this listing were selected because they were suggested by
colleagues of the editors, seemed timeless, and/or had late copyright
dates. The listing is by no means exhaustive.

The producer's name appears immediately following the entry's title,
after which are noted the year of production, the running time, and "col-
or," where applicable. (All entries are 16 millimeter, black and white,
sound, unless otherwise indicated.) Rental sources appear last, abbreviated. Full names, along with addresses, are listed at the end of the
chapter. If no rental sources are listed, the producer is also the distributor.

Perhaps a word of caution is in order. It is often assumed that a
film will provide adequate context for its subject matter, but frequently
the task may fall to the teacher. Previews may help to determine whether
the teacher will need to supplement a film's coverage or will want to
show only portions of a film relevant to particular course content.

COMMUNICATION AND LANGUAGE

Baboon Behavior. University of California, Los Angeles, S. L. Washburn
   & I. DeVore, 1961, 31 min., color. UC, IU, UMich, UMinn, NYU, and
   PSU.

A Communications Model. National Educational Television, 1967, 30 min.
   BU, IU, and PSU.

Communications Revolution. Ohio State University, 1961, 22 min. IU,
   UMich, NYU, and PSU.

Communication: The Nonverbal Agenda. CRM Productions, 1975, 30 min.,
   color. BU, UC, CRM/MHF, UI, KSU, UMich, and UMinn.

Exploring Nonverbal Communication (two-part filmstrip). Center for
   Advanced Study of Human Communication.

Language and Linguistics, Nos. 1-13. National Educational Television &
   H. L. Smith, Jr., 1957, each 29-30 min. UC, UI, IU, and UMinn.

Language by Gesture. University of Michigan, 1966, 28 min. UMich and
   PSU.

Nonverbal Behavior. Harper & Row Media, 1977, 22 min.

EMOTIONS AND MOTIVATION

Acquisition of the Token-Reward Habit in the Cat. K. U. Smith, 1937, 17
    min., silent. PSU.

Anxiety (filmstrip). Denoyer-Geppert Audio Visuals, 1966, color.

Baboon Ecology. University of California, Los Angeles, S. L. Washburn &
    I. DeVore, 1963, 21 min., color. UC, UMich, UMinn, NYU, and PSU.

Brakes and Misbehavior. National Educational Television, 1957, 30 min.
    UC, IU, and PSU.

Childhood Aggression: A Social Learning Approach to Family Therapy.
    Oregon Research Institute, 1974, 31 min., color. UMich and RP.

The City and the Self. Stanley Milgram and Harry From, 1973, 52 min. (or
    as two-part program), color. UI and TLM.

Coping with Conflict: As Expressed in Literature (two-part filmstrip).
    Sunburst Communications, 1973, color.

Coping with Life: The Role of Self-Control (two-part filmstrip). The
    Center for Humanities, 1975, color. SC.

David and Hazel: A Story in Communications. National Film Board of
    Canada, 1965, 29 min. BU, UI, KSU, UMich, UMinn, and NYU.

Dealing with Stress (two-part filmstrip). Human Relations Media, 1976,
    color. SC.

Emotional Maturity. Contemporary Films/McGraw-Hill, 1958, 20 min. BU,
    UI, KSU, UMich, UMinn, and NYU.

Emotions: Friend or Enemy. National Educational Television & Hofstra
    University, 1954, 30 min. IU.

Feelings. John Tracy Clinic, 1961, 11 min. KSU.

Frustration and Fixation. R. S. Feldman, P. Ellen, & R. H. Barrett,
    1951, 19 min. PSU.

The Game. National Film Board of Canada, 1967, 28 min. BU, UC, IU, KSU,
    MHF, UMich, UMinn, NYU, and PSU.

How Can I Understand Other People (filmstrip). Denoyer-Geppert Audio
    Visuals, 1956, color.

Masks: How We Hide Our Emotions (two-part filmstrip). Human Relations
     Media, 1976, color. HARM and SC.

Motivation and Reward in Learning. N. E. Miller & G. Hart, 1948, 15
     min. UC, UI, IU, KSU, UMich, UMinn, NYU, and PSU.

The Need to Achieve. National Educational Television, 1963, 30 min. BU,
     UC, UI, IU, KSU, UMich, UMinn, and PSU.

Personal Problem Solving (filmstrip). Denoyer-Geppert Audio Visuals,
     1965, color.

Personality: Roles You Play (two-part filmstrip). Sunburst
     Communications, 1974, color.

Psychosomatic Conditions--Obesity. Robert Anderson Associates, 1964, 28
     min. NYU.

Shyness: Reasons and Remedies (two-part filmstrip). Human Relations
     Media, 1975, color. SC.

Who Did What to Whom? Mager Associates, 1972, 17 min., color. UMich,
     UMinn, PSU, and RP.

GROWTH AND DEVELOPMENT, MATURATION

Achieving Sexual Maturity. Filmfair Communications, 1973, 8 mm., 21
     min., color. BU, PSU, and JW.

Adolescence to Adulthood: Rites of Passage (two-part filmstrip).
     Sunburst Communications, 1974, color.

Aging: Pre-Retirement. CRM Productions, 1973, 22 min., color. BU,
     CRM/MHF, UI, KSU, UMich, and PSU.

Behavior of Animals and Human Infants in Response to a Visual Cliff. R.
     D. Walk & E. J. Gibson, 1959, 15 min. UC, UMinn, and PSU.

Between Man and Woman. Psychological Films, Inc., 1973, 33 min., color.

Bright Side. Mental Health Film Board, I. Jacoby, R. Leacock, & H. Rome,
     1958, 23 min. UI, UMich, NYU, and PSU.

Childhood Aggression: A Social Learning Approach to Family Therapy.
     Oregon Research Institute, 1974, 31 min., color. UMich and RP.

Childhood: The Enchanted Years. N. L. Noxon & I. Rosten, 1971, 52 min.,
     color. IU, KSU, UMich, UMinn, and PFI.

Children Growing Up with Other People. British Information Services,
    1948, 24 min. UI, UMich, NYU, and PSU.

Cognition. Harper & Row Media, 1971, 28 min. HARM, UI, IU, KSU, UMinn,
    NYU, and PSU.

The Conscience of a Child. National Educational Television, 1963, 30
    min. BU, UC, UI, IU, KSU, UMich, UMinn, and PSU.

Death and Dying: Closing the Circle (three-part filmstrip). Guidance
    Associates, 1975, color.

Developing Self-Respect (two-part filmstrip). Sunburst Communications,
    1976, color.

Development. CRM Productions, 1971, 33 min., color. BU, CRM/MHF, UI,
    IU, KSU, and UMinn.

Development of the Smile and Fear of Strangers in the First Year of
    Life. Langley Porter Neuropsychiatric Clinic & D. G. Freedman, 1963,
    22 min. PSU.

Early Reading and Writing. Wm. B. Mathews and Co., 1966, 49 min.

Early Sibling Relationships. Curriculum Consultants, 1971, 8 mm., 45 min.

Emotional Ties in Infancy. L. J. Stone & Vassar College, Department of
    Psychology, 1969, 12 min. NYU.

The Ending (filmstrip). Schloat Productions of Prentice-Hall Media,
    1973, color.

Experiment No. 6--Childhood of the Chimpanzee. National Educational
    Television, Delta Primate Research Center, & W. Mason, 1967, 30 min.
    BU, UC, UI, IU, KSU, UMinn, and PSU.

Gramp: A Man Ages and Dies (filmstrip). Sunburst Communications, 1977,
    color. HARM and SC.

The Growing Mind: I. Sensori-Motor Development. British Broadcasting
    Corporation, 1970, 30 min. TLM.

Growing Up Female: As Six Become One. J. Reichert & J. Klein, 1971, 60
    min. KSU and NDF.

Guiding Environmental Discovery I: Mark, Six Months. R. Formanek, A.
    Gurian, & S. Greenberg, 1972, 8 mm., 20 min. CC.

How Babies Learn. United States Public Health Service, United States
    Children's Bureau, B. M. Caldwell, & H. B. Richmond, 1966, 35 min.,
    color. UC, IU, KSU, NYU, and PSU.

Infancy. Harper & Row Media, 1971, 20 min. HARM, UI, IU, KSU, UMinn, NYU, and PSU.

Intellectual Development of Babies. R. Formanek & G. Morine, 1965, 8 mm., 36 min., color. HU.

Learning to Learn in Infancy. L. J. Stone & Vassar College, Department of Psychology, 1970, 30 min. NYU.

Life Goals: Setting Personal Priorities (three-part filmstrip). Human Relations Media, 1976, color. SC.

Living with Dying (two-part filmstrip). Sunburst Communications, 1977, color. HARM and SC.

Long Time to Grow, Parts 1-3. Vassar College, Child Study Department; Part 1--Two- and Three-Year-Olds in Nursery School, 1951, 35 min.; Part 2--Four- and Five-Year-Olds in School, 1954, 40 min.; Part 3--Six-, Seven-, Eight-Year-Olds--Society of Children, 1957, 30 min. UC, UI, IU, KSU, UMich, UMinn, NYU, and PSU.

Masks: How We Hide Our Emotions (two-part filmstrip). Human Relations Media, 1976, color. HARM and SC.

Mate Selection: Making the Best Choice (two-part filmstrip). Human Relations Media, 1975, color. SC.

Men's Lives. New Day Films, 1974, 43 min., color. UMinn and NDF.

Moral Development. CRM Productions, 1973, 28 min., color. BU, CRM/MHF, UI, IU, KSU, and PSU.

On Being an Effective Parent, Parts 1 & 2. American Personnel and Guidance Association, 1973, 45 min., color.

Person to Person in Infancy. L. J. Stone & Vassar College, Department of Psychology, 1970, 22 min. NYU.

Personality: Roles You Play (two-part filmstrip). Sunburst Communications, 1974, color.

Perspectives on Death (two-part filmstrip). Sunburst Communications, 1977, color. HARM and SC.

Preparation for Parenthood (three-part filmstrip). Sunburst Communications, 1975, color.

Psychological Adjustment to College. Indiana University, 1971, 43 min. UC, UI, and IU.

Psychological Hazards in Infancy. L. J. Stone & Vassar College, Department of Psychology, 1970, 22 min. NYU.

Rock-A-Bye Baby. British Broadcasting Corporation, 1971, 30 min., color. UC, IU, UMich, UMinn, NYU, PSU, and TLM.

Sixteen in Webster Groves. Columbia Broadcasting System, 1966, 47 min. UC, UI, IU, KSU, UMich, UMinn, NYU, and PSU.

Study in Human Development, Parts 3-4. H. D. Behrens, silent; Part 3--Nineteen Months to Two Years and Eight Months, 1946, 19 min.; Part 4--Three Years to Five Years, 1948, 18 min. PSU.

Study of Twins, Parts 1-4. H. D. Behrens, silent; Parts 1 & 2, 1947, each 17 min.; Part 3, 1949, 18 min.; Part 4, 1951, 19 min. IU and PSU.

Thirty-Six Weeks Behavior Day. A. Gesell, 1953, 11 min. IU, KSU, UMich, UMinn, and PSU.

365 Days with Your Baby. Moringa Milk Industry, Japan, 1954, 28 min. PSU. (The narrative is in Japanese, but content is easy to follow.)

Values for Dating (four-part filmstrip). Sunburst Communications, 1974, color.

What About Marriage? (three-part filmstrip). Sunburst Communications, 1973, color.

LEARNING AND TESTING

Acquisition of the Token-Reward Habit in the Cat. K. U. Smith, 1937, 17 min., silent. PSU.

Analysis of the Forms of Animal Learning, Parts 1-4. K. U. Smith & W. E. Kappauf, 1940, silent; Parts 1 & 2, each 17 min.; Parts 3 & 4, each 13 min. UC and PSU.

Animal Reasoning. National Educational Television & Tulane University, 1967, 9 min. IU and PSU.

Aspects of Behavior. CRM Productions, 1971, 31 min., color. BU, CRM/MHF, UI, IU, and KSU.

Behavior Theory in Practice, Parts 1-4. E. P. Reese, 1966, each 20 min., color. UI, IU, KSU, UMich, PSU, and PH.

Biofeedback: The Yoga of the West. Hartley Film Foundation, 1974, 40 min, color. HFF, UI, and UMinn.

Brain and Behavior. National Educational Television, 1963, 30 min. BU, UC, UI, IU, KSU, UMich, UMinn, and PSU.

The Brain: Creating a Mental Elite. Document Associates, 1971, 22 min., color. UC, DA, NYU, and PSU.

Brainwashing, Parts 1 & 2. Columbia Broadcasting System, 1957, each 26 min. AF.

Children Learning by Experience. British Information Services, 1948, 32 min. IU, UMich, and NYU.

Computers and Human Behavior. National Educational Television, 1963, 30 min. BU, UC, UI, IU, KSU, UMich, UMinn, and PSU.

Demonstration in Human Learning. R. L. Karen & San Diego Junior College, 1957, 18 min. PSU.

Dynamics of an Experimental Neurosis, Parts 1-4. J. H. Masserman, 1944, silent; Part 1--Conditioned Feeding Behavior and Induction of Experimental Neurosis in Cats, 21 min.; Part 2--Effects of Environmental Frustrations and Intensification of Conflict in Neurotic Cats, 16 min.; Part 3--Experimental Diminution of Neurotic Behavior in Cats, 19 min.; Part 4--Active Participation in Establishing More Satisfactory Adjustment, 20 min. UMinn and PSU.

Dynamics of Competition in Cats: Inter-Cat Relationships in a Manipulative Feeding Situation. J. H. Masserman, 1944, 15 min., silent. PSU.

Exercise in Operant Conditioning. L. Aarons, 1966, 19 min. PSU.

How Babies Learn. United States Public Health Service, United States Children's Bureau, B. M. Caldwell, & H. B. Richmond, 1966, 35 min., color. UC, IU, KSU, NYU, and PSU.

Inside the World of Your Dreams. Independent Television Corporation, 1976, 28 min., color. UI and ITC.

Involuntary Control. N. Miller, 1971, 21 min., color. BU, IU, and JW.

The I.Q. Myth, Parts 1 & 2. Carousel Films, 1975, 51 min., color. BU, UC, CF, UI, KSU, and UMich.

Learning. CRM Productions, 1971, 30 min., color. BU, CRM/MHF, UI, IU, KSU, UMich, UMinn, and PSU.

Learning, Parts 1-3. K. C. Montgomery, R. J. Herrnstein, & W. H. Morse, 1956; Part 1--Reinforcement in Learning and Extinction, 8 min.; Part 2--Learning Discrimination and Skills, 14 min.; Part 3--Controlling Behavior Through Reinforcement, 16 min. BU, UC, UI, IU, KSU, UMich, UMinn, NYU, and PSU.

Learning About Learning. National Educational Television, 1963, 30 min.
  BU, UC, UI, IU, KSU, UMich, UMinn, and PSU.

Learning and Behavior. B. F. Skinner & R. J. Herrnstein, 1960, 26 min.
  UC, UI, IU, UMich, UMinn, NYU, and PSU.

Long Time to Grow, Parts 1-3. Vassar College, Child Study Department;
  Part 1--Two- and Three-Year-Olds in Nursery School, 1951, 35 min.;
  Part 2--Four- and Five-Year-Olds in School, 1954, 40 min.; Part
  3--Six-, Seven-, Eight-Year-Olds--Society of Children, 1957, 30 min.
  UC, UI, IU, KSU, UMich, UMinn, NYU, and PSU.

Man As He Behaves. National Educational Television, Harvard University,
  & O. Lindsley, 1967, 30 min. IU and PSU.

Methodology: The Psychologist and the Experiment. CRM Productions,
  1975, 31 min., color. CRM/MHF, UI, and KSU.

Moral Development. CRM Productions, 1973, 28 min., color. BU, CRM/MHF,
  UI, IU, KSU, and PSU.

Of Men and Machines. National Educational Television, 1963, 30 min. BU,
  UC, UI, IU, KSU, UMich, UMinn, and PSU.

Operation Reentry. WWTW, Chicago, & National Educational Television,
  1969, 30 min. UC, IU, and PSU.

A Psychology of Creativity. R. I. Evans & Center for Creative
  Leadership, 1972, 28 min., color. UI and MAC.

Reinforcement Control of a Young Child's Behavior. Weisberg, 1968, 15
  min. PSU.

Reinforcement Therapy. Smith, Kline, & French, 1966, 45 min. AF, UMich,
  UMinn, NYU, and PSU.

Rewards and Reinforcements in Learning. Behavior Modification
  Productions & L. Meyerson, 1969, 26 min. UC and UMich.

Spruce House. WWTW, Chicago, & National Educational Television, 1969, 29
  min. UC and IU.

Techniques of Non-Verbal Psychological Testing. C. J. Ross, 1964, 20
  min., color. BU, UI, IFB, KSU, and PSU.

To Alter Human Behavior . . . Without Mind Control. Document Associates,
  20 min. UC, DA, and NYU.

To Discover Your Body's Time Clock: Anticipate the Rhythms of Your
  Ecstasy and Blues. Document Associates, 1976, 20 min., color. UC,
  DA, KSU, and NYU.

Token Economy: Behaviorism Applied. CRM Productions, 1972, 23 min.,
    color. BU, UC, CRM/MHF, UI, IU, KSU, and PSU.

Understanding Aggression. R. Ulrich, 1972, 29 min., color. PH.

What Time is Your Body? British Broadcasting Corporation, 1975, 23 min.,
    color. UC, UMinn, and TLM.

MENTAL DEFICIENCY

Care of the Young Retarded Child. International Film Bureau, 1965, 18
    min., color. BU, IFB, KSU, UMich, UMinn, and PSU.

Color Her Sunshine. WCET, Cincinnati, 1969, 21 min. BU, UC, and IU.

Geel: A Changing Tradition. University of California, Extension Media
    Center, 1973, 41 min. UC, NYU, and PSU.

Mental Retardation, Parts 1 & 2. University of Wisconsin & United States
    Children's Bureau, 1967, each 30 min., color. UMinn and PSU.

Michael--A Mongoloid Child. British Film Institute, 1961, 14 min. NYU
    and PSU.

Not Without Hope. Marshall Faber, 1964, 23 min., color. PSU.

PKU--Preventable Mental Retardation (2nd ed.). International Film
    Bureau, 1967, 16 min., color.

Report on Down's Syndrome. University of Southern California School of
    Medicine, Los Angeles Children's Hospital, C. Ross, & R. Koch, 1963,
    21 min., color. BU, UC, IFB, KSU, UMinn, and PSU.

Selling One Guy Named Larry. National Association for Retarded Children,
    1966, 17 min. NYU and PSU.

There Was a Door. Green Park Productions, 1959, 30 min. UMich, NYU, and
    PSU.

Time's Lost Children. Indiana University, 1973, 29 min., color. UC, UI,
    and IU.

To Lighten the Shadows. Southern Illinois University, 1963, 21 min. BU,
    IFB, and PSU.

Training the Mentally Retarded Child at Home (filmstrip). National Film
    Board of Canada, 1965, color. IFB.

PERSONALITY DEVELOPMENT AND MENTAL DISORDERS

Abnormal Behavior. CRM Productions, 1971, 28 min., color. BU, CRM/MHF, UI, and KSU.

Activity for Schizophrenia. United States Veterans Administration, 1951, 25 min. PSU.

Angry Boy. Mental Health Film Board, 1951, 28 min., color. BU, UC, UI, IU, KSU, UMich, UMinn, NYU, and PSU.

Aphasia: The Road Back. National Educational Television, 1965, 20 min. BU, IU, UMinn, and PSU.

Autism's Lonely Children. National Educational Television, University of California, Los Angeles, Neuropsychiatric School, & F. Hewett, 1967, 20 min. BU, UC, IU, UMinn, and PSU.

Case Study of Multiple Personality. C. H. Thigpen & H. M. Cleckley, 1957, 30 min., b & w, color. UC, UMich, and PSU.

Children in Search of a Self. Memorial Guidance Clinic of Virginia, H. Gordon, & W. M. Lordi, 1961, 21 min. PSU.

Come Out, Come Out. Whoever You Are. WWTW, Chicago, 1969, 59 min. UC and IU.

The Conscience of a Child. National Educational Television, 1963, 30 min. BU, UC, UI, IU, KSU, UMich, UMinn, and PSU.

Depression. Robert Anderson Associates, H. B. Durost, & H. E. Lehmann, 1961, 30 min. BU, UC, UMich, NYU, and PSU.

Development of an Infantile Psychosis. University of Washington, 1963, 18 min. PSU.

Development of the Smile and Fear of Strangers in the First Year of Life. Langley Porter Neuropsychiatric Clinic & D. G. Freedman, 1963, 22 min. PSU.

Dynamics of an Experimental Neurosis, Parts 1-4. J. H. Masserman, 1944, silent; Part 1--Conditioned Feeding Behavior and Induction of Experimental Neurosis in Cats, 21 min.; Part 2--Effects of Environmental Frustrations and Intensification of Conflict in Neurotic Cats, 16 min.; Part 3--Experimental Diminution of Neurotic Behavior in Cats, 19 min.; Part 4--Active Participation in Establishing More Satisfactory Adjustment, 20 min. UMinn and PSU.

Emotional Illness. National Educational Television, 1967, 30 min. UC, IU, KSU, UMinn, and PSU.

Epileptic Seizure Patterns. Indiana University, 1967, 25 min. UC, IU, UMinn, and PSU.

Experimental Neuroses by Control of Emotions. J. T. Barendregt & F. S. A. M. van Dam, 1969, 30 min. PFI.

The Feeling of Hostility. National Film Board of Canada, 1948, 27 min. BU, UC, UI, IU, KSU, UMinn, NYU, and PSU.

The Feeling of Rejection. National Film Board of Canada, 1948, 23 min. BU, UC, UI, IU, KSU, UMich, UMinn, NYU, and PSU.

Fountain House. WWTW, Chicago, & National Educational Television, 1969, 29 min. IU.

Freud: The Hidden Nature of Man. H. Kravitz, 1970, 29 min., color. BU, UI, IU, KSU, LCA, and UMinn.

Frustration and Fixation. R. S. Feldman, P. Ellen, & R. H. Barrett, 1951, 19 min. PSU.

Games People Play: The Practice. National Educational Television, 1967, 30 min. BU, UC, UI, IU, UMinn, NYU, and PSU.

Geel: A Changing Tradition. University of California, Extension Media Center, 1974, 41 min. UC, NYU, and PSU.

Horizon House. WWTW, Chicago, & National Educational Television, 1969, 29 min. IU.

The Human Side. Mental Health Materials Center, D. C. Cameron, H. Rome, M. Karlins, & N. K. Kjenass, 1957, 24 min. UMinn, NYU, and PSU.

"I'm OK--You're OK": Can T. A. (Transactional Analysis) Free the Child in Us? Document Associates, 1973, 18 min., color. UC, DA, KSU, NYU, and PSU.

Lonely Night. Mental Health Film Board & I. Jacoby, 1955, 62 min. BU, UC, IU, NYU, and PSU.

Man As He Behaves. National Educational Television, Harvard University, & O. Lindsley, 1967, 30 min. IU and PSU.

A Man with a Problem. University of Adelaide, South Australia, W. A. Cramond, F. M. M. Mai, J. H. Court, & J. Morley, 1967, 17 min. UC and PSU.

The Maze. J. B. Maas, R. Young, & D. Gruben, 1971, 30 min., color. UC, HM, IU, and PSU.

Mental Health: New Frontiers of Sanity. Document Associates, 1971, 22
    min., color. UC, DA, and NYU.

Pathological Anxiety. Robert Anderson Associates, Montreal General
    Hospital, N. B. Epstein, H. E. Lehmann, & A. M. Marcus, 1961, 30
    min. BU, UC, UMich, NYU, and PSU.

Personality. CRM Productions, 1971, 30 min., color. BU, CRM/MHF, UI,
    and KSU.

Primal Therapy: In Search of the Real You. Document Associates, 1976,
    19 min., color. DA, KSU, NYU, and PSU.

Psychological Defenses (two series, each a three-part filmstrip). Human
    Relations Media, 1975, color. HARM and SC.

Psychopath. Robert Anderson Associates, Andra Verdun Protestant
    Hospital, H. B. Durost, & H. E. Lehmann, 1961, 30 min. BU, UMich,
    NYU, and PSU.

The Quiet One. J. Loeb & W. Levitt, 1948, 68 min. UC, UI, IU, KSU,
    UMich, NYU, and PSU.

Referred for Underachievement: A Family Intake Interview. E. A. Mason,
    1966, 35 min. UC, UI, and NYU.

Shades of Gray. United States Army, 1948, 66 min. IU, UMich, UMinn, and
    PSU.

Suicide: Causes and Prevention (two-part filmstrip). Human Relations
    Media, 1977, color. HARM and SC.

They're Your People. WWTW, Chicago, & National Educational Television,
    1969, 29 min. IU.

To Live and Move According to Your Nature Is Called Love. WWTW, Chicago,
    & National Educational Television, 1969, 29 min. UC and IU.

Wellmet House. WWTW, Chicago, & National Educational Television, 1969,
    30 min. IU.

Who's OK, Who's Not OK: An Introduction to Abnormal Psychology
    (three-part filmstrip). Human Relations Media, 1976, color. HARM
    and SC.

Working and Playing to Health. Mental Health Materials Center, 1954, 36
    min. BU, UMich, and NYU.

You Are There: Dr. Pinel Unchains the Insane. Columbia Broadcasting
    System, 1956, 27 min. UI, IU, UMich, and PSU.

PSYCHOLOGY AS A SCIENCE AND SCHOOLS OF PSYCHOLOGY

Being Abraham Maslow. W. Bennis & L. Zweig, 1972, 30 min. FL and PSU.

B. F. Skinner and Behavior Change. Research Press, 1975, 45 min.,
    color. UC, UMich, and RP.

B. F. Skinner on Counseling. American Personnel and Guidance
    Association, 1972, 25 min., color.

B. F. Skinner on Education, Parts 1 & 2. American Personnel and Guidance
    Association, 1972, each 25 min., color.

Carl Rogers on Education, Parts 1 & 2. American Personnel and Guidance
    Association, 1973, each 30 min., color.

A Conversation with Carl Rogers, Parts 1 & 2. Film Center, each 30 min.
    PFI.

Dr. Carl Gustav Jung. J. Freeman & H. Burnett, 1967, 38 min. PSU.

Dr. Ernest Jones. National Broadcasting Corporation, 1958, 27 min. UI,
    UMich, UMinn, and PSU.

ESP: The Human 'X' Factor. National Educational Television, D. Prowitt,
    & J. B. Rhine, 1967, 30 min. UC, UI, IU, UMinn, and PSU.

The Humanistic Revolution. Psychological Films, Inc., 1971, 32 min.

Inside the World of Your Dreams. Independent Television Corporation,
    1976, 28 min., color. UI and ITC.

Jung Speaks of Freud. R. I. Evans & J. W. Meany, 1957, 29 min. UC and
    PSU.

Landmarks in Psychology (three-part filmstrip). Human Relations Media,
    1976, color. HARM and SC.

Notable Contributors to the Psychology of Personality. National Science
    Foundation & R. I. Evans. MAC and PSU.
    Dr. Gordon Allport, Parts 1 & 2, 1966, each 50 min.
    Dr. Raymond Cattell, Parts 1 & 2, 1966, each 50 min.
    Dr. Erik Erikson, Parts 1 & 2, 1966, each 50 min.
    Dr. Hans Eysenck, 1971, 30 min., color.
    Dr. Erich Fromm, Parts 1 & 2, 1966, each 50 min.
    Dr. Ernest Hilgard, Parts 1 & 2, 1966; Part 1--27 min.; Part 2--30
        min.
    Dr. Carl G. Jung, 1966, 32 min.
    Dr. R. D. Laing, Parts 1 & 2, 1966, each 30 min., color.
    Dr. Konrad Lorenz, Parts 1-4, 1966, each 30 min., color.

Dr. Arthur Miller, Parts 1 & 2, 1966, each 50 min.
Dr. Gardner Murphy, Parts 1 & 2, 1966, each 50 min.
Dr. Henry Murray, Parts 1 & 2, 1966, each 50 min.
Dr. Jean Piaget with Dr. Barbel Inhelder, Parts 1 & 2, 1971, each 40
    min., color.
Dr. J. B. Rhine, Parts 1 & 2, 1971, each 45 min., color.
Dr. Carl Rogers, Parts 1 & 2, 1971, each 50 min., color.
Dr. Nevitt Sanford, Parts 1 & 2, 1966; Part 1--31 min.; Part 2--25
    min.
Dr. B. F. Skinner, Parts 1 & 2, 1966, each 50 min.

R. D. Laing: A Dialogue on Mental Illness and Its Treatment. Harper &
    Row Media, 1977, 22 min.

R. D. Laing on R. D. Laing. Harper & Row Media, 1977, 15 min.

Search and Research: Psychology in Perspective. Psychological Films,
    Inc., 1963, 30 min.

The Story of Carl Gustav Jung, Parts 1-3. British Broadcasting
    Corporation, 1972, each 30 min., color. UC, UI, UMich, and TLM.

Together, Parts 1 & 2. F. S. Keller and B. F. Skinner, 1972, color; Part
    1--The Early Years, 33 min.; Part 2--1930 to Tomorrow, 28 min. PH.

PSYCHOTHERAPY

Actualization Therapy: An Integration of Rogers, Perls and Ellis.
    Psychological Films, Inc., 1974, 27 min., color.

Actualization Through Assertion. Research Press, 28 min.

Albert Ellis: Rational Emotive Psychotherapy, Parts 1-5. American
    Personnel and Guidance Association, 1972, each 30 min., color; Part
    1--Rational Emotive Psychotherapy; Part 2--Rational Emotive Psycho-
    therapy Applied to Groups; Part 3--Demonstration with an Elementary
    School Age Child; Part 4--Demonstration with a Young Divorced Woman;
    Part 5--Demonstration with a Woman Fearful of Expressing Emotion.

Because That's My Way. W. McGaw, 16 mm. or videotape, 60 min., color.
    GP.

Carl Rogers Conducts an Encounter Group. J. M. Whiteley, 1970, 70 min.,
    color. APGA.

Carl Rogers on Facilitating a Group. American Personnel and Guidance
    Association, 1971, 30 min., color.

Carl Rogers on Marriage, Parts 1-5. American Personnel and Guidance
    Association, 1973, color; Part 1--Persons as Partners, 28 min.; Part
    2--An Interview with Hal and Jane, 44 min.; Part 3-- An Interview
    with Bob and Carol, 44 min.; Part 4--An Interview with Nancy and
    John, 42 min.; Part 5--An Interview with Jane and Jerry, 44 min.

Childhood Aggression: A Social Learning Approach to Family Therapy.
    Oregon Research Institute, 1974, 31 min., color. UMich and RP.

Cry Help! National Broadcasting Corporation, 1970, 90 min., color. UC,
    UI, UMinn, and PSU.

Emotional Dilemma. National Educational Television, 1967, 60 min. BU,
    UC, IU, KSU, UMinn, and PSU.

Encounter: To Make a Start. Psychological Films, Inc., 1974, 31 min.

The Farthest Frontier. Columbia Broadcasting System, 1967, 47 min. UC,
    UI, UMich, UMinn, and PSU.

Fat Fighters. Brigham Young University, Department of Motion Picture
    Production, 1971, 21 min. UMinn and PSU.

Fighting Fear with Fear. McGraw-Hill Films, 1968, 27 min. UI, KSU, and
    UMinn.

Frankl and the Search for Meaning. Psychological Films, Inc., 1973, 30
    min., color.

Full Circle. Mental Health Film Board & I. Jacoby, 1964, 29 min. BU,
    UI, IFB, NYU, and PSU.

Games People Play: The Theory. National Educational Television, 1967,
    30 min. BU, UC, UI, IU, UMinn, NYU, and PSU.

Gestalt Dream Analysis. Psychological Films, Inc., 60 min.

Gramp: A Man Ages and Dies (filmstrip). Sunburst Communications, 1977,
    color. HARM and SC.

Group Worker. University of Michigan, 1967, 30 min. PSU.

The Human Potential Movement: Journey to the Center of the Self.
    Document Associates, 17 min., color. UC, DA, and NYU.

"I'm OK--You're OK": Can T. A. (Transactional Analysis) Free the Child
    in Us? Document Associates, 1973, 18 min., color. UC, DA, KSU, NYU,
    and PSU.

In the Now: An Individual Application of Gestalt Therapy. Psychological
    Films, Inc., 45 min.

Living with Dying (two-part filmstrip). Sunburst Communications, 1977,
     color. HARM and SC.

Lowen and Bioenergetic Therapy. Psychological Films, Inc., 1973, 48
     min., color.

Meditation: Yoga, T'ai Chi and Other Spiritual Trips. Document
     Associates, 1975, 21 min., color. UC, DA, KSU, and NYU.

Mind over Body. British Broadcasting Corporation and Time-Life Films,
     1972, 35 min., color. UI, UMich, PSU, and TLM.

Perspectives on Death (two-part filmstrip). Sunburst Communications,
     1977, color. HARM and SC.

Primal Therapy: In Search of the Real You. Document Associates, 1976,
     19 min., color. DA, KSU, NYU, and PSU.

Progressive Relaxation Training. Research Press, 21 min.

Psychiatry in Action. Contemporary Films, 1943, 60 min. PSU.

Reinforcement Therapy. Smith, Kline, & French, 1966, 45 min. AF, UMich,
     UMinn, NYU, and PSU.

Suicide: Causes and Prevention (two-part filmstrip). Human Relations
     Media, 1977, color. HARM and SC.

The Suicide Clinic: A Cry for Help. National Educational Television,
     1969, 28 min. UC, UI, and IU.

Three Approaches to Psychotherapy, Parts 1-3. E. L. Shostrom, 1965, b &
     w, color; Part 1--48 min.; Part 2--32 min.; Part 3--37 min. BU, KSU,
     UMich, UMinn, NYU, and PFI.

Touching. Psychological Films, Inc., 1975, 35 min., color.

Trouble in the Family. National Educational Television, 1965, 90 min.
     UC, UI, IU, KSU, UMinn, NYU, and PSU.

Two Faces of Group Leadership. Psychological Films, Inc., 30 min.

SENSE ORGANS AND THE NERVOUS SYSTEM

Autonomic Nervous System. National Foundation and Duke University School
     of Medicine, 1953, 40 min., color. BU and PSU.

Behavior Disturbances After Bilateral Removal of the Frontal Areas of the
     Cortex in Cats. K. U. Smith, 1938, 16 min., silent. PSU.

Biofeedback: Listening to Your Head. Document Associates, 19 min.,
    color. UC, DA, NYU, and PSU.

Biofeedback: The Yoga of the West. Hartley Film Foundation, 1974, 40
    min., color. HFF, UI, and UMinn.

Brain and Behavior. National Educational Television, 1963, 30 min. BU,
    UC, UI, IU, KSU, UMich, UMinn, and PSU.

The Change from Visible to Invisible: A Study of Optical Transitions.
    J. J. Gibson, 1969, 10 min., silent. PSU.

Dangerous Noise. Pennsylvania State University, Psychological Cinema
    Register, 1968, 15 min.

Drugs and the Nervous System. Churchill Films, 1966, 18 min., color.
    BU, UC, UI, IU, KSU, UMich, UMinn, and NYU.

Experimental Psychology of Vision. Center for Mass Communication & G. M.
    Gilbert, 1941, 16 min., silent. UI, UMich, and PSU.

Fidelity of Report. W. S. Ray, 1946, 6 min., silent. BU, UC, and PSU.

Functions of the Nervous System. K. K. Bosse, 1949, 13 min. BU, UI, and
    PSU.

Genetics and Behavior. J. Antonitis & J. P. Scott, 1953, 18 min., b & w,
    color, silent. PSU.

Holistic Health: The New Medicine. Hartley Film Foundation, 35 min.

Information Processing. CRM Productions, 1971, 28 min., color. BU,
    CRM/MHF, UI, KSU, UMich, and PSU.

Inside the World of Your Dreams. Independent Television Corporation,
    1976, 28 min., color. UI and ITC.

Involuntary Control. N. Miller, 1971, 21 min., color. BU, IU, and JW.

Learning to Live with Stress: Programming the Body for Health.
    Document Associates, 19 min.

Living in a Reversed World. E. J. Mauthner & Professor Erismann, 1958,
    12 min. PSU.

Meditation: Yoga, T'ai Chi and Other Spiritual Trips. Document
    Associates, 1975, 21 min., color. UC, DA, KSU, and NYU.

The Mind of Man. National Educational Television, 1970, 119 min.,
    color. BU, UC, UI, IU, UMich, UMinn, and PSU.

Miracle of the Mind. Columbia Broadcasting System, 1968, 26 min.,
    color. BU, UI, IU, MHF, and UMinn.

Motion Perception, Parts 1 & 2. J. B. Maas, 1971, color; Part
    1--2-Dimensional Motion Perception, 7 min.; Part 2--3-Dimensional
    Motion Perception, 11 min. HM, UI, and PSU.

Neurological Examination of the Newborn. Wexler Film Production & United
    States Department of Health, Education, and Welfare, National Insti-
    tute of Health, 1960, 30 min., color. PSU.

Neurological Examination of the One-Year-Old. Wexler Film Production &
    United States Department of Health, Education, and Welfare, National
    Institute of Health, 1960, 30 min., color. PSU.

Role of the Hypothalamus in Emotion and Behavior. J. H. Masserman, 1943,
    27 min., silent. UC and PSU.

A Rough Sketch for a Proposed Film Dealing with the Powers of Ten and the
    Relative Size of Things in the Universe. Pyramid Films, 1968, 8 min.

Secrets of Sleep. WGBH and British Broadcasting Corporation, 1976, 52
    min., color. TLM.

Seizure: The Medical Treatment and Social Problems of Epilepsy. United
    States Veterans Administration, 1951, 47 min. BU, KSU, UMinn, and
    PSU.

The Senses. American Institute of Biological Sciences, 1961, 30 min.
    IU, KSU, and UMich.

The Sensory World. CRM Productions, 1971, 33 min., color. BU, CRM/MHF,
    UI, KSU, and PSU.

Sleep and Dreaming in Humans. J. B. Maas, 1971, 14 min., color. HM, IU,
    and PSU.

The Sleeping Brain. J. B. Maas, 1971, 23 min., color. HM, IU, UMinn,
    and PSU.

Strange Sleep. WGBH, 1976, 59 min., color. TLM.

To Discover Your Body's Time Clock: Anticipate the Rhythms of Your
    Ecstasy and Blues. Document Associates, 1976, 20 min., color. UC,
    DA, KSU, and NYU.

Upright Vision Through Inverting Spectacles. E. J. Mauthner, Professor
    Erismann, & I. Kohler, 1953, 11 min., silent. PSU.

Visual Perception. Educational Testing Service, 1959, 20 min., color.
    UC, UI, IU, KSU, UMich, and PSU.

What Time Is Your Body? British Broadcasting Corporation, 1975, 23 min.,
    color. UC, UMinn, and TLM.

A World To Perceive. National Educational Television, 1963, 30 min. BU,
    UC, UI, IU, KSU, UMich, UMinn, and PSU.

SOCIAL AND ANTISOCIAL BEHAVIOR

Alcoholism: A Model of Drug Dependency. CRM Productions, 1972, 20 min.,
    color. UC, CRM/MHF, UI, IU, KSU, UMinn, and PSU.

All the Lonely People: A Study of Alienation (two-part filmstrip).
    Schloat Productions of Prentice-Hall Media, 1973, color.

America on the Rocks. National Audiovisual Center, 1973, 15- and
    28-min. versions, color.

Baboon Social Organization. University of California, Los Angeles, S. L.
    Washburn, & I. DeVore, 1963, 17 min., color. UC, UMinn, NYU, and PSU.

Behavioral Interviewing with Couples. Research Press, 14 min. (Also
    available in videocassette.)

Biochemedical Revolution: Moods of the Future. Document Associates, 17
    min. UC and DA.

The Black Woman. National Educational Television, 1970, 52 min. UC, IU,
    UMich, and PSU.

Bold New Approach. Mental Health Film Board & I. Jacoby, 1966, 52 min.
    UI, IU, IFB, UMich, UMinn, NYU, and PSU.

Business, Behaviorism and the Bottom Line. CRM Productions, 1972, 23
    min., color. BU, UC, CRM/MHF, UI, IU, KSU, UMich, UMinn, and PSU.

Childhood Aggression: A Social Learning Approach to Family Therapy.
    Oregon Research Institute, 1974, 31 min., color. UMich and RP.

The City and the Self. Stanley Milgram and Harry From, 1973, 52 min. (or
    as a two-part program), color. UI and TLM.

Competitive Values (two-part filmstrip). Human Relations Media, 1975,
    color. SC.

Conformity and Independence. Harper & Row Media, 1975, 23 min., color.
    HARM, UMich, UMinn, and NYU.

The Delinquents, Parts 1 & 2. Columbia Broadcasting System, 1959, each
    30 min.; Part 1--A Boy Named Bob; Part 2--The Highfields Story. AF.

The Detached Americans. WCAU, Philadelphia, 1964, 33 min. BU, UC, KSU, and UMinn.

Drug Abuse: Bennies and Goofballs. United States Public Health Service, Food and Drug Administration, 1966, 19 min. PSU.

Drugs and the Nervous System. Churchill Films, 1966, 18 min., color. BU, UC, UI, IU, KSU, UMich, UMinn, and NYU.

The Eye of the Storm. American Broadcasting Corporation, 1970, 25 min., color. UC, UI, IU, KSU, UMich, UMinn, and PSU.

The Family (four-part filmstrip). Schloat Productions of Prentice-Hall Media, color.

Games People Play: The Theory. National Educational Television, 1967, 30 min. BU, UC, UI, IU, UMinn, NYU, and PSU.

Group Dynamics: "Groupthink." CRM Productions, 1973, 22 min., color. BU, UC, CRM/MHF, UI, KSU, UMich, and UMinn.

Growing Up Female: As Six Become One. J. Reichert & J. Klein, 1971, 60 min. KSU and NDF.

Human Aggression. Harper & Row Media, 1977, 22 min.

If You Want It Done Right. Roundtable Films, 1975, 20 min., color.

I'm Dependent, You're Addicted. British Broadcasting Corporation, 1973, 51 min., color. TLM.

Invitation to Social Psychology. Harper & Row Media, 1977, 25 min., color. HARM and NYU.

John Kenneth Galbraith: The Idea of the City. University-at-Large, 1968, 29 min., color. UI, KSU, UMich, and PSU.

Leadership: Style or Circumstance? CRM Productions, 1975, 27 min., color. BU, UC, CRM/MHF, UI, KSU, UMich, and UMinn.

LSD--Insight or Insanity? M. Miller & R. S. Scott, 1968, 28 min., color. BFA, BU, UC, UI, IU, KSU, UMich, NYU, and PSU.

LSD--The Spring Grove Experiment. Columbia Broadcasting System, 1966, 54 min. BU, UI, IU, KSU, UMich, UMinn, and PSU.

Maggie Kuhn: Wrinkled Radical. Indiana University, 1975, 27 min., color.

Masculinity (four-part filmstrip). Schloat Productions of Prentice-Hall Media, color.

Maybe Tomorrow. Spring Hill College, 1969, 19 min., color. IU.

Men in Cages. Columbia Broadcasting System, 1966, 52 min. BU, UC, KSU, UMinn, and PSU.

Men's Lives. New Day Films, 1974, 43 min., color. UMinn and NDF.

My Parents Are Getting a Divorce (two-part filmstrip). Human Relations Media, 1976, color. SC.

The Neglected. Mental Health Film Board & I. Jacoby, 1965, 30 min. BU, UC, UI, IU, IFB, UMich, UMinn, NYU, and PSU.

The New Morality: Challenge of the Student Generation. Columbia Broadcasting System, 1967, 37 min. UC, UI, and UMinn.

No Gun Towers, No Fences. WWVU, West Virginia University, 1969, 30 min., color. UC, UI, IU, and KSU.

Obedience. S. Milgram, 1965, 45 min. BU, UC, UMich, NYU, and PSU.

Odyssey of a Dropout. Coronet Films, 1966, 20 min. UI, KSU, and UMinn.

Patterns of Human Conflict (three-part filmstrip). Schloat Productions of Prentice-Hall Media, 1973, color.

Prison. National Educational Television, 1971, 59 min. UC, IU, and PSU.

Productivity and the Self-Fulfilling Prophecy: The Pygmalion Effect. CRM Productions, 1975, 31 min., color. BU, UC, CRM/MHF, UI, KSU, UMich, and UMinn.

Rosedale: The Way It Is. Indiana University, 1976, 57 min., color.

Seeds of Hate: An Examination of Prejudice (two-part filmstrip). Schloat Productions of Prentice-Hall Media, 1972, color.

The Social Animal. National Educational Television, 1963, 30 min. BU, UC, UI, IU, KSU, UMich, UMinn, and PSU.

Social Psychology. CRM Productions, 1971, 33 min., color. BU, CRM/MHF, UI, KSU, and PSU.

Story of Joe: Recollections of Drug Abuse (six-part filmstrip). Richard Bruner Productions, 1970, color. SC.

Three Styles of Marital Conflict. Research Press, 14 min. (Also available in videocassette.)

Transactional Analysis. CRM Productions, 1975, 31 min., color. BU, UC, CRM/MHF, UI, KSU, UMich, and UMinn.

Values for Dating (four-part filmstrip). Sunburst Communications, 1974, color.

Violence: Will It Ever End? Document Associates, 1973, 19 min., color. UC, DA, and NYU.

What About Marriage? (three-part filmstrip). Sunburst Communications, 1973, color.

Who Did What to Whom? Mager Associates, 1972, 17 min., color. UMich, UMinn, PSU, and RP.

Why Do We Obey Laws? (two-part filmstrip). Sunburst Communications, 1974, color.

Women and Health/Mental Health (seven-part microfilm). Women's History Research Center.

Women In Management: Threat or Opportunity? CRM Productions, 1975, 29 min., color. BU, UC, CRM/MHF, UI, KSU, and UMinn.

A Woman's Place (four-part filmstrip). Schloat Productions of Prentice-Hall Media, color.

Women's Work: America, 1620-1920 (four-part filmstrip). Schloat Productions of Prentice-Hall Media, color.

STATISTICS

Statistics at a Glance. Helios Films, 1972, 20 min., color. BU and JW.

Meanings of Abbreviations

AF	Association Films
AIT	Agency for Instructional Television
APGA	American Personnel and Guidance Association
ARF	Addiction Research Foundation
BF	Biofilm
BFA	BFA Educational Media
BU	Boston University
CC	Curriculum Consultants
CF	Carousel Films
CHF	Churchill Films
CM	Carol Media
CRM/MHF	CRM/McGraw-Hill Films
DA	Document Associates
DAFL	Du Art Film Labs
DF	Dimension Films
FI	Films Incorporated
FL	Filmakers Library

GA	Guidance Associates
GP	Great Plains National Instructional Television Library
HARM	Harper & Row Media
HBJ	Harcourt Brace Jovanovich
HFF	Hartley Film Foundation
HM	Houghton Mifflin
HU	Hofstra University
IFB	International Film Bureau
IU	Indiana University
ITC	Independent Television Corporation
JW	John Wiley and Sons
KSU	Kent State University
LCA	Learning Corporation of America
MAC	Macmillan Films, Inc.
MHB	McGraw-Hill Book Co.
MHF	McGraw Hill Films
MHMC	Mental Health Media Center
MTPS	Modern Talking Picture Service
NAC	National Audiovisual Center
NDF	New Day Films
NMAC	National Medical Audiovisual Center
NYU	New York University
P	Pyramid
PE	Perennial Education, Inc.
PFI	Psychological Films, Inc.
PH	Prentice-Hall Film Library
PMF	Parents' Magazine Films
PSU	Pennsylvania State University
RM	Research Media
RP	Research Press
SC	Sunburst Communications
SF	Scott, Foresman, and Co.
TLM	Time-Life Multimedia
UC	California, University of
UI	Illinois, University of
UMich	Michigan, University of
UMinn	Minnesota, University of
WC	Wisconsin Clearinghouse on Alcohol and Other Drug Information

Addresses of Distributors

Addiction Research Foundation, 36 Russell Street, Toronto, Ontario, Canada M5S 2S1

Agency For Instructional Television, Box A, Bloomington, IN 47401

American Academy of Psychotherapists, Tape Library, c/o Dr. Herbert Roth, 2175 N. W. 86th Street, Suite 7, Des Moines, IA 50322

American Association for the Advancement of Science, 1515 Massachusetts
    Avenue, N. W., Washington, DC 20005

American Personnel and Guidance Association, 1607 New Hampshire Avenue,
    N. W., Washington, DC 20009

Anti-Defamation League of B'nai B'rith, 315 Lexington Avenue, New York,
    NY 10016

Aspect IV Educational Films, 41 Riverside Avenue, Westport CT 06880

Association Films, 600 Grand Avenue, Ridgefield, NJ 07657

Audio-Forum, 901 North Washington Street, Suite 200, Alexandria, VA 22314

BFA Educational Media, 2211 Michigan Avenue, P. O. Box 1795, Santa
    Monica, CA 90406

BioFilm, RFD #1, P. O. Box 192, Easton, MD 21601

BMA Audio Cassette Programs, 270 Madison Avenue, New York, NY 10016

Boston University, Krasker Memorial Film Library, School of Education,
    765 Commonwealth Avenue, Boston, MA 02215

California, University of, Extension Media Center, Berkeley, CA 94720

Carol Media, East 36A Midland Avenue, Paramus, NJ 07652

Carousel Films, 1501 Broadway, New York, NY 10036

Center for Advanced Study of Human Communication, P. O. Box 14461,
    Columbus, OH 43214

Center for the Study of Democratic Institutions, P. O. Box 4068, Santa
    Barbara, CA 93103

Churchill Films, 662 North Robertson Boulevard, Los Angeles, CA 90069

CRM/McGraw-Hill Films, 110 Fifteenth Street, Del Mar, CA 92014

Curriculum Consultants, 13 Oak Brook Lane, Merrick, NY 11566

Dimension Films, 666 North Robertson Boulevard, Los Angeles, CA 90069

Denoyer-Geppert Audio Visuals, 5235 Ravenswood Avenue, Chicago, IL 60640

Document Associates, 211 East 43rd Street, New York, NY 10022

Du Art Film Labs, 245 West 55th Street, New York, NY 10019

Filmakers Library, 290 West End Avenue, New York, NY   10023

Films Incorporated, 1144 Wilmette Avenue, Wilmette, IL   60091

Florida State University, Film Library, Tallahassee, FL   32306

Florida, University of, College of Education, Institute for Development
    of Human Resources, 513 Weil Hall, Gainesville, FL   32601

Great Plains National Instructional Television Library, P. O. Box 80669,
    Lincoln, NE 68501

Guidance Associates, 757 Third Avenue, New York, NY   10017

Harcourt Brace Jovanovich, 757 Third Avenue, New York, NY   10017

Harper & Row Media, 10 East 53rd Street, New York, NY   10022

Hartley Film Foundation, Cat Rock Road, Cos Cob, CT   06807

Hofstra University, Hempstead, Long Island, NY   11550

Houghton Mifflin Co., New Media, One Beacon Street, Boston, MA   02107

Human Relations Media, 343 Manville Road, Pleasantville, NY   10570

Illinois, University of, Visual Aids Service, Champaign, IL   61820

Independent Television Corporation, 555 Madison Avenue, New York, NY
    10022

Indiana University, Audio-Visual Center, Bloomington, IN   47401

Instructional Dynamics, Inc., 450 East Ohio, Chicago, IL   60611

International Film Bureau, 323 South Michigan Avenue, Chicago, IL   60604

Jeffrey Norton Publishers, Audio Division, 145 East 49th Street, New
    York, NY   10017

Kent State University, Audio Visual Services, Kent, OH   44242

Lansford Publishing Co., P. O. Box 8711, Department QQ, San Jose, CA
    95155

Learning Corporation of America, 1350 Avenue of the Americas, New York,
    NY   10019

Life Science Associates, One Fenimore Road, P. O. Box 500, Bayport, NY
    11705

Listening Library, Inc., One Park Avenue, Old Greenwich, CT   06870

Macmillan Films, Inc., 34 MacQuesten Parkway South, Mt. Vernon, NY 10550

Maine, University of, Instructional Systems Center, Film Rental Library,
     Orono, ME   04473

Wm. B. Mathews and Co., 130 Seventh Street, Pittsburgh, PA   15229

McGraw-Hill Films, 1221 Avenue of the Americas, New York 10020 (for
     purchase information) or Princeton Road, Hightstown, NJ 08520 (for
     rental information)

McGraw-Hill Book Co., Trade Order Services, College Division, Princeton
     Road, Hightstown, NJ 08520

Mental Health Materials Center, 419 Park Avenue South, New York, NY   10016

Mental Health Media Center, 4907 Cordell Avenue, Bethesda, MD   20014

Michigan, University of, Audio-Visual Education Center, 416 Fourth
     Street, Ann Arbor, MI   48109

Minnesota, University of, Audio-Visual Library Services, 3300 University
     Avenue, S. E., Minneapolis, MN 55414

Modern Talking Picture Service, 2323 New Hyde Park Road, New Hyde Park,
     NY   11040

National Audiovisual Center, National Archives and Records Service,
     General Services Administration, Washington, DC 20409

National Center for Audio Tapes, Stadium 348, University of Colorado,
     Boulder, CO   80309

National Film and Video Center, 4321 Sykesville Road, Finksburg, MD   21048

National Film Board of Canada, 1251 Avenue of the Americas, New York, NY
     10020

National Information Center for Educational Media, University of Southern
     California, University Park, Los Angeles, CA   90007

National Medical Audiovisual Center (Annex), Station K, Atlanta, GA   30324

National School Public Relations Association, 1801 North Moore Street,
     Arlington, VA 22209

New Day Films, P.O. Box 315, Franklin Lakes, NJ   07417

New York University, Film Library, 26 Washington Place, New York, NY
     10003

Pacifica Tape Library, Department P, 5316 Venice Boulevard, Los Angeles,
     CA 90019

Parents' Magazine Films, 52 Vanderbilt Avenue, New York, NY 10017

Pennsylvania State University, Audio-Visual Department, Special Services
     Building, University Park, PA 16802

Perennial Education, Inc., 477 Roger Williams, P. O. Box 855/Ravinia,
     Highland Park, IL 60035

Prentice-Hall Film Library, Englewood Cliffs, NJ 07632

Psychological Films, Inc., 110 North Wheeler Street, Orange, CA 92669

Psychotherapy Tape Library, 59 Fourth Avenue, New York, NY 10003

Pyramid, 7101 Wisconsin Avenue, N. W., Bethesda, MD 20014

Pyramid Films, Division of Adams Productions, P. O. Box 1048, Santa
     Monica, CA 90406

Reel Research, Box 6037, Albany, CA 94706

Research Media, 96 Mount Auburn Street, Cambridge, MA 02138

Research Press, 2612 North Mattis Avenue, Champaign, Il 61820

Roundtable Films, 113 North San Vicente Boulevard, Beverly Hills, CA
     90211

W. B. Saunders Company, West Washington Square, Philadelphia, PA 19105

Schloat Productions of Prentice-Hall Media, 150 White Plains Road,
     Tarrytown, NY 10591

Scott, Foresman, and Co., 1900 East Lake Avenue, Glenview, IL 60025

Society for Visual Education, 1345 Diversey Parkway, Chicago, IL 60614

Sunburst Communications, 41 Washington Avenue, Pleasantville, NY 10570

Time-Life Multimedia, Time & Life Building, New York, NY 10020

John Wiley & Sons, 605 Third Avenue, New York, NY 10016 and/or 512
     Burlington Avenue, LaGrange, IL 60525

Wisconsin Clearinghouse on Alcohol and Other Drug Information, 420 North
     Lake Street, Madison, WI 53703

Women's History Research Center, 2325 Oak Street, Berkeley, CA 94708

Ziff-Davis Publishing Co., Consumer Products Division, 595 Broadway, New
     York, NY 10012

Chapter 7

Reference Materials

Richard A. Kasschau

What follows is a nonexhaustive list of books that teachers of psychology may wish to use to supplement their usual sources of information. The range of topics is traditional. The books vary considerably
in reading level; many may be appropriate for high school or undergraduate students. Brief annotations have been added to focus on each book's
strengths.

Insofar as possible, a balance has been provided with regard to
positions on controversial issues. However, due to the vastness of
in-print resources, few original sources have been cited. Rather, secondary sources that include extensive bibliographies have been given pre-
ference. With few exceptions, the books are currently in print; thus,
the list can be used as a guide to develop a collection for a school
library.

General Introduction

Source Materials

Bell, J. E. A guide to library research in psychology. Dubuque, Iowa:
   Wm. C. Brown, 1971. $2.95 paper. Identification and discussion of
   numerous library resources for students of psychology; coverage of
   both reference volumes and nonreference volumes.

English, H. B., & English, A. C. The comprehensive dictionary of
   psychological and psychoanalytical terms: A guide to usage. New
   York: David McKay, 1958. Out of print. The most comprehensive
   source of definitions of traditional terms that psychologists use.

Eysenck, H. J. Fact and fiction in psychology. Baltimore: Penguin,
   1965. Out of print. A discussion of the interaction of personality
   with neuroses, accidents, criminal behavior, and other social ex-
   changes; one of a series of books that examine contributions of
   psychology to understanding various human problems.

Keller, F. S., & Sherman, J. G. The Keller Plan handbook: Essays on a
   personalized system of instruction. Menlo Park, Calif.: W. A.
   Benjamin, 1974. $4.25 paper. Introductory information on organiza-
   tion, use, and behavioral theory underpinnings of the Personalized
   System of Instruction (PSI).

Woods, P. J. (Ed.). Sourcebook on the teaching of psychology. Roanoke,
   Va.: Scholars' Press, 1973. $22.50 cloth. Course outlines and
   teaching bibliographies in traditional content areas of psychology.

Zimbardo, P. G., & Newton, J. W. Instructor's resource book to accompany
Psychology and life (9th ed.) Glenview, Ill.: Scott, Foresman,
1975. No price available. A mixture of teaching tips, resources for
movies, equipment and demonstrations, and challenging aids for the
improvement of instruction.

Series Publications

Annual Reviews, Inc. Annual Review of Psychology.
The Bobbs-Merrill Co. Bobbs-Merrill Reprint Series in Psychology.
Brooks/Cole Publishing Co. Basic Concepts in Psychology series.
CRM/Random House. Psychology Today series.
W. H. Freeman & Co. Scientific American Offprint series.
Little, Brown & Co. Time-Life Human Behavior series.
Macmillan Publishing Co. Macmillan series (paperbacks).
Prentice-Hall, Inc. Foundations of Modern Psychology series.
Scott, Foresman & Co. Basic Psychological Concepts series.

Miscellany

Evans, R. I. The making of psychology: Discussions with creative
contributors. New York: Alfred A. Knopf, 1976. $5.95 cloth.
Interviews with 28 famous recent and current research psychologists,
who discuss their research and aspects of their personal and professional lives.

Siegel, M. H., & Zeigler, H. P. (Eds.). Psychological research: The
inside story. New York: Harper & Row, 1976. $7.95 paper. Famous
psychologists' personal accounts of how they conducted their research.

Skinner, B. F. The technology of teaching. Englewood Cliffs, N. J.:
Prentice-Hall, 1968. $4.95 paper. A series of 11 essays applying
the principles of operant conditioning to teaching, student motivation, and classroom management.

History and Systems

Boring, E. G. A history of experimental psychology (2nd ed.). Englewood
Cliffs, N. J.: Prentice-Hall, 1950. $16.95 cloth. The classic
text; a difficult and very scholarly book, yet readable; a good
source of details, dates.

Chaplin, J. P., & Krawiec, T. S. Systems and theories of psychology (3rd
ed.). New York: Holt, Rinehart & Winston, 1974. $15.95 cloth. A
lengthy topical treatment of schools of psychology as related to
sensation/perception, learning, motivation, personality, etc.

Evans, R. I. B. F. Skinner: The man and his ideas. New York: E. P.
Dutton, 1968. $2.95 paper. A presentation, in interview format, of

Skinner's reactions to a series of challenging questions about various psychological topics, positive versus aversive control of behavior, teaching machines, etc.; one of a series of interviews with various psychologists published by Dutton, Harcourt Brace Jovanovich, and Harper & Row.

Marx, M. H., & Hillix, W. A. Systems and theories in psychology (2nd ed.). New York: McGraw-Hill, 1973. $15.95 cloth. A discussion of the place of psychology in science and a review of many "systematic" organizations of the discipline--associationism to math models.

Misiak, H., & Sexton, V. S. A history of psychology: An overview. New York: Grune & Stratton, 1966. $18.25 cloth. The long view of psychology: an analysis of major intellectual views, especially over the past 100 years.

Murphy, G., & Kovach, J. K. Historical introduction to modern psychology (3rd ed.). New York: Harcourt Brace Jovanovich, 1972. $15.95 cloth. A coherent discussion of evolving research, theory, systems, and methods throughout the history of psychology.

Schultz, D. P. A history of modern psychology (2nd ed.). New York: Academic Press, 1974. $14.95 cloth. A detailed examination of structuralism, functionalism, behaviorism, and psychoanalysis in historical perspective.

Watson, R. I. The great psychologists (4th ed.). Philadelphia: J. B. Lippincott, 1978. $9.25 paper. A third-person biographical account of the works and impact of important psychologists.

Wertheimer, M. A brief history of psychology (Rev. ed.). New York: Holt, Rinehart & Winston, 1979. No price available. A discussion of the major schools of psychology, setting them in the broader context of science and philosophy.

Methods and Data

Agnew, N. M., & Pyke, S. W. The science game: An introduction to research in the behavioral sciences (2nd ed.). Englewood Cliffs, N. J.: Prentice-Hall, 1978. $7.95 paper. A design perspective on the conduct of research, including a chapter on writing research reports.

Anderson, D. C., & Borkowski, J. G. Experimental psychology: Research tactics and their applications. Glenview, Ill.: Scott, Foresman, 1978. $12.95 cloth. Coverage of experimental design in early chapters, followed by a focus on applications in four content areas.

Bradley, J. I., & McClelland, J. N. Basic statistical concepts: A self-instructional text (2nd ed.). Glenview, Ill.: Scott, Foresman,

1978. $5.25 paper. A programmed-learning text covering descriptive statistics, correlation, and the basics of decision-making with statistics.

Bruning, J. L., & Kintz, B. L. Computational handbook of statistics (2nd ed.). Glenview, Ill.: Scott, Foresman, 1977. $8.95 paper. "Cookbook" of psychological statistics, with examples of many statistical calculations.

Deese, J. Psychology as science and art. New York: Harcourt Brace Jovanovich, 1972. $5.95 paper. An issues-oriented analysis of how psychological knowledge is a mix of science and myth.

Doherty, M. E., & Shemberg, K. M. Asking questions about behavior: An introduction to what psychologists do (2nd ed.). Glenview, Ill.: Scott, Foresman, 1978. $3.95 paper. A discussion of how to formulate researchable questions, starting with questions that students might ask in their first psychology class and later focusing on, as a specific example, the study of stress.

Guilford, J. P., & Fruchter, B. Fundamental statistics in psychology and education (6th ed.). New York: McGraw-Hill, 1978. $14.95 cloth. A treatment of descriptive statistics, analysis of variance, and correlation/prediction.

Huff, D., & Geis, I. How to lie with statistics. New York: W. W. Norton, 1954. $5.95 cloth; $1.95 paper. Light reading; an excellent source of funny examples of use/misuse of statistics.

Martin, D. W. Doing psychology experiments. Monterey, Calif.: Brooks/Cole, 1977. $6.95 paper. A how-to manual offering readable advice on experimental design and analysis.

McGuigan, F. J. Experimental psychology (3rd ed). Englewood Cliffs, N. J.: Prentice-Hall, 1978. $13.95 cloth. A view of research from the design perspective; a discussion of many different basic experimental problems and designs for studying those problems.

Ray, W. S. Statistics in psychological research. New York: Macmillan, 1962. $8.95 cloth. An unusual statistics book, with content organized in terms of the language of science; review of algebra; statistics presented as syntactic, semantic, and pragmatic.

Rosenthal, R. Experimenter effects in behavioral research (Enlarged ed.). New York: Irvington Publishers, 1976. $15.95 cloth. An explanation of the nature of experimenter expectancy effects and a discussion of related studies, methodological implications, and recent research.

Spence, J. T., Cotton, J. W., Underwood, B. J., & Duncan, C. P. Elementary statistics (3rd ed.). Englewood Cliffs, N. J.: Prentice-Hall,

1976. $11.95 cloth. A tightly written book covering descriptive and inferential statistics, and including nonparametric statistics; an emphasis on hypothesis-testing.

Underwood, B. J. Experimental psychology (2nd ed.). Englewood Cliffs, N. J.: Prentice-Hall, 1966. $14.95 cloth. A sound methodological text, with broad coverage of traditional experimental topics; a valuable source of research ideas that can be studied with minimal equipment.

Wood, G. Fundamentals of psychological research (2nd ed.). Boston: Little, Brown, 1966. $14.95 paper. A presentation of the basic design and research strategies of psychologists, with a heavy emphasis on and a discussion of basic statistics.

Developmental Psychology

Aldous, J. Family careers: Developmental change in families. New York: John Wiley, 1978. $12.95 cloth. A discussion of changes in families from the time they are formed until they disappear; an analysis of marriage, parents and children, and siblings as "careers."

Bijou, S. W., & Baer, D. M. Behavior analysis and child development. Englewood Cliffs, N. J.: Prentice-Hall, 1978. $5.95 paper. An application of a theory of behavior analysis to child development; a treatment of complex processes (problem-solving, thinking, etc.)

Brackbill, Y., & Thompson, G. C. (Eds.). Behavior in infancy and early childhood. New York: Free Press, 1967. $10.95 cloth. Sixty-three papers addressing growth/motor development and developmental aspects of sensory/perceptual skills, conditioning/learning, language, intelligence, and social/emotional skills.

Fisher, S., & Fisher, R. L. What we really know about child rearing: Science in support of effective parenting. New York: Basic Books, 1977. $12.50 cloth. How-to advice to parents on childrearing, based on laboratory and clinical research on the emotional and physical development of children.

Fitzgerald, H. E., Strommen, E. A., & McKinney, J. P. Developmental psychology: The infant and young child. Homewood, Ill.: Dorsey Press, 1977. $6.50 paper. The first in a series of four books offering a life-span (infant, child, adolescent/adult) view of development; a summary of research, emphasizing cognitive, social, and personality development.

Horrocks, J. E. The psychology of adolescence (4th ed.). Boston: Houghton Mifflin, 1976. $14.50 cloth. An analysis of a series of topics (ranging from motivation and direction to vocational development) in relation to adolescent development.

Hurlock, E. B. Developmental psychology (4th ed.). New York: McGraw-Hill, 1975. $15.50 cloth. Balanced coverage of early, middle, and late life development, including death; a discussion of the development of specific capacities and behavior patterns at each age. The author also has Child Development (6th ed., 1978), and Adolescent Development (4th ed., 1973), with the same publisher.

Jersild, A. J., Telford, C. W., & Sawrey, J. W. Child psychology (7th ed.). Englewood Cliffs, N. J.: Prentice-Hall, 1975. $14.95 cloth. A review of research with an eye toward implications for the child's perspective; extensive coverage of Piaget.

Lamb, M. E. (Ed.). Social and personality development. New York: Holt, Rinehart & Winston, 1978. $13.95 cloth. A "chronological perspective" of skills developed in childhood and adolescence; treatment of gender role and moral development.

Liebert, R. M., Poulos, R. W., & Marmor, G. S. Developmental psychology (2nd ed.). Englewood Cliffs, N. J.: Prentice-Hall, 1977. $14.95 cloth. A focus on child development in a broad range of areas (perception, learning, language, etc.); some coverage of adolescent and adult developmental processes.

Mussen, P. H., Conger, J. J., & Kagan, J. Child development and personality (4th ed.). New York: Harper & Row, 1974. $14.95 cloth. One of the classic texts in the field of child development; research oriented, but with a broad view of the implications for each child's development.

Newman, B. M., & Newman, P. R. Infancy and childhood: Development and its contexts. New York: John Wiley, 1978. $13.95 cloth. Coverage of life-span development in early chapters; in later chapters, a focus on social institutions' impact on the child (school, day-care centers, etc.).

Phillips, J. L. The origins of intellect: Piaget's theory (2nd ed.). San Francisco: W. H. Freeman, 1975. $10.00 cloth; $5.00 paper. A review of evidence and demonstrations of phenomena typical of Piaget's four stages; a closing section on educational implications/applications.

Rice, F. P. The adolescent: Development, relationships and culture. Boston: Allyn & Bacon, 1975. $14.95 cloth. A "topics" approach to adolescent development, from physical and moral capabilities to ethnic characteristics.

Stone, L. J., & Church, J. Childhood and adolescence: A psychology of the growing person. New York: Random House, 1973. $13.95 cloth. Coverage of development through the teenage years; integration of laboratory findings with "real world" experiences.

Physiological and Comparative Psychology

General

Gardner, E. Fundamentals of neurology (6th ed.). Philadelphia: W. B. Saunders, 1975. $12.00 cloth. An illustrated discussion of basic neural transmission, functional anatomy, and its relation to behavior.

Gardner, H. The shattered mind: The person after brain damage. New York: Alfred A. Knopf, 1976. $12.95 cloth. An examination of investigations of brain-damaged patients and the implications for the study of normal thought processes. An added benefit: use of first-person narrations.

Grossman, S. P. A textbook of physiological psychology. New York: John Wiley, 1967. $22.50 cloth. A discussion of: neuronal and anatomical features; visual and motor functions, reactions such as hunger, thirst, emotion; correlates of learning; consolidation; and theories of brain operation; heavy reading. The author has also published Essentials of Physiological Psychology (1973).

Hebb, D. O. Textbook of psychology (3rd ed.). Philadelphia: W. B. Saunders, 1972. $9.25 cloth. An "introductory" book reducing many explanations of perception, learning, emotion, etc., to basic physiology; a classic in its field.

Morgan, C. T. Physiological psychology (3rd ed.). New York: McGraw-Hill, 1965. $17.50 cloth. A discussion of the physiology of the peripheral and central nervous systems and the senses, also the physiological aspects of a variety of behaviors (emotion, sleep, hunger, conditioning, etc.); good on basics, but growing dated.

Netter, F. H. The Ciba collection of medical illustrations. Vol. 1, Nervous system. Newark, N. J.: Ciba Pharmaceutical Co., 1958. $17.00 cloth. A peerless source of detailed, enlarged drawings of many aspects of the appearance and distribution of the nervous system.

Rose, S. The conscious brain. New York: Alfred A. Knopf, 1973. $10.00 cloth. (Vintage Books, $4.95 paper.) An issues approach to physiological functioning, addressing the major problems of memory, emotion, and sleep and placing physiological psychology in historical perspective; fun reading, moderately illustrated.

Schneider, A. M., & Tarshis, B. An introduction to physiological psychology. New York: Random House, 1975. $14.95 cloth. A good book for students not familiar with physiological psychology; technical terms well explained.

Thompson, R. F. <u>Introduction to physiological psychology</u>. New York: Harper & Row, 1975. $16.95 cloth. A presentation of neuroanatomy as a basis for behavior and awareness; treatment of evolution, genetics, behavioral biology, thought, and language.

Wooldridge, D. E. <u>The machinery of the brain</u>. New York: McGraw-Hill, 1963. $2.45 paper. A nontechnical description of the major areas/functions of the brain; highly readable.

Drugs and Altered States

Geller, A., & Boas, M. <u>Drug beat</u> (2nd ed.). New York: McGraw-Hill, 1971. $2.95 paper. Detail on the history, distribution, uses, and dangers of marijuana, LSD, and the amphetamines; coverage limited to these drugs.

Green, H. I., & Levy, M. H. <u>Drug misuse . . . human abuse</u>. New York: Marcel Dekker, 1976. $19.75 cloth. A guide for parents/teachers on problems of misuse, legal status, signs of abuse; 12 chapters of facts about a wide variety of drugs.

Hilgard, E. R. <u>Divided consciousness: Multiple controls in human thought and action</u>. New York: John Wiley, 1977. $16.95 cloth. An unusual view of consciousness; integration of research on hypnosis; analysis of a wide range of research on amnesia, dreams, hallucinations, and multiple personalities.

Jones, K. L., Shainberg, L. W., & Byer, C. O. <u>Drugs and alcohol</u> (2nd ed.). New York: Harper & Row, 1973. $4.95 paper. A discussion of the sources and effects of drugs and alcohol, comparing physiological and psychological reactions; technical language minimized.

Julien, R. M. <u>A primer of drug actions</u> (2nd ed.). San Francisco: W. H. Freeman, 1978. $14.00 cloth; $6.50 paper. A presentation of actions, uses, limitations, and side effects of drugs that affect central nervous system functioning.

Laurie, P. <u>Drugs: Medical, psychological and social facts</u> (2nd ed.). Baltimore: Penguin, 1971. Out of print. A book with a self-explanatory title.

Longo, V. G. <u>Neuropharmacology and behavior</u>. San Francisco: W. H. Freeman, 1972. $8.00 cloth; $3.95 paper. A discussion of the chemical and pharmacological properties and the effects of major psychotropic drugs.

McConnell, R. A. <u>ESP curriculum guide</u>. New York: Simon & Schuster, 1971. $5.95 paper. A look at the lessons for science of the ESP phenomenon, listing books/articles (annotated), presenting a course syllabus, and suggesting experiments for classroom teaching.

Oswald, I. Sleep (2nd ed.). Baltimore: Penguin, 1970. $2.50 paper. A review of brain mechanisms and sleep; coverage of mental functions during and near sleep, sleep deprivation, hypnosis, and insomnia.

Ray, O. S. Drugs, society and human behavior. St. Louis, Mo.: C. V. Mosby, 1972. $8.75 cloth. A discussion of drug use and regulation, fundamentals of drug actions, nondrug drugs (coffee, etc.), psychotherapeutic drugs, narcotics, and "phantasticants"; identification of a variety of sources of information for teaching.

Snyder, S. H. Madness and the brain. New York: McGraw-Hill, 1975. $3.95 paper. An examination of "madness" and what goes on in the brain of a severely disturbed person; extensive treatment of schizophrenia.

Animal Behavior

DeVore, I. (Ed.). Primate behavior: Field studies of monkeys and apes. New York: Holt, Rinehart & Winston, 1965. $12.95 cloth. Primarily papers based on naturalistic observation; contributions from anthropology, psychology, zoology, linguistics, and psychiatry.

Dewsbury, D. Comparative animal behavior. New York: McGraw-Hill, 1978. $14.95 cloth. An explanation of the development, mechanisms, evolution, and adaptive significance of animal behavior.

Dewsbury, D. A., & Rethlingshafer, D. (Eds.). Comparative psychology: A modern approach. New York: McGraw-Hill, 1973. $20.00 cloth. A collection of papers examining the patterns, origins, correlates, modification, and evolution of animal behavior.

Hinde, R. A. Animal behaviour: A synthesis of ethology and comparative psychology (2nd ed.). New York: McGraw-Hill, 1970. $22.50 cloth. A far-ranging text reviewing findings in the study of animal behavior from both ethological and psychological laboratories.

Lorenz, K. King Solomon's ring. New York: Thomas Y. Crowell, 1952. $6.95 cloth. (Apollo Editions, $1.95 paper.) An illustrated description, by a leading ethologist, of the processes of naturalistic observation.

Rumbaugh, D. M. (Ed.). Language learning by a chimpanzee. New York: Academic Press, 1977. $19.25 cloth. Issues raised by and findings of one of several projects studying communication possibilities between humans and other animals.

Schein, M. W. (Ed.). Benchmark papers in animal behavior. New York: Academic Press, 1974-. A continuing series of volumes on selected topics (e.g., territoriality, imprinting); collections of the most critical papers in the area.

Tinbergen, N. The study of instinct. New York: Oxford University Press, 1969. $4.00 paper. An introduction to the ethologist's techniques for studying behavior; a discussion of behavior as reaction to external stimuli, internal factors, and spontaneity; an explanation of the development, adaptiveness, and evolution of behavior.

Sensation/Perception

Bartley, S. H. Principles of perception (2nd ed.). New York: Harper & Row, 1969. $16.95 cloth. Expansive coverage of the visual sense--development, acuity, constancies, perception of movement, etc.; less detailed coverage of the other senses.

Fried, P. A. (Ed.). Readings in perception: Principle and practice. Lexington, Mass.: D. C. Heath, 1974. $8.95 paper. A collection of readings addressing everything from "learning to love" to "auditory backward inhibition in concert halls"; a wide range of interesting topics.

Geldard, F. The human senses (2nd ed.). New York: John Wiley, 1972. $18.25 cloth. The classic in this area; information about the sensory apparatus and functions and functioning of each of the human senses.

Gibson, J. J. The senses considered as perceptual systems. Boston: Houghton Mifflin, 1966. $15.95 cloth. Treatments of aspects of the environment, perceptual systems, orientation and scanning, and information pick-up and deficiencies in the senses.

Gregory, R. L. The intelligent eye. New York: McGraw-Hill, 1971. $8.95 cloth. Fun reading about a complex process, vision; good illustrations supporting well-written commentary about the eye and visual perception.

Gross, C. G., & Zeigler, H. P. Readings in physiological psychology: Neurophysiology/sensory processes. New York: Harper & Row, 1969. Out of print. A book in three parts: neurophysiological foundations, processing of sensory information, and central control of sensory input; heavy reading.

Held, R., & Richards, W. (Eds.). Recent progress in perception: Readings from Scientific American. San Francisco: W. H. Freeman, 1976. $12.00 cloth; $7.50 paper. One of a number of books of readings collected by the authors from Scientific American, featuring theories and mechanisms of perception; richly illustrated.

Leibowitz, H. W. Visual perception. New York: Macmillan, 1965. $3.50 paper. An unusual book; coverage of problems of perception (adaptation, innate aspects, selectivity, illusions, etc.) in early chapters, followed by reprints of eight famous papers on perceptual problems.

Ludel, J. <u>Introduction to sensory processes</u>. San Francisco: W. H.
   Freeman, 1978. $17.00 cloth; $9.00 paper. A primary focus on the
   physiological aspects of each sensory system, but including some
   information about functions/functioning; well illustrated.

McBurney, D. H., & Collings, V. B. <u>Introduction to sensation/perception</u>.
   Englewood Cliffs, N. J.: Prentice-Hall, 1977. $12.95 cloth. A
   little bit of everything: research, how-to-do-it advice, data analysis, cognitive factors as they affect perception, and pattern perception.

Scharf, B. (Ed.). <u>Experimental sensory psychology</u>. Glenview, Ill.:
   Scott, Foresman, 1975. $14.95 cloth. A general introduction to the
   field, including a discussion of the physiological sensory system and
   the interaction between physiology and behavior/perception.

Uttal, W. <u>The psychobiology of sensory coding</u>. New York: Harper & Row,
   1973. $22.50 cloth. An integration of psychology and neurophysiolo-
   gy, tracing stimulus information from initial input to its registra-
   tion in the central nervous system; a treatment of dimensions of experience and neural codes, not individual senses.

Von Fieandt, K., & Moustgaard, I. K. <u>The perceptual world</u>. New York:
   Academic Press, 1978. $62.50 cloth. A historical perspective,
   discussing problems common to all perceptual systems and dealing with
   personal factors in perception.

<u>Learning/Memory</u>

Adams, J. A. <u>Learning and memory: An introduction</u>. Homewood, Ill.:
   Dorsey Press, 1976. $14.50 cloth. A discussion, in equal parts, of
   learning and memory; interrelation of laboratory phenomena and
   theory, as appropriate.

Cofer, C. N. (Ed.). <u>The structure of human memory</u>. San Francisco:
   W. H. Freeman, 1976. $10.00 cloth; $5.50 paper. A variety of papers
   by leading experts interrelating contemporary research with theories;
   short, but heavy reading.

Ferster, C. B., Culbertson, S., & Perrott, M. C. <u>Behavior principles</u> (2nd
   ed.). Englewood Cliffs, N. J.: Prentice-Hall, 1975. $13.95 cloth.
   An explanation of the principles of operant conditioning; a discussion of laboratory demonstrations and a wide range of operant behavioral techniques.

Hergenhahn, B. R. <u>An introduction to theories of learning</u>. Englewood
   Cliffs, N. J.: Prentice-Hall, 1976. $12.95 cloth. A review of
   cognitive and associative theories of learning, placing each in
   historical perspective.

Hilgard, E. R., & Bower, G. H. Theories of learning (4th ed.). Englewood Cliffs, N. J.: Prentice-Hall, 1974. $14.95 cloth. A classic text, covering everything from Skinner to neurophysiology, from Guthrie to Hull to Tolman.

Hill, W. F. Learning: A survey of psychological interpretations (3rd ed.). New York: Harper & Row, 1977. No price available. An explanation of the principles of learning; broad coverage of a variety of contemporary theories and theorists.

Hulse, S. H., Deese, J., & Egeth, H. E. The psychology of learning (4th ed.). New York: McGraw-Hill, 1975. $14.95 cloth. Topical treatment of the full range of animal and human learning phenomena, especially recent advances in cognitive theory.

Kimble, G. A. Hilgard and Marquis's conditioning and learning (2nd ed.). Englewood Cliffs, N. J.: Prentice-Hall, 1961. $13.95 cloth. A classic text, discussing classical conditioning and operant conditioning in all their forms.

Marx, M. H. (Ed.). Learning. New York: Macmillan. Vol. 1, Processes, 1969, $16.95 cloth; Vol. 2, Interactions, 1970, $16.95 cloth; Vol. 3, Theories, 1970, out of print. Three volumes containing experts' summaries of research in each content area on a wide variety of learned behaviors.

Millenson, J. R. Principles of behavioral analysis. New York: Macmillan, 1967. $13.95 cloth. A data-oriented introduction to behavioral psychology, including fundamental and compounded units of analysis and complex contingencies and reinforcement.

Pavlov, I. P. Conditioned reflexes. Gloucester, Mass.: Peter Smith, undated. $7.00 cloth. (Dover, $4.00 paper.) An English translation of the work originating the study of classical conditioning.

Pennypacker, H. S., Koenig, C. H., & Lindsley, O. R. Handbook of the standard behavior chart. Kansas City, Kans.: Precision Media (c/o Behavior Research Co.), 1972. No price available. Instructions for standardized plotting of the frequency of human behavior; plotting of daily data in the form of counts/minute.

Reynolds, G. S. A primer of operant conditioning (Rev. ed.). Glenview, Ill.: Scott, Foresman, 1975. $8.95 cloth. A brief synopsis of the principles of operant conditioning; well illustrated with performance curves.

Skinner, B. F. Cumulative record: A selection of papers (3rd ed.). New York: Meredith Corporation, 1972. No price available. A collection of papers--some theory, some philosophy, some practical applications.

Staats, A. W. Human learning: Studies extending conditioning principles to complex behavior. New York: Holt, Rinehart & Winston, 1964. $11.00 cloth. One of the early efforts to extend basic learning principles into complex learning situations such as language and verbal behavior.

Tarpy, R. M., & Mayer, R. E. Foundations of learning and memory. Glenview, Ill.: Scott, Foresman, 1978. $10.95 cloth. Broad coverage of traditional topics in both animal and human learning.

Motivation/Emotion

Arnold, M. (Ed.). Feelings and emotions. New York: Academic Press, 1970. $21.95 cloth. One of the Personality and Psychopathology volumes on motivational phenomena; research papers on physiological and cognitive theories of emotion.

Beck, R. C. Motivation: Theories and principles. Englewood Cliffs, N. J.: Prentice-Hall, 1978. No price available. Coverage of both animal and human motivation, divided into analysis of biological, behavioral, and social factors.

Bolles, R. C. Theory of motivation (2nd ed.). New York: Harper & Row, 1975. $16.95 cloth. A presentation of various theories of motivation; an extensive analysis of the role of reinforcement; a discussion of the physiological correlates of motivated states; a good reference section.

Candland, D. K., Fell, J. P., Keen, E., Leshner, A. I., Plutchik, R., & Tarpy, R. M. Emotion. Monterey, Calif.: Brooks/Cole, 1977. $11.95 cloth. A series of papers emphasizing theoretical treatments of emotion as a topic; a review of environmental factors in some depth.

Cofer, C. N., & Appley, M. H. Motivation: Theory and research. New York: John Wiley, 1964. $19.95 cloth. A classic text; an excellent summary of the literature prior to publication, covering physiological factors, behavioral results, and the theoretical impact of motivation/emotion.

Darwin, C. The expression of the emotions in man and animals. Philadelphia: Richard West, 1873. $20 cloth. (University of Chicago Press, 1965, $10.00 cloth, $3.95 paper.) A review of the general principles of emotional expression, including the means of expressing emotions; an examination of various emotions (anxiety, grief, joy, hatred, anger, etc.).

Deci, E. L. Intrinsic motivation. New York: Plenum Press, 1975. $14.95 cloth. A summary of various approaches to motivation, based on experimental research; cognitive analyses of internal (intrinsic) motivational factors.

Dollard, J., Miller, N. E., Doob, L. W., Mowrer, O. H., & Sears, R. R. Frustration and aggression. New Haven, Conn.: Yale University Press, 1939. $7.50 cloth. A classic study of an important phenomenon: the relation between environmental outcomes (success or failure) and resultant behavior.

Ferguson, E. D. Motivation: An experimental approach. New York: Holt, Rinehart & Winston, 1976. $14.50 cloth. Coverage of both physiological and learned factors that influence motivation; a research-based treatment, with suggestions for classroom-based experiments to study motivation.

Kroman, A. The psychology of motivation. Englewood Cliffs, N. J.: Prentice-Hall, 1977. No price available. A presentation of behaviorist, psychoanalytic, cognitive, and consistency views of motivation in historical context.

Lorenz, K. On aggression. New York: Harcourt Brace Jovanovich, 1966. $9.50 cloth; $3.50 paper. An ethologist's report on naturalistic observations of aggression as expressed in nature by a variety of organisms.

Nebraska Symposium on Motivation. Lincoln: University of Nebraska Press, 1953-. A yearly symposium with six to eight invited papers addressing various aspects of motivation/emotion broadly interpreted.

Stein, D. G., & Rosen, J. F. Motivation and emotion. New York: MacMillan, 1974. $6.25 paper. A series of papers mainly emphasizing physiological factors in motivation and emotion.

Valle, F. P. Motivation: Theories and issues. Monterey, Calif.: Brooks/Cole, 1975. $10.95 cloth. A theoretical analysis of the physiological factors influencing motivation.

Weiner, B. Theories of motivation: From mechanism to cognition. Chicago: Rand McNally, 1972. $13.50 cloth. A review of the many theories of motivation--from useless to in use, from a century ago to now; a good review of the literature.

Cognitive Psychology (Language, Thinking, and Problem-Solving)

Bourne, L. E., Jr., Ekstrand, B. R., & Dominowski, R. L. The psychology of thinking. Englewood Cliffs, N. J.: Prentice-Hall, 1971. $13.95 cloth. A conceptual/empirical analysis of human thinking, in terms of its components; an extension of empirical work into theories and complex problems.

Chomsky, N. Language and mind (Enlarged ed.). New York: Harcourt Brace Jovanovich, 1972. $7.95 paper. An expanded version of one of the

signal books in the establishment of psycholinguistics as a field of
intellectual endeavor; very difficult reading, but challenging; a
presentation of the theory of transformational grammar.

Clark, H. H., & Clark, E. V. Psychology and language: An introduction
to psycholinguistics. New York: Harcourt Brace Jovanovich, 1977.
$15.95 cloth. A discussion of language as an object of study--com-
prehension, production and acquisition, meaning and thought; tough
reading, but well illustrated.

Deese, J. Psycholinguistics. Boston: Allyn & Bacon, 1970. $3.95
paper. An intriguing brief essay by an associationist turned cognitive psychologist, delineating his reasons for switching.

Foss, D. J., & Hakes, D. T. Psycholinguistics: An introduction to the
psychology of language. Englewood Cliffs, N. J.: Prentice-Hall,
1978. $15.95 cloth. Coverage of the understanding, production, and
development of language, starting with a simple introduction to the
study of it.

Linden, E. Apes, men, and language. New York: E. P. Dutton, 1975.
$8.95 cloth. (Penguin, $2.95 paper.) Lessons drawn from experience
gained in teaching sign language to chimps, extended to show their
implications for understanding more of how humans communicate.

Miller, G. A. The psychology of communication: Seven essays. New York:
Basic Books, 1967. $3.95 paper. Essays covering everything from
cybernetics and automation to psychical research--problems at the
overlap of psychology and communication theory.

Neisser, U. Cognitive psychology. Englewood Cliffs, N. J.: Prentice-
Hall, 1967. $12.95 cloth. A seminal text following stimuli through
the organism from the initial stimulation of a sense organ through
many transformations to eventual use/storage in memory and thought.

Pollio, H. R. The psychology of symbolic activity. Reading, Mass.:
Addison-Wesley, 1974. $15.75 cloth. An illustrated, far-ranging
discussion of symbolic activity from associationist and information-processing perspectives.

Reynolds, A. G., & Flagg, P. W. Cognitive psychology. Cambridge, Mass.:
Winthrop Publishers, 1977. $13.95 cloth. A review of the history
and methods of cognitive psychology; coverage of the processing of
information, dwelling on models of memory; also a discussion of
language acquisition and bilingualism.

Vinacke, W. E. Psychology of thinking (2nd ed.). New York: McGraw-Hill,
1974. $18.50 cloth. A history of the topic leading to a discussion
of modern theoretical interpretations; an extension of basics to an
analysis of fantasy and dreams, creativity, and even internalized
concepts of self.

Individual Differences/Testing

Anastasi, A. <u>Individual differences</u>. New York: John Wiley, 1965. $8.50
paper. A historical perspective on the psychological study of individual differences; coverage of the measurement and nature of intelligence, behavioral genetics, and cultural deprivation and genius.

Anastasi, A. <u>Psychological testing</u> (4th ed.). New York: Macmillan,
1976. $15.95 cloth. A classic text, dealing with the context of
test usage and the principles of tests; a presentation of tests of
intellectual level, separate abilities, and personality.

Ciminero, A. R., Calhoun, K. S., & Adams, H. E. (Eds.). <u>Handbook of</u>
<u>behavioral assessment</u>. New York: John Wiley, 1977. $27.00 cloth.
A compendium of research in three sections: general issues in,
approaches to, and examples of behavioral assessment.

Covington, M. V., & Beery, R. G. <u>Self-worth and school learning.</u>. New
York: Holt, Rinehart & Winston, 1976. $2.95 paper. A discussion of
the issue of effective rewards for students of differing ability
levels; a review of individual differences in learning, and different
reactions of students to successes and failures.

Cronbach, L. J. <u>Essentials of psychological testing</u> (3rd ed.). New
York: Harper & Row, 1970. $16.95 cloth. A review of the basic
issues in test development and administration; a discussion of a
large array of tests, some with sample items.

Loehlin, J. C., Lindzey, G., & Spuhler, J. N. <u>Race differences in</u>
<u>intelligence</u>. San Francisco: W. H. Freeman, 1975. $14.00 cloth;
$5.95 paper. A review of the evidence--hereditary and environment-
al--available through the mid 1970s; carefully researched conclusions
based solely on the evidence examined.

Stanley, J. C., & Hopkins, K. D. <u>Educational and psychological measure-</u>
<u>ment and evaluation</u> (5th ed.). Englewood Cliffs, N. J.:
Prentice-Hall, 1972. $13.95 cloth. Coverage of the development of
educational measures and standardized measures; knowledge of statistics required for full benefit of text.

Thorndike, R. L., & Hagen, E. P. <u>Measurement and evaluation in psychology</u>
<u>and education</u> (4th ed.). New York: John Wiley, 1977. $16.95
cloth. An explanation of the basics of testing and measurement,
types of tests, and environments in which tests may be used; also a
discussion of social and political issues in testing.

Tyler, L. E. <u>Individual differences: Abilities and motivational</u>
<u>directions</u>. Englewood Cliffs, N. J.: Prentice-Hall, 1974. $6.95
paper. A simple, straightforward account of what psychologists have
learned about individual differences and how to assess them.

Tyler, L. E. <u>The psychology of human differences</u> (3rd ed.). Englewood
    Cliffs, N. J.: Prentice-Hall, 1965. $14.95 cloth. An analysis and
    description of the nature and extent of measurable differences in
    individuals and groups, stressing methodological considerations and
    factors influencing differences.

Tyler, L. E. <u>Tests and measurements</u> (2nd ed.). Englewood Cliffs, N. J.:
    Prentice-Hall, 1971. $3.95 paper. A presentation of basic measure-
    ment concepts, statistical techniques, and principles of test con-
    struction, in a context of concern about fairness and privacy.

Personality

Theories

Barron, F. <u>Human personality in conflict and growth: A book for
    beginners</u>. New York: Harper & Row, 1978. No price available. A
    humanistic approach based on theories of pragmatism, gestalt psy-
    chology, and creative evolution; a summary of data collected from
    clinical, life-story, and assessment methodology.

Byrne, D. <u>An introduction to personality</u> (2nd ed.). Englewood Cliffs,
    N. J.: Prentice-Hall, 1974. $15.95 cloth. A research-oriented
    introduction, tracing origins of ideas, translation of ideas into
    research, and the interconnection of theory and research.

Hall, C. S. <u>A primer of Freudian psychology</u>. New York: New American
    Library, 1973. $1.25 paper. A general review of Freud, psychoana-
    lysis, and its impact on contemporary personality theory; references
    to earlier work by Freud.

Hall, C. S., & Lindzey, G. <u>Theories of personality</u> (3rd ed.). New
    York: John Wiley, 1978. $15.95 cloth. A classic text; a general
    introduction to personality theory, followed by analysis of most
    current theories, each presented in terms of structure, dynamics,
    development and characteristic research.

Hurlock, E. B. <u>Personality development</u>. New York: McGraw-Hill, 1974.
    $14.95 cloth. A text in three major sections: the meaning of per-
    sonality, personality determinants, and evaluation of personality; an
    analysis and critique of theories in terms of research findings.

Liebert, R. M., & Spiegler, M. D. <u>Personality: Strategies and issues</u>
    (3rd ed.). Homewood, Ill.: Dorsey Press, 1978. $15.95 cloth. A
    summary of four strategies of studying personality (psychoanalytic,
    dispositional, phenomenological, and behavioral); also a comparison
    of theories.

Mischel, W. <u>Introduction to personality</u> (2nd ed.). New York: Holt,
    Rinehart & Winston, 1976. $14.95 cloth. A discussion of major

theoretical approaches to personality; a good review of many contemporary issues—for example, televised aggression, sex bias, and the interaction of assessment and therapy.

Stagner, R. Psychology of personality (4th ed.). New York: McGraw-Hill, 1974. $15.50 cloth. A discussion focusing on the normal adult personality; an integration of theories of personality, developmental data, measurement and assessment, and personal behavior with studies of biological and social influences.

Szasz, T. S. The myth of mental illness (Rev. ed.). New York: Harper & Row, 1974. $10.95 cloth; $2.50 paper. An intriguing "counter-culture" challenge to society's traditional techniques of diagnosing and treating personality disorders.

Psychopathology (Abnormal Psychology)

Coleman, J. C. Abnormal psychology and modern life (5th ed.). Glenview, Ill.: Scott, Foresman, 1976. $16.95 cloth. A review of the causative factors (biological, psychosocial, sociocultural) of abnormal behavior; a discussion of patterns of abnormal behavior, and methods of assessment, treatment, and prevention.

Davison, G. C., & Neale, J. M. Abnormal psychology (2nd ed.). New York: John Wiley, 1978. $15.95 cloth. An introduction to basic issues; sections on anxiety/depression, social problems, schizophrenia, organic syndromes, and treatment.

Freud, S. Psychopathology of everyday life. New York: W. W. Norton, 1971. $3.95 paper. Fascinating reading; examples of everyday behavior examined, dissected, and analyzed by Freud in terms of psychoanalytic theory.

Kaplan, B. (Ed.). The inner world of mental illness: A series of first-person accounts of what it was like. New York: Harper & Row, 1964. $10.95 paper. A book whose contents are well explained by its title.

Maser, J. D., & Seligman, M. E. P. Psychopathology: Experimental methods. San Francisco: W. H. Freeman, 1977. $18.50 cloth; $8.95 paper. Thirteen chapters presenting experimental work and clinical evidence related to a specific kind of psychopathology.

Stone, S., & Stone, A. Abnormal personality through literature. Englewood Cliffs, N. J.: Prentice-Hall, 1966. $9.50 paper. A brief description of a variety of disorders, using examples from literature to illustrate each disorder or symptom.

Ullman, L. P., & Krasner, L. A psychological approach to abnormal behavior (2nd ed.). Englewood Cliffs, N. J.: Prentice-Hall, 1975.

$15.95 cloth. A tracing of the development of abnormal behavior, showing its susceptibility to normal behavioral controls; a behavioral explanation for abnormal behavior.

White, R. W., & Watt, N. F. The abnormal personality (4th ed.). New York: John Wiley, 1973. (Originally published by Ronald Press, New York.) $12.75 cloth. Use of social and historical perspectives to place case histories and analyses in context; a discussion of the origins, development, and results of abnormal personality.

Zax, M., & Cowen, E. L. Abnormal psychology: Changing conceptions (2nd ed.). New York: Holt, Rinehart & Winston, 1976. $15.95 cloth. A historical approach, from traditional to modern; a comparison of various theories of abnormal psychology; a review of recent issues (e.g., mental health programs, electroshock).

Psychotherapy

Bandura, A. Principles of behavior modification. New York: Holt, Rinehart & Winston, 1969. $14.95 cloth. An application of a social-learning perspective in forming a theory of behavioral change; an emphasis on vicarious, symbolic, and self-regulatory behaviors.

Corsini, R. J. (Ed.). Current psychotherapies (2nd ed.). Itasca, Ill.: F. E. Peacock, 1979. No price available. A survey of the 13 major types of psychotherapy by leading practitioners of them.

Garfield, S. L., & Bergin, A. E. (Eds.). The handbook of psychotherapy and behavior change: An empirical analysis (2nd ed.). New York: John Wiley, 1978. $35.00 cloth. A survey of research relating to the effectiveness of psychotherapy.

Goffman, E. Asylums: Essays on the social situation of mental patients and other inmates. Chicago: Aldine-Atherton, 1961. $19.50 cloth. (Doubleday, $2.95 paper.) A book whose title adequately describes its contents.

Goldfried, M. R., & Davison, G. C. Clinical behavior therapy. New York: Holt, Rinehart & Winston, 1976. $12.95 cloth. A comprehensive behavioral background, providing a framework for review of current behavioral therapies and decisions for specific clinical applications.

Kovel, J. A complete guide to therapy: From psychoanalysis to behavior modification. New York: Pantheon Books, 1976. $10.00 cloth; $3.95 paper. Answers to all the questions that the consumer asks about psychotherapy but usually can't find the answers to.

Lazarus, R. S. Patterns of adjustment (3rd ed.). New York: McGraw-Hill, 1976. $14.50 cloth. A discussion of successes/failures and models of adjustment and treatment strategies, from a perspective of normal adjustment strategies.

Malott, R., Tillema, M., & Glenn, S. Behavior analysis and behavior
    modification: An introduction. Kalamazoo, Mich.: Behaviordelia,
    1978. $8.50 paper. A discussion of the techniques of behavior
    modification, starting with an analysis of behavior; also a treatment
    of ethical issues.

Martin, D. G. Introduction to psychotherapy. Monterey, Calif.:
    Brooks/Cole, 1971. $4.95 paper. A short introduction to four major
    schools of psychotherapy: psychoanalysis, client-centered therapy,
    existential approaches, and learning approaches.

Martin, G., & Pear, J. Behavior modification: What it is and how to do
    it. Englewood Cliffs, N. J.: Prentice-Hall, 1978. $12.95 cloth. A
    presentation of principles of behavior modification, in increasing
    order of difficulty; coverage of skills of observation and recording.

Price, R. H., & Denner, B. (Eds.). The making of a mental patient. New
    York: Holt, Rinehart & Winston, 1973. $6.95 paper. A discussion of
    the role of social forces and psychiatric ideology in shaping the
    reaction of the "mentally ill"; a tracing of a new patient from
    detection through commitment through strategies for survival.

Social Psychology

Aronson, E. The social animal (2nd ed.). San Francisco: W. H. Freeman,
    1976. $12.50 cloth; $5.50 paper. Easy reading on propaganda/persua-
    sion, aggression/prejudice, attraction, and communication.

Berkowitz, L. A survey of social psychology. New York: Holt, Rinehart
    & Winston, 1975. $13.95 cloth. A well-illustrated review of a wide
    variety of social problems--prejudice, crime/violence, social devi-
    ance, and riots--as well as altruism and sensitivity training.

Berscheid, E., & Walster, E. Interpersonal attraction. Reading, Mass.:
    Addison-Wesley, 1969. $2.95 paper. An examination of conditions
    affecting attraction in situations ranging from attraction/rejection
    in a group to romantic love.

Evans, R. I., & Rozelle, R. M. (Eds.). Social psychology in life (2nd
    ed.). Boston: Allyn & Bacon, 1973. $7.95 paper. A collection of
    readings including a number of classic studies/analyses grouped to
    "set the stage," analyze measurement techniques, and illustrate
    experimental manipulations in social psychology.

Hollander, E. P. Principles and methods of social psychology (3rd ed.).
    New York: Oxford University Press, 1976. $13.00 cloth. Use of
    "cases" to illustrate content and methodology, covering socializa-
    tion, interaction, communication, group functioning, and leadership.

Ittelson, W. H., Proshansky, H. M., Rivlin, L. G., & Winkel, G. H. _Introduction to environmental psychology_. New York: Holt, Rinehart & Winston, 1974. $11.95 cloth. An analysis of human relations in terms of our relationship to our environment.

Krech, D., Crutchfield, R. S., & Ballachey, E. L. _Individual in society_. New York: McGraw-Hill, 1962. $13.50 cloth. Somewhat dated but excellent coverage of attitudes, social/cultural habitat, and groups/organizations.

Martinez, J. L. (Ed.). _Chicano psychology_. New York: Academic Press, 1978. $10.00 cloth. Research on Chicanos, divided into social psychology, bilingualism, psychological testing, and mental health and psychotherapy.

Rubin, Z. _Liking and loving: An invitation to social psychology_. New York: Holt, Rinehart & Winston, 1973. $6.50 paper. The use of interpersonal relations as a vehicle to present theory and research on traditional topics of social psychology.

Secord, P. F., & Backman, C. W. _Social psychology_ (2nd ed.). New York: McGraw-Hill, 1974. $14.95 cloth. A topical organization of concepts drawn from psychology and sociology; coverage of social influence processes, group structure and process, the individual, and socialization processes.

Wrightsman, L. S. _Social psychology_ (2nd ed.). Monterey, Calif.: Brooks/Cole, 1977. $14.95 cloth. Topical coverage, including forming relationships, behavior toward others, attitudes, group differences, and environmental and group influences.

General Topics of Interest

Psychology as a Vocation/Profession

American Psychological Association. _Careers in psychology_. Washington, D. C.: Author, 1978. Single copy free. Responses to a variety of questions concerning teaching, research, and service careers; identification of many other sources of career information.

Miller, G. A. _Spontaneous apprentices: Children and language_. New York: Seabury, 1977. $9.95 cloth. A book specifically about the study of language development, but offering a lively comment on the "business" of doing research: funding, starting, striving, and sometimes failing.

Super, D. E., & Super, C. _Opportunities in psychology careers today_. Skokie, Ill.: Vocational Guidance Manuals (c/o National Textbook Co.), 1976. $4.75 cloth; $2.95 paper. A definition of psychology; employment prospects and rewards; fields; education and training required; advice on starting and advancing a career.

Woods, P. J. (Ed.). <u>Career opportunities for psychologists: Expanding and emerging areas</u>. Washington, D. C.: American Psychological Association, 1976. $5.00 paper. Papers on job prospects and advice for PhD candidates in psychology; summary statistics, focused mainly on doctoral-level training.

Woods, P. J. (Ed.). <u>The psychology major: Training and employment strategies</u>. Washington, D. C.: American Psychological Association, 1979. A complete analysis of and suggestions for formulation of educational goals, jobs for which to train, and strategies for finding a rewarding job once educated.

Practical Applications

Flanders, J. P. <u>Practical psychology</u>. New York: Harper & Row, 1976. $11.95 cloth. A discussion of strategies and procedures for building lasting and effective relationships; suggestions for a large variety of interesting activities, aimed at, for example, clarifying values or changing emotions and reducing fears.

Grasha, A. F. <u>Practical applications of psychology</u>. Cambridge, Mass.: Winthrop Publishers, 1978. $9.95 paper. A book on the understanding, development, and modification of personal skills and the application of those skills in interpersonal (social) settings.

Morgan, C. T., & Deese, J. <u>How to study</u> (2nd ed.). New York: McGraw-Hill, 1969. $3.95 paper. A book addressed to students, explaining how to apply the principles of learning and conditioning to improve study and retention skills.

Chapter 8

Instruments and Supplies for
Teaching and Research

Joseph B. Sidowski

The purpose of this chapter is to provide the reader with an abbreviated listing of companies that market instruments, supplies, and animals for use in class demonstrations or laboratory research. A list of readings covering electronics, methods, and instruments is also provided.

Most equipment or systems designed for laboratory research can also be used for class demonstrations; however, demonstration items generally are not designed to meet stringent research requirements. The American Psychological Association publication High School Psychology Teacher (and its predecessor Periodically) often contains examples of inexpensive materials and methods suitable for class demonstrations; these are seldom suitable for scientifically rigorous laboratory research although they may be used to demonstrate experimental methodologies and/or designs. Some of the equipment sold by firms specializing in psychological equipment is designed for teaching purposes but offers most of the characteristics of the more expensive research systems. Some companies sell systems that can be built up from relatively simple and inexpensive items to more complex systems suitable for both teaching and research.

Teachers or administrators interested in purchasing equipment are advised to obtain catalogs from all of the firms listed under the appropriate category below, particularly "Psychological Equipment and Supplies: General." Firms listed under the General category sell various types of equipment for psychology. Some of the equipment is compatible; that is, an item from one company can easily be connected to an item from another company. A careful reading of the company brochures will indicate those marketing compatible equipment. It is also advisable to keep one's name on the mailing list for announcements, price changes, instructional material, etc. Occasionally instrument companies distribute instructional material or hints that are valuable and very clearly written.

Before purchasing equipment or animals from commercial sources, one should check local organizations. Members of university or college departments of psychology are often very willing to loan equipment to local high school teachers; in some instances a great deal of help may accompany the loan. Also, as researchers purchase or build new systems to keep up with modern technology, older but very usable equipment is often stored; owners may be willing to give such equipment to anyone showing an interest, a need, and a high school affiliation. Research animals such as rats, mice, or pigeons may also be available. Small animals are sometimes purchased for use in one or two experiments and then destroyed. Many of the experiments merely involve learning or conditioning, and the animals are very usable for teaching purposes. Of course, adherence to APA's Guidelines for the Use of Animals in School Science Behavior Projects is absolutely necessary (see Chapter 11).

If equipment purchases are necessary, it is advisable to check with an individual experienced in using instrumented systems like those one desires. If teachers desire operant conditioning equipment, for example, they can phone a local psychology department and ask for the name of someone who might provide purchasing advice. One should ask about the reputation of the companies. How well do they support guarantees? What maintenance or trade-in service is offered? How much work will be required to set up the equipment? What electronics sophistication is required? What discounts are offered to educational institutions? Bids should be requested. Although the telephone is a fast means of obtaining information from a company, all bids and guarantees should be in writing.

Teachers who are interested in building equipment or in learning about the types of instruments and systems used in various areas of psychology, including clinical psychology, should refer to the list of readings at the end of this chapter. The two special issues of the American Psychologist (Sidowski, 1969, 1975) are excellent sources of information concerning the state and uses of technology in various areas of the profession. High school students and the lay public generally do not think of psychologists as users of electronic equipment, instrumented systems, and computers. Most are surprised and often awed when introduced to the activities of psychologists involved in applying modern technology to the investigation and solution of problems associated with human and animal behavior. The two instrumentation issues of the American Psychologist are readable and enlightening publications in this respect. The references also include relatively easy-to-read publications on basic electronics and instrumentation specific to psychology.

The remainder of this chapter contains the following: a Product Directory of animals, supplies, and equipment; addresses of companies marketing the above; and a list of reference books and manuals.

PRODUCT DIRECTORY
ANIMALS AND ANIMAL CARE

Animals, Laboratory

Amphibians, Fish, and Marine Invertebrates

Carolina Biological Supply
Neptune Wholesale Scientific Division
West Jersey Biological Farms

Gerbils and Hamsters (also try local animal stores)

Ancare Corp.
Hilltop Lab Animals, Inc.
West Jersey Biological Farms

Mice and Rats

ARS/Sprague-Dawley
Charles River Breeding Laboratories
Holtzman Co., Inc.
Timco Breeding Laboratories, Inc.

Pigeons

Palmetto Pigeon Plant

Planaria, Protozoa, Earthworms, and Mealworms

Carolina Biological Supply
Mogul-Ed

Activity Measurement

Columbus Instruments
Lafayette Instruments
Stoelting Co.
Tech Serv Inc.

Cages and Caging Materials
(Plastic and/or Metal)

Ancare Corp.
Bio-Science Industries
Hazelton Systems, Inc.
Lab Products
Plas-Labs

Food

The simplest way to obtain food for laboratory animals is to contact local feed stores listed in the yellow pages of the telephone book.

Food Pellets (Various Sizes)

P. J. Noyes

Research Equipment

See "Psychological Equipment and Supplies: General." A number of the companies listed market various kinds of animal research instruments and systems.

ELECTRONIC EQUIPMENT AND SUPPLIES

General

Olson Electronics and Radio Shack stores are often located locally. Refer to the local telephone directory.

Allied Electronics
Herbach & Rademan, Inc.
Lafayette Radio Electronics
Newark Electronics
Olson Electronics
Poly-Paks
Radio Shack

Counters and Timers

Counters and interval timers of various types are also available from some of the companies listed under "Psychological Equipment and Supplies: General."
Conroc, Cramer Division
Dimco-Gray Co.
Standard Electric Time Corp.
Veeder-Root

Instrument Kits

Some of the companies listed under "Electronic Equipment and Supplies: General" also sell kits. Although kits are less expensive than assembled instruments, assembling equipment is time consuming and error prone.
EICO Electronic Instrument Co.
Heath Co.

Scientific: General

Edmund Scientific Co.

PSYCHOLOGICAL EQUIPMENT AND SUPPLIES

General

Behavioral Controls
Coulbourn Instruments
Davis Scientific Instruments
Farrall Instrument Co.
GenRad
Ralph Gerbrands Co.
Harvard Apparatus Co.
Lafayette Instruments

LVB Corporation
Marietta Apparatus Co.
Psychological Instruments Co.
Scientific Prototype Mfg. Co.
Stoelting Co.
Tech Serv Inc.

Biofeedback Instruments

Autogenic Systems
Behavioral Controls
Biofeedback Research
Coulbourn Instruments
Cyborg
Edmund Scientific Co.
Lafayette Instruments
Tech Serv Inc.
Thought Technology, Ltd.

Biopsychology

Instruments for studies in biopsychology are generally expensive, and many require substantial knowledge of electronics for operational understanding. The interested teacher or student is advised to contact an experienced researcher for advice. Listings of specific supplies, equipment, and systems may be found in Science's annual Guide to Scientific Instruments and in the "Buyer's Guide" of the special issue of the American Psychologist on "Instrumentation in Psychology" (Sidowski, 1975). Suppliers listed under "Biofeedback Instruments" market equipment that allows the user to employ body-surface electrodes to feed back human biological signals associated with muscle action potential, brain waves, and galvanic skin responses. Companies that supply most of the sophisticated laboratory equipment and systems used in psychophysiological research--for example, Grass Instruments--are listed in the same two publications.

Conditioning Apparatus

See "Psychological Equipment and Supplies: General."

Operant Devices and Systems

See also "Psychological Equipment and Supplies: General."

Sunrise Systems, Inc. (microcomputer-controlled operant systems)

Perceptual and Motor Skills

Lafayette Instruments
Marietta Apparatus Co.
Research Media, Inc.
Stoelting Co.

Projecting Stimuli

Various methods are available for projecting and/or presenting stimuli in studies of learning, information processing, or perception. A popular and relatively inexpensive method now employed in learning research uses the Kodak Carousel Projector. Stimuli are merely photographed and presented on slides. The projector can be programmed to advance by simple timing/programming techniques. The Kodak Carousel Projector is generally available at local photography stores. Commercial automatic projection systems are available from some of the suppliers noted under "Psychological Equipment and Supplies: General."

Eastman Kodak Corp.

Reaction Time

For demonstration purposes a simple reaction-time system can be constructed easily with a Standard Electric clock, a lantern battery, and a switch. Minimum knowledge of electrical circuitry is required.
See also "Psychological Equipment and Supplies: General."

Standard Electric Time Corp.

Psychoacoustics/Audition

B & K Instruments
Coulbourn Instruments
GenRad
Hearing Laboratories, Inc.
Lafayette Instruments
Starkey Labs
Stoelting Co.

Vision Research

Color Materials: General

Munsell Color Corp.

Color Mixers

Ralph Gerbrands Co.
Lafayette Instruments
Marietta Apparatus Co.
Stoelting Co.

Perception (Depth, Illusions, Phi Phenomenon)

Lafayette Instruments
Psychological Instruments Co.
Research Media, Inc.
Stoelting Co.

Tachistoscopes

Ralph Gerbrands Co.
Lafayette Instruments
Polymetric
Scientific Prototype Mfg. Co.
Stoelting Co.

REFERENCES AND REFERENCE BOOKS

Instrumentation in psychology, as in all professions, continues to change as the state of technology advances. In the 1960s relay circuits were common; many of the teaching and research systems built around these switching devices are still in use. With the introduction of the transistor and other solid-state electronics, psychological equipment became more compact, and the emphasis in circuitry turned to the use of these components. Within the past 10 years, also, minicomputers moved into many psychology departments for teaching and research purposes. Some psychology departments now have as many as 20 small computers used for various purposes. Within recent years integrated circuits have simplified many aspects of equipment design and construction, so they are now popular components of many systems. The most recent advances influencing the design, construction, and/or purchase of equipment in psychology evolve from the development of microprocessors and microcomputers. Microprocessor developments have led to smaller and more intelligent instruments at a tremendously low cost. Persons interested in constructing new systems for teaching or research should orient their thinking along these lines. A commercial microcomputer system can be purchased for as low as $650, which includes a TV display, an alphanumeric keyboard, cassette, BASIC language built in, and reasonable memory.

BASIC ELECTRONICS

Commercial bookstores carry a variety of hardcover and softcover books that introduce the novice to basic modern electronics in a simple and clear fashion. Many local electronics stores carry softcover publications covering various aspects of electronics.

Brophy, J. J. Basic electronics for scientists (3rd ed.). New York:
    McGraw-Hill, 1977. No price available.

Crawford, M. Basic electricity and basic electronics. Blue Ridge Summit,
    Pa.: TAB Books, 1973. No price available.

Crowhurst, N. H. Basic electronics course. Blue Ridge Summit, Pa.: TAB
    Books, 1972. $9.95 paper.

Diefenderfer, A. J. Principles of electronic instrumentation.
    Philadelphia, Pa.: W. B. Saunders, 1972. $16.95 cloth.

Hoenig, S. A., & Payne, F. L. How to build and use electronic devices without frustration, panic, mountains of money, or an engineering degree. Boston: Little, Brown, 1973. $9.95 cloth.

Lancaster, D. TTL cookbook. Indianapolis: Howard W. Sams, 1974. $8.95 paper. A widely used reference in psychological laboratories because it provides a guide to understanding and using transistor-transistor logic (TTL) integrated circuits. Lancaster also has authored Sams's books on resistor-transistor logic (RTL) and diode-transistor logic (DTL). The TTL Cookbook describes a number of useful integrated circuits.

Sands, L. G., & Mackenroth, D. R. Encyclopedia of electronic circuits: Latest digital circuits. West Nyack, N. Y.: Parker Publishing Co., 1976. No price available.

Sessions, K. W. (Ed.). Master handbook of 1001 practical electronic circuits. Blue Ridge Summit, Pa.: TAB Books, 1975. $9.95 paper.

Manuals

The companies listed below publish a number of handbooks and manuals covering the use of transistors, diodes, integrated circuits, and solid-state electronics.

General Electric Corp.
Electronics Park
Syracuse, NY 13201

Texas Instruments, Inc.
P. O. Box 5012
M/S 54
Dallas, TX 75222

Motorola Semiconductor Products
5005 East McDowell Road
Phoenix, AZ 85008

Westinghouse Electric Corp.
Semiconductor Division
Youngwood, PA 15697

ELECTRONICS AND INSTRUMENTATION IN PSYCHOLOGY

Cleary, A. Instrumentation for psychology. New York: John Wiley, 1977. $17.50 cloth.

Hetzel, M. L., & Hetzel, C. W. Relay circuits for psychology. Englewood Cliffs, N. J.: Prentice-Hall, 1969. (Originally published by Appleton-Century-Crofts.) $8.95 paper. A very dated reference, strictly for the individual who has inherited the older relay equipment marketed by the general psychological equipment suppliers of the 1960s; not a guide for building a new system; easy to understand if relay equipment is used.

Schwitzgebel, R. L., & Schwitzgebel, R. K. Psychotechnology: Electronic control of mind and behavior. New York: Holt, Rinehart & Winston, 1973. $6.95 paper.

Science. Guide to scientific instruments. Washington, D. C.: American
Association for the Advancement of Science. Issued annually.

Sidowski, J. B. (Ed.). Experimental methods and instrumentation in psychology. New York: McGraw-Hill, 1966. $23.00 cloth. Somewhat
dated in details of circuitry and state of electronics, but a very
useful reference source for methods used in research laboratories;
written in how-to-do-it fashion by scientists from the major experimental areas of psychology.

Sidowski, J. B. (Ed.). Special issue: Instrumentation in psychology.
American Psychologist, 1969, 24, 185-408 (entire March issue). An
interesting collection of articles describing instrumented systems in
use in 1969; a useful look at technology as used by psychologists
studying various aspects of human and animal behavior.

Sidowski, J. B. (Ed.). Special issue: Instrumentation in psychology.
American Psychologist, 1975, 30, 191-468 (entire March issue). A
collection of articles describing instrumented systems used in the
study of biofeedback, human space flight, learning, sleep, mental
health care, and other areas of research and application; a strong
emphasis on computers, reflecting the rapid influence of these
machines on developments in psychology; like the 1969 instrumentation
issue, an excellent and inexpensive reference for introducing teachers and students to the manner in which the revolutions in electronics and computer technology have affected and continue to influence
the field of psychology.

Udolf, R. Logic design for behavioral scientists. Chicago: Nelson-
Hall, 1973. $12.95 cloth.

Zucker, M. H. Electronic circuits for the behavioral and biomedical sciences: A reference book of useful solid-state circuits. San Francisco: W. H. Freeman, 1969. $12.50 cloth. Somewhat dated but still
useful.

Psychobiology/Psychophysiology

Buckstein, E. Introduction to biomedical electronics. Indianapolis:
Howard W. Sams, 1973. $5.95 paper.

Hassett, J. A primer of psychophysiology. San Francisco: W. H. Freeman, 1978. No price available. A clear introduction to the area,
containing a simply written section on recording human physiological
responses.

Singh, D., & Avery, D. D. Physiological techniques in behavioral research. Monterey, Calif.: Brooks/Cole, 1975. $8.95 paper. An
easy-to-read and inexpensive introduction with drawn illustrations to
help students learn the techniques and tools of physiological psychology; descriptions of surgical methods, etc., at a level that is
extremely easy to follow.

Wilsoncroft, W. E., & Law, O. T. Laboratory manual for physiological psy-
    chology. Austin, Texas: Psychonomic Society, 1967. $1.50 paper.
    In spite of the publication date, an extremely useful book for the
    student interested in learning the techniques used in physiological
    psychology; sections dealing with the handling and care of lab ani-
    mals, anesthesia, electronics, recording, methods of implanting and
    stimulation, etc.

ADDRESSES OF SUPPLIERS

Allied Electronics
401 East Eighth Street
Fort Worth, TX   76101

Ancare Corp.
47 Manhasset Avenue
Manhasset, NY   11030

ARS/Sprague-Dawley
P. O. Box 4220
Madison, WI   53711

Autogenic Systems
809 Allston Way
Berkeley, CA   94710

B & K Instruments, Inc.
5111 West 164th Street
Cleveland, OH   44142

Behavioral Controls
P. O. Box 480
Milwaukee, WI   53201

Biofeedback Research
6325 Wilshire Boulevard
Los Angeles, California 90048

Bio-Science Industries
1200 Memorial Drive
Asbury Park, NJ   07712

Carolina Biological Supply
2700 York Road
Burlington, NC   27215

Charles River Breeding Laboratories
251 Ballardvale Street
Wilmington, MA   01887

Columbus Instruments
950 North Hague Avenue
Columbus, OH   43204

Conroc, Cramer Division
Mill Rock Road
Old Saybrook, CT   06475

Coulbourn Instruments
P. O. Box 2551
Lehigh Valley, PA   18001

Cyborg
342 Western Avenue
Boston, MA   02135

Davis Scientific Instruments
12137 Cantura Street
Studio City, CA   91604

Dimco-Gray Co.
8200 South Suburban Road
Centerville, OH   45459

Eastman Kodak Corp.
343 State Street
Rochester, NY   14650

Edmund Scientific Co.
7782 Edscorp Building
Barrington, NJ   08007

EICO Electronic Instrument Co.
108 New South Road
Hicksville, NY   11801

Farrall Instrument Co.
P. O. Box 1037
Grand Island, NE   68801

GenRad
300 Baker Avenue
Concord, MA 01742

Ralph Gerbrands Co.
Eight Beck Road
Arlington, MA 02174

Harvard Apparatus Co.
150 Dover Road
Millis, MA 02054

Hazelton Systems, Inc.
P. O. Box 700
Aberdeen, MD 21001

Hearing Laboratories, Inc.
P. O. Box 9457
Minneapolis, MN 55440

Heath Co.
Benton Harbor, MI 49022

Herbach & Rademan, Inc.
401 East Erie Avenue
Philadelphia, PA 19134

Hilltop Lab Animals, Inc.
P. O. Box 25
Chatsworth, CA 91311
&
P. O. Box 195
Scottsdale, PA 15683

Holtzman Co., Inc.
P. O. Box 9509
Madison, WI 53715

Lab Products
635 Midland Avenue
Garfield, NJ 07026

Lafayette Instruments
P. O. Box 1279
Lafayette, IN 47902

Lafayette Radio Electronics
P. O. Box 450
Syosset, Long Island, NY 11791

LVB Corporation
P. O. Box 2221
Lehigh Valley, PA 18001

Marietta Apparatus Co.
118 Maple Street
Marietta, OH 45750

Mogul-Ed
1222 West South Park Avenue
Oshkosh, WI 54903

Munsell Color Corp.
2441 North Calvert Street
Baltimore, MD 21218

Neptune Wholesale Scientific
   Division
1911 Colonial Avenue
Norfolk, VA 23517

Newark Electronics
500 North Pulaski Road
Chicago, IL 60624

P. J. Noyes
Whitefield Road
Lancaster, NH 03584

Olson Electronics
260 South Forge Street
Akron, OH 44327

Palmetto Pigeon Plant
P. O. Box 1585
Sumter, SC 29150

Plas-Labs
917 East Chilson Street
Lansing, MI 48906

Polymetric
463 Salem Street
Wilmington, MA 01887

Poly-Paks
P. O. Box 942E
Lynnfield, MA 01940

Psychological Instruments Co.
1733 Arlington Boulevard
Richmond, VA 23230

Radio Shack
1500 One Tandy Center
Fort Worth, TX   76102

Research Media, Inc.
Four Midland Avenue
Hicksville, NY   11801

Scientific Prototype Mfg. Co.
615 West 131st Street
New York, NY   10027

Standard Electric Time Corp.
89 Logan Street
Springfield, MA   01101

Starkey Labs
Auditory Research Division
6700 Washington Avenue South
Eden Prairie, MN   55344

Stoelting Co.
1350 South Kostner Avenue
Chicago, IL   60623

Sunrise Systems, Inc.
Fourteen Booth Hill Road
North Scituate, MA   02060

Tech Serv Inc.
BRS/LVE Division
5301 Holland Drive
Beltsville, MD   20705

Thought Technology, Ltd.
2193 Clifton Avenue
Montreal, Quebec, Canada   H4A 2N5

Timco Breeding Laboratories, Inc.
305 Almeda-Genoa Road
Houston, TX   77047

Veeder-Root
70 Sargent Street
Hartford, CT   06102

West Jersey Biological Farms
P. O. Box 6
Wenonah, NJ   08090

Chapter 9

Addresses of National Organizations

Organizations are included in the present list for a variety of reasons:

1. They may provide (usually without cost and sometimes in quantity) booklets, pamphlets, fact sheets, brochures, newsletters, and similar materials that could be useful for various segments of a high school psychology course.

2. They may provide information about or experimental materials of curriculum development projects relating to the study of human behavior.

3. They may provide information useful to students who are in the process of exploring career possibilities in areas directly or indirectly related to psychology.

4. They may provide information, primarily for teachers, relating to the existence of formal training opportunities, availability of funds, etc.

5. They may provide information relevant to personal problems, handicaps, or difficulties and are often able to suggest local helping facilities--both to inform teachers further and to assist students who may have, for one reason or another, particular concerns.

There is considerable overlap. Most organizations listed fulfill at least two of the foregoing functions. Some fulfill all five. Some exist almost exclusively for the dissemination of information to the lay public; others are much more specifically oriented toward their professional members (although all have some kind of ongoing public information activity). If the name of an organization gives few or no clues to its function, its major concern has been indicated parenthetically. The list is as exhaustive as present resources permit but very probably has important omissions. Many organizations have local chapters to which they may refer inquiries.

The most important source of information directly relevant to high school psychology teachers is:

American Psychological Association
Clearinghouse on Precollege Psychology
1200 Seventeenth Street, N. W.
Washington, DC 20036

175

Organization Address List

Addiction Research Foundation
33 Russell Street
Toronto, Ontario, Canada   M5S 2S1

Administration for Children, Youth
  and Families
United States Department of Health,
  Education and Welfare
P. O. Box 1182
Washington, DC   20013

Al-Anon Family Group Headquarters, Inc.
P. O. Box 182
New York, NY   10010

American Alliance for Health,
  Physical Education, and Recreation
1201 Sixteenth Street, N. W.
Washington, DC   20036

American Anthropological Association
1703 New Hampshire Avenue, N. W.
Washington, DC   20009

American Association for
  Laboratory Animal Science
2317 West Jefferson Street, Suite 208
Joliet, IL   60435

American Association for the
  Advancement of Science
1515 Massachusetts Avenue, N. W.
Washington, DC   20005

American Association of Criminology
P. O. Box 321
Harvard Square Station
Cambridge, MA   02138

American Association of Marriage
  and Family Counselors
225 Yale Avenue
Claremont, CA   91711

American Association of Religious
  Therapists
5800 Southwest 130th Avenue
Fort Lauderdale, FL   33330

American Association on Mental
  Deficiency
5201 Connecticut Avenue, N. W.
Washington, DC   20015

American Correctional Association
  (crime)
4321 Hartwick Road, Suite L208
College Park, MD   20740

American Educational Research
  Association
1126 Sixteenth Street, N. W., Room 110
Washington, DC   20036

American Ethnological Society
c/o Dr. June Collins, Corresponding Secretary
State University College at Buffalo
1300 Elmwood Avenue
Buffalo, NY   14222

American Genetic Association
1028 Connecticut Avenue, N. W.
Washington, DC   20036

American Group Psychotherapy
  Association, Inc.
1995 Broadway, Fourteenth Floor
New York, NY   10023

American Humane Association
Child Protection Division
5351 South Roslyn Street
Englewood, CO   80110

American Institutes for Research
  in the Behavioral Sciences
Fairfax Building
4614 Fifth Avenue
Pittsburgh, PA   15213

American Medical Association
535 North Dearborn Street
Chicago, IL   60610

The American Museum of Natural
  History
Central Park West at 79th Street
New York, NY   10024

American Nurses Association, Inc.
2420 Pershing Road
Kansas City, MO   64108

American Orthopsychiatric Association
1775 Broadway
New York, NY   10019

American Personnel and Guidance Association
1607 New Hampshire Avenue, N. W.
Washington, DC   20009

American Political Science Association
1527 New Hampshire Avenue, N. W.
Washington, DC   20036

American Psychiatric Association
1700 Eighteenth Street, N. W.
Washington, DC   20009

American Psychoanalytic Association
One East 57th Street
New York, NY   10022

American Psychological Association
1200 Seventeenth Street, N. W.
Washington, DC   20036

American Society for Psychical Research
Five West 73rd Street
New York, NY   10023

American Society of Clinical Hypnosis
2400 East Devon Avenue, Suite 218
Des Plaines, IL   60018

American Society of Criminology
c/o Harry E. Allen
Ohio State University
1314 Kinnear Road
Columbus, OH   43212

American Sociological Association
1722 N Street, N. W.
Washington, DC   20036

American Speech and Hearing Association
10801 Rockville Pike
Rockville, MD   20852

American Statistical Association
806 Fifteenth Street, N. W.
Washington, DC   20005

Animal Behavior Society
Dr. Devra Kleiman, Secretary
Office of Zoological Research
National Zoological Park
Washington, DC   20009

Animal Welfare Institute
P. O. Box 3650
Washington, DC   20007

Association for Computing Machinery
1133 Avenue of the Americas
New York, NY   10036

Association for Education of the
   Visually Handicapped
919 Walnut Street, Fourth Floor
Philadelphia, PA   19107

Association for Educational Communication
   and Technology
1126 Sixteenth Street, N. W., Room 311
Washington, DC   20036

Association for Humanistic Psychology
325 Ninth Street
San Francisco, CA   94103

Association for the Education of
   Teachers in Science
c/o Dr. Joyce Swartney, Secretary-Treasurer
State University College at Buffalo
1300 Elmwood Avenue
Buffalo, NY   14222

Association for the Gifted
   (children)
c/o Dr. John C. Gowan
1426 South Southwind Circle
Westlake Village, CA   91361

Association for the Sociology of
   Religion
Robert McNamara, Executive Secretary
Loyola University of Chicago
6525 North Sheridan Road
Chicago, IL   60626

Association of Rehabilitation Facilities
   (handicapped)
5530 Wisconsin Avenue, N. W., Suite 955
Washington, DC   20015

Big Brothers/Big Sisters of America
   (family)
220 Suburban Station Building
Philadelphia, PA   19103

The Big Sisters, Inc. (family)
60 Lafayette Street
New York, NY   10013

Biological Sciences Curriculum Study
P. O. Box 930
Boulder, CO   80306

B'nai B'rith Career and Counseling
  Services
1640 Rhode Island Avenue, N. W.
Washington, DC   20036

Brain Research Foundation
An Affiliate of the University of Chicago
343 South Dearborn Street
Chicago, IL 60604

Catholic Big Brothers (family)
1011 First Avenue
New York, NY   10022

Center for Personalized Instruction
Georgetown University
Washington, DC 20057

Child Study Association of America/
  WEL-MET, Inc.
50 Madison Avenue
New York, NY   10010

Child Welfare League of America, Inc.
67 Irving Place
New York, NY   10003

Council for Exceptional Children
1920 Association Drive
Reston, VA   22091

Council on Adoptable Children
1813 Glendora Drive
District Heights, MD 20028

Council on Social Work Education
345 East 46th Street
New York, NY   10017

Daughters of Bilitis
  (female homosexuality)
330 Grove Street
San Francisco, CA   94102

Do It Now Foundation (chemical
  awareness)
Institute for Chemical Survival
P. O. Box 5115
Phoenix, AZ 85010

Drug Enforcement Administration
United States Department of Justice
1405 I Street, N. W.
Washington, DC   20537

Education Development Center
  (Exploring Human Nature and
  Exploring Childhood)
School and Society Programs
55 Chapel Street
Newton, MA   02160

Education for Parenthood Project
Office of Education
400 Maryland Avenue, S. W., Room 2089-G
Washington, DC   20202

Educational Research Council of America
Rockefeller Building
Cleveland, OH 44113

Educational Testing Service
Princeton, NJ   08540

Epilepsy Foundation of America
1828 L Street, N. W.
Washington, DC   20036

ERIC Clearinghouse for Social
  Studies/Social Science Education
855 Broadway
Boulder, CO   80302

ERIC Clearinghouse on Science,
  Mathematics, and Environmental
  Education
The Ohio State University
1800 Cannon Drive
400 Lincoln Tower
Columbus, OH   43210

Family Life Bureau
United States Catholic Conference
1312 Massachusetts Avenue, N. W.
Washington, DC   20005

Family Service Association of
  America
44 East 23rd Street
New York, NY   10010

Foundation for Research on Human
  Behavior
630 City Center Building
Ann Arbor, MI   48108

Fund for the Improvement of Post-Secondary
  Education
United States Department of Health,
  Education and Welfare
400 Maryland Avenue, S. W., Room 3123
Washington, DC   20202

Future Scientists of America
  (clubs for high school students)
c/o National Science Teachers
  Association
1742 Connecticut Avenue, N. W.
Washington, DC   20009

Gam-Anon, National Service Office, Inc.
  (for relatives of gamblers)
P. O. Box 4549
Downey, CA   90241

Gamblers Anonymous
P. O. Box 17173
Los Angeles, CA   90017

General Service Board of Alcoholics
  Anonymous
P. O. Box 459
Grand Central Station
New York, NY   10017

Genetics Society of America
c/o Business Office
P. O. Drawer U
University Station
Austin, TX   78712

Goodwill Industries of America, Inc.
  (rehabilitation)
9200 Wisconsin Avenue
Bethesda, MD   20014

High School Political Science
  Curriculum Project
Social Studies Development Center
Indiana University
513 North Park Avenue
Bloomington, IN   47401

History of Science Society
c/o Professor Roger H. Stuewer
School of Physics and Astronomy
University of Minnesota
116 Church Street, S. E.
Minneapolis, MN   55455

Human Behavior Curriculum Project
c/o American Psychological Association
1200 Seventeenth Street, N. W.
Washington, DC   20036

Human Factors Society, Inc.
P. O. Box 1369
Santa Monica, CA   90406

Human Sciences Program
c/o Biological Sciences Curriculum
  Study
P. O. Box 930
Boulder, CO   80306

Humane Society of the United States
2100 L Street, N. W.
Washington, DC   20037

Individualized Science Instruc-
  tional System
College of Education
Florida State University
Tallahassee, FL   32306

Institutes of Religion and Health
Three West 29th Street
New York, NY   10001

International Reading Association
800 Barksdale Road
Newark, DE   19711

Mental Health Association
1800 North Kent Street
Arlington, VA   22209

Mental Health Materials Center, Inc.
419 Park Avenue South
New York, NY   10016

National Academy of Sciences
National Research Council
2101 Constitution Avenue, N. W.
Washington, DC   20418

National Alliance Concerned with
  School-Age Parents
7315 Wisconsin Avenue, N. W., Suite 211-W
Washington, DC   20014

National Association for Music
  Therapy, Inc.
c/o Ms. Margaret Sears, Executive
  Director
P. O. Box 610
Lawrence, KS   66044

National Association for Retarded
  Citizens
2709 Avenue E East
Arlington, TX   76011

National Association of Biology
  Teachers
11250 Roger Bacon Drive
Reston, VA   22090

National Association of Social
  Workers
1425 H Street, N. W.
Washington, DC   20005

National Association of the Deaf
814 Thayer Avenue
Silver Spring, MD   20910

National Center on Educational
  Media and Materials for the
  Handicapped
The Ohio State University
Columbus, OH   43210

National Clearinghouse for Alcohol
  Information
Annex
P. O. Box 2345
Rockville, MD   20852

National Clearinghouse for Drug
  Abuse Information
5600 Fishers Lane
Rockville, MD   20852

National Commission on
  Resources for Youth
36 West 44th Street
New York, NY   10036

National Council for the Social
  Studies
2030 M Street, N. W., Suite 406
Washington, DC   20036

National Council on Alcoholism
733 Third Avenue
New York, NY   10017

National Council on Crime and
  Delinquency
Continental Plaza
411 Hackensack Avenue
Hackensack, NJ   07601

National Council on Family Relations
1219 University Avenue, S. E.
Minneapolis, MN   55414

National Education Association
1201 Sixteenth Street, N. W.
Washington, DC   20036

National Endowment for the
  Humanities
806 Fifteenth Street, N. W.
Washington, DC   20506

National Epilepsy League
6 North Michigan Avenue
Chicago, IL   60602

National Institute of Education
1832 M Street, N. W.
Washington, DC   20208

National Institute of Mental Health
5600 Fishers Lane
Rockville, MD   20857

National Institute of Science
c/o Dr. L. Shelbert Smith
Department of Chemistry
Central State University
Wilberforce, OH   45384

National League for Nursing
Ten Columbus Circle
New York, NY   10019

National Organization for Non-Parents
Three North Liberty Street
Baltimore, MD   21201

National Organization for Women
425 Thirteenth Street, N. W.
Washington, DC   20004

National Rehabilitation Association
1522 K Street, N. W.
Washington, DC   20005

National Science Foundation
1800 G Street, N. W.
Washington, DC   20550

National Science Teachers Association
1742 Connecticut Avenue, N. W.
Washington, DC   20009

National Society for Autistic Children
169 Tampa Avenue
Albany, NY   12208

National Therapeutic Recreation Association
1601 North Kent Street
Arlington, VA 22209

National Urban League
  (black concerns)
500 East 62nd Street
New York, NY 10021

NTL Institute for Applied
  Behavioral Science
1501 Wilson Boulevard
Arlington, VA 22209

Office of Education
United States Department of
  Health, Education and Welfare
400 Maryland Avenue, S. W.
Washington, DC 20202

Parapsychological Association
c/o Executive Secretariat
P. O. Box 7503
Alexandria, VA 22307

Parapsychology Foundation, Inc.
29 West 57th Street
New York, NY 10019

Philosophy of Science Association
c/o Dr. Peter D. Asquith, Executive Secretary
Department of Philosophy
Michigan State University
East Lansing, MI 48824

Population Reference Bureau, Inc.
1337 Connecticut Avenue, N. W.
Washington, DC 20036

President's Committee on Employment
  of the Handicapped
c/o Mr. Bernard Posner, Executive Secretary
Washington, DC 20210

Prime Time School TV
120 South Lasalle Street
Chicago, IL 60603

Psychology Educators Special Interest Group
National Council for the Social Studies
c/o Barry Beerman
George D. Hewlitt High School
60 Everett Avenue
Hewlitt, NY 11557

Public Affairs Committee
381 Park Avenue South
New York, NY 10016

Recovery, Incorporated, The Association of
  Nervous and Former Mental Patients
116 South Michigan Avenue
Chicago, IL 60603

Resource Center on Sex Roles
  in Education
National Foundation for the Improvement
  of Education
1201 Sixteenth Street, N. W., Suite 701
Washington, DC 20036

Rural Sociological Society
c/o Frank O. Leuthold, Treasurer
325 Morgan Hall
University of Tennessee
Knoxville, TN 37916

Rutgers Center of Alcohol Studies
Rutgers--The State University
New Brunswick, NJ 08903

Salvation Army (rehabilitation,
  social service)
120 West Fourteenth Street
New York, NY 10011

Science Clubs of America
1719 N Street, N. W.
Washington, DC 20036

Science Service
1719 N Street, N. W.
Washington, DC 20036

Scientists' Institute for Public
  Information
355 Lexington Avenue
New York, NY 10017

Sex Information and Education Council
  of the United States, Inc.
137 North Franklin Street
Hempstead, NY 11550

Social Science Education Consortium, Inc.
855 Broadway
Boulder, CO 80302

Society for Experimental Biology and
  Medicine
630 West 168th Street
New York, NY   10032

Society for the Scientific Study
  of Sex
Twelve East 41st Street, Suite 1104
New York, NY   10017

STASH, Inc. (chemical awareness)
118 South Bedford Street
Madison, WI   53703

Summerhill Society (education)
c/o Mr. Edward P. Gottlieb
339 Lafayette Street
New York, NY   10012

United Cerebral Palsy Association, Inc.
66 East 34th Street New York, NY   10016

Women's Educational Equity
  Communications Network
Far West Laboratory for Educational
  Research and Development
1855 Folsom Street
San Francisco, CA   94103

Chapter 10

Putting It All Together in the Classroom

Maxine Warnath

In preceding chapters specific information has been provided on background materials and resources for the high school course in psychology.
This chapter focuses on some of the ways in which that information might
be used. There is no intention to illustrate a right or perfect approach
to teaching psychology; rather, alternatives are discussed, and the final
decision is left to the individual teacher.

In some ways teaching a high school psychology course is not very
different from teaching other high school subjects. In other ways there
are some very definite differences. Some of the basic issues that cut
across all disciplines are:

Grading, measurement, and evaluation. What methods should be used to
measure achievement, growth, etc., in the students? Will there be sufficient objective measures to assure that the assessment is not overly subjective? On the other hand, is there room for professional judgment to
play a role in the assessment process? The fundamental question is, What
form of assessment is appropriate for a particular course and its objectives, and where is that form located on the continuum between objective
and subjective?

Structure, organization, and format. As with most other subject
areas, careful advance planning for a psychology course is a must. Sequence and scope should be determined, as well as the mechanics necessary
for a successful teaching experience. One of the areas to be considered
is the form of classroom activities. Once again there is a continuum
involved, ranging from the straight lecture to the "What will we do today?" style of conducting class. Between these two ends of the continuum
is a variety of methods that allow differing levels of student involvement in the learning process. Psychology lends itself quite easily to
student involvement. In Chapter 6 on Audiovisual Materials there is a
partially annotated list of films and filmstrips that can help to illustrate vividly certain psychological principles and concepts. High School
Psychology Teacher (formerly Periodically), a newsletter published by the
American Psychological Association, regularly publishes AIDs (Activities,
Inquiries, and Demonstrations) that involve the student in the learning
process. Existing AIDs and gimmicks (as they were called in Periodically) cover many subareas and topics in psychology and can be selected to
fit the specific orientation of a course. Gimmicks published through May
1977 are available as Manuscript Number 1754 ($30 paper, $6 fiche) from
APA's Journal Supplement Abstract Service. AIDs are available from the
APA Clearinghouse on Precollege Psychology.

In preparing for the high school psychology course the teacher has at
least one very important positive factor functioning in his or her
favor--the ever-apparent intrinsic interest in the content areas of psychology. Psychology is, by its very nature, a fascinating subject to

study, particularly so during adolescence when there are such questions
as: Why do I act the way I do? Why do others react to me the way they
do? How can I learn to relate to others so that I can feel better about
the outcomes? Why do I feel the way I do? All this suggests that psychology should be taught with a personal-growth/experiential approach.
At the same time, there are those who believe that psychology should take
a data/methodology/principles approach, paying less attention to personal
application.

There are many supporting arguments for each side. Among those in
support of the personal-growth/experiential approach are: (a) According
to theories of development, the high school age is the appropriate time
for learning about one's self and one's sense of identity. (b) Affective
development at the high school level is neglected in the current emphasis
on cognitive development. (c) Facts are of little value unless the individual learns how to apply those facts; we spend far too much time on
rote memorization.

Arguments for the data/methodology/principles approach are: (a) Psychology is a discipline based on some fundamental laws and theories that
provide structure and meaning. A course should not carry the label "psychology" unless it provides the student with some appreciation for this
foundation. (b) The self-knowledge gained by the individual through
personal-growth/experiential courses will quickly be lost unless it is
supported by understanding of some of the basic psychological phenomena.
(c) We all build our own "psychology of individual and interpersonal behavior" based on our own experiences and society's collective experiences
passed on by way of folklore and myths. It is important to know how to
determine the validity of the various aspects of this "personally developed psychology." Increasing this validity will enable the individual to
function more effectively in school, job, family, etc.

The debate about the proper approach for the high school psychology
course has gone on for years. The difficulty of finding a middle ground
between the two approaches was expressed most aptly by Bare (1971):

> Shall what is taught be knowledge of self or knowledge of others,
> principles or applications to personal and social problems, precision
> or significance, hard or soft? Viewing the issue as knowledge of
> self or knowledge of others, one sees a problem unique to psycholo-
> gy: the subject matter is both objective and subjective, and the
> explanations for phenomena must be satisfying not only scientifically
> but experientially. Psychology has been trying to bridge these poles
> since its inception. The study of consciousness was the study of me
> with the hope of understanding you; the study of behavior is the
> study of you with the hope of understanding me. (pp. 5-6)

It appeared for a long time that the two approaches were mutually
exclusive. More recently, however, there seems to have been some mellow-
ing. The approaches do not appear to be so dichotomous as they once
seemed. A course can provide the student with research data, methodological skills, and basic principles while enabling the student to make appropriate personal applications. Much of the research data available,

except in the most extreme cases, is easily presented in such a way that both advocates of psychology as a science and advocates of psychology as personal growth and understanding can be satisfied. Consider the following subareas of psychology, for example:

● personality: The three major views on personality (behavioral/learning, psychoanalytic, and humanistic) can be presented in theoretical form and structure with accompanying exercises or experiential materials to help students make application to individual situations.

● social psychology: The research data on affiliation, liking, and loving can be used as the basis for a discussion on teenage dating, early marriage, how we choose friends, etc. The data on dyadic and group communication patterns, decision-making processes under varying conditions, conflict resolution, etc., can easily be used to help students understand interactions in the classroom as well as in other areas of the students' lives such as within the family, on the job, and so on.

● development: Theories and data can be presented on the stages that we have each gone through in developing to where we are now and those we are likely to go through in the future. The treatment can include, for example, why our younger brother or sister is behaving in a certain way, whether the behavior is usual, and whether it is likely to change.

● physiological psychology: Data can be presented on the interaction between "body and mind," along with research findings on the control of behavior through mental processes. Also, students can look at studies of the biological bases of behavior, including some biological processes that are not known to be controlled by mental processes. Another avenue of exploration is biofeedback and ways of using it in everyday life.

● methodology in psychology: Among the possible subjects of study in this area are methods of producing scientific information, ways of determining if the folklore and myths passed down through generations regarding human behavior are reliable and valid, ways of looking at behavior more objectively so as to reduce personal bias in a situation, the potential problem of becoming so objective that the human being is lost in a collection of objective data, ethical problems involved in research with human and/or animal subjects, and the dangers of pushing ethical limits in the name of science and research.

These are only samples of how various subareas in psychology can be used as a focal point for both data and personal aspects. A valuable resource for the teacher in this regard will be the study units being prepared through the Human Behavior Curriculum Project, sponsored by the American Psychological Association. In the near future, study units in the following areas will be published and available for classroom use:

changing attitudes, conditioning and learning, language and communication, natural behaviors, personality, school life and organizational psychology, social influences on behavior, and states of consciousness. Each study unit is a two- to three-week module that gives detailed outlines for instruction, along with most of the materials to back it up. A student reading is also provided. The orientation is that of combining basic data and principles with activities to involve the student both in and out of the classroom.

A helpful reference on the broad issue of teaching psychology as a discipline versus teaching psychology for personal growth is Teaching Psychology in Secondary Schools by Kasschau and Wertheimer (1974). It discusses the issue in depth and also provides information on curriculum materials, teacher training and certification, and the history of high school psychology.

The remainder of this chapter will discuss a variety of ways to supplement the class lecture or, if one prefers, supplant the lecture altogether. The listing is not exhaustive; it is intended to serve as a stimulus for further ideas. Publications that pursue some of these areas in more depth are:

Gronlund, N. E. Individualizing classroom instruction. New York: Macmillan, 1974. $2.75 paper.

Johnson, K. R., & Ruskin, R. S. Behavioral instruction. Washington, D. C.: American Psychological Association, 1977. $5.00 paper.

Maas, J. B., & Kleiber, D. A. (Eds.). Directory of teaching innovations in psychology. Washington, D. C.: American Psychological Association, 1975. $15.00 paper. Some of the ideas presented in this chapter can be found in expanded form in the Directory, along with references for additional information. Although the plans discussed are from college-level courses, a few minor changes make many of them applicable to the high school.

McKeachie, W. J. Teaching tips: A guidebook for the beginning college teacher (7th ed.). Lexington, Mass.: D. C. Heath, 1978. $4.95 paper.

Mosher, R. L., & Sprinthall, N. A. Psychological education in secondary schools: A program to promote individual and human development. American Psychologist, 1970, 25, 911-924.

Walker, E. L., & McKeachie, W. J. Teaching the beginning course in psychology. Monterey, Calif.: Brooks/Cole, 1967. $4.95 paper.

Role-Playing and Simulation Games

Role-playing is a technique whereby participants take the role of a designated person in a situation described by the teacher. The role player attempts to portray the way that person would act and feel in that particular situation. The technique has been used for many years in schools, workshops, organizational development training programs, etc. Although role-playing episodes may be planned in advance, they often are developed spontaneously out of the specific problem area under discussion.

Simulation games, an approach developed in recent years, provide a more structured total experience than the short sequences used in role-playing. Simulations may cover one class period or involve units of a week or even several weeks in length. Students can and do become very involved in the simulated experience and begin to understand how people who are actually in those situations feel and perceive their world. Because the feelings can sometimes be rather intense, sufficient time should be planned after the exercise is completed to discuss thoroughly all the feelings that may have arisen during the exercise. Some of the games currently available have been developed with an economics, political science, or general social science orientation; however, minor changes in the orientation section of the game and the post-game discussion questions can make the games applicable to psychology classes, particularly in the area of social psychology. For example, a simulation game that portrays life in the inner city can be used to illustrate the differing impacts of cooperation and competition in the development of community stability, attitude formation and change, intergroup communication, etc.

After students have had experience with one or more simulation games, another class activity to involve students in a different way is that of developing their own games. The activity requires understanding the concept to be emphasized and determining how the concept will be translated into the structure of the game. Although the activity is complex, it does allow for a variety of experience in the classroom and is a direct attempt to translate concepts and theory into "reality."

Following are some publications that discuss the use of games. The Abt book and the Taylor and Walford book contain descriptions of and instructions for several games. The Taylor and Walford book also contains a section on sources of materials for the classroom. The Social Science Education Consortium's Data Book contains a large section on games, describing them according to objectives, rationale, intended user characteristics, content, and procedures, and specifying source and cost. The Horn book is a compendium of hundreds of games and simulations, categorized by field, with summary descriptions, playing data, lists of materials, and sources.

Abt, C. C. Serious games. New York: Viking Press, 1970. $5.95 cloth.

Boocock, S. S., & Schild, E. O. (Eds.). Simulation games in learning. Beverly Hills, Calif.: Sage Publications, 1968. Out of print.

Carlson, E. Learning through games. Washington, D. C.: Public Affairs Press, 1969. $6.00 cloth.

Horn, R. E. (Ed.). The guide to simulations/games for education and training (3rd ed.) (Vol. 1). Cranford, N. J.: Didactic Systems, 1977. $23.00 cloth.

Social Science Education Consortium. Social studies curriculum materials
    data book. Boulder, Colo.: Author, 1971. Supplemented biannually,
    1972 through 1977; annually, 1978-. $75.00 for the basic book;
    $10.00 for the annual supplement.

Taylor, J. L., & Walford, R. Simulation in the classroom. Baltimore:
    Penguin, 1972. Out of print.

Observations in Class Using "Borrowed" Children

During the study of child development, children of the particular age
under discussion can be brought to class for direct observation. The
children may be younger brothers and sisters of students, or children of
neighbor families who are "borrowed" along with their parents and some of
their more portable toys. Prior to the observation day the students can
develop forms for recording behaviors that are considered typical of the
age to be observed and for noting additional behaviors. Simple notations
can be agreed on so that after the observation is completed, the students
will be able to compare the data they have collected. Tasks appropriate
to the age can be planned in advance and presented to the child (or children) for a more structured observation, if desired.

In addition to the obvious advantage of seeing "real, live human beings" of the age being studied, the students also have the experience of
developing data forms, determining what items should be included, actually noting down their behavioral observations, and compiling data--an experience that can lead to discussion of one of the research methods used
in developmental psychology.

Problems-and-Issues Approach

Environmental issues and the quality of life are of increasing concern to all of us. Classroom units can be developed around either a specific local issue (pollution of the river running through town, roadside
chemical spraying of weeds, etc.) or a more general global issue (e.g.,
population growth), using it as a focal point for exploration and application of basic psychological principles. Social psychological approaches to problem-solving are appropriate here, but there are also possibilities for involving theories and data from developmental psychology,
learning, personality, etc. Areas in social psychology such as opinion
formation and change, social change, cooperation and competition,
win-lose and synergy, social influence, and communication processes can
all be involved in a force-field analysis of the problem area. The process of force-field analysis (see Lewin, 1951) will be discussed here to
show how the field of social psychology can be used in a problems-and-is-
sues approach.

1. define the problem by determining the actual conditions and the
    preferred conditions;
2. identify forces acting for and against the changes necessary to
    reach the preferred condition, to illustrate the balance or
    counterbalance of forces in a system;

3. determine the relative strengths of the forces for and against
    the changes necessary to reach the preferred condition;
4. develop strategies to reduce resistance to change and encourage
    movement toward the goal;
5. develop proposals for implementation.

There is a good discussion of force-field analysis and the psychology
of social change in Watson and Johnson's Social Psychology: Issues and
Insights (1972, pp. 422-454). In most cases (particularly when the class
is considering global problems) the exercise will be largely theoretical
in nature. However, if the problem is local, the class may actually become involved with community government agencies or citizen groups that
are working on the problem by doing some background research and analysis.

Use of Observed Incidents in Class Discussion

Daily incidents outside the classroom are a rich resource for class
discussions. Sources of the incidents can be newspaper or magazine clip-
pings, radio or television news broadcasts, incidents observed first-hand
by students, etc. Class discussion involves a description of the behavior and analysis of it using a specific theoretical approach (attribution
theory, Freudian, behavioristic, etc.) currently being studied. For example, an incident might be considered in which a three-year-old was
playing with some blocks, a five-year-old entered the scene, and some
vigorous interaction ensued between the two children. The incident could
be discussed in terms of Erikson's and/or Piaget's developmental stages.
By the end of the term, the class should be able to analyze ordinary
day-to-day situations from many perspectives, an advantage in helping
them learn how better to understand and respond to events affecting them
in their own settings.

Experimental "Labs" in the Classroom

When we think of laboratory programs, we often assume that we must
have elaborately equipped space available (preferably including animals)
if we are to conduct psychological experiments. Not so! Although some
teachers do have access to well-equipped experimental psychology labs, it
is possible to develop an experimental approach in the classroom using
minimal equipment and simple tasks, such as measuring reaction time or
mirror tracing. Emphasis is on assembling of the equipment (much of
which can be constructed in cooperation with the school's shop classes),
experimental design (independent variables, dependent variables, experimental and control groups, etc.), collection of data, writing of reports
using a modified APA style, and one of the most important aspects, the
ethical questions involved in the specific experiment and in experimentation in general (see Chapter 11). Two especially useful laboratory manuals (see Chapter 3 for a list of additional ones) are:

Debold, R. C. Manual of contemporary experiments in psychology.
    Englewood Cliffs, N. J.: Prentice-Hall, 1968. Out of print. All
    exercises can be performed outside of class with friends as subjects.

Jung, J., & Bailey, J. H. Contemporary psychology experiments: Adaptations for laboratory (2nd ed). New York: John Wiley, 1976. $6.95 paper. All exercises require students to observe behavior of subjects their own age in out-of-class situations.

Use of Media and Movement by Students in the Classroom

To a large degree our classrooms are verbal and cognitive in nature, stressing information transfer and repetition, either oral or written. The recent explorations into the implications of right-brain/left-brain research for educational processes may encourage use of other approaches to the acquisition and processing of knowledge. Paints, crayons, paper, glue, scissors, film, slides, magazine pictures, etc., can be used by students to represent their understanding of concepts in perception, motivation, and interpersonal interaction, among many other possible concepts. In conjunction with the high school dance teacher, use of the body can be explored, along with tension and stress reduction and the relationship between body control and feelings. An interdisciplinary media-and-movement show illustrating psychological concepts could be an end-of-the term product.

Classroom Use of Media and Books

Annotated lists of books and media are found in other chapters of this volume. In this chapter the emphasis is on some ways to use the items included on those lists.

Videotapes of Current Television Programs

Contingent on copyright laws and local station restrictions, temporary recordings can be made of popular television "sitcoms" and dramas with video recording equipment available in schools. Segments of programs can be brought into the classroom for use as a stimulus for discussion and analysis of behavior according to the theoretical approach of one's choice. Some areas that can be studied in this way include social influence, communication patterns, nonverbal communication, attribution theory, Freudian psychoanalysis, and developmental patterns. Such sequences can also be used to provide a common experience to train students in behavioral observation using recording forms developed by the class itself. Videotapes (like film) have the advantage of being able to be viewed repeatedly so that accuracy of recording can be checked. Videotapes of television programs have the added advantage of being very current and familiar to most students. Using familiar material for analysis may help students more effectively transfer skills to their real-life situations.

Another use for the videotape recorder and playback machine is reproduction of selected commercials for analysis and discussion of motivation, persuasion, communication, and sex-role socialization. Saturday morning cartoons provide abundant material for the study of aggression and violence, the "con" game, and interpersonal interactions of many kinds.

Fiction and Science Fiction

Novels and science fiction often seem more interesting to the high school student than the usually assigned textbook. Some teachers take advantage of this intrinsic interest and use science fiction and novels as an integral part of their course (see Chapter 5). Carefully selected novels or short stories can be used as outside-of-class assignments, with basic psychological principles explained in class by the teacher and class discussion of examples of those principles as found in the assigned readings. Adolescent psychology, personality development, and many aspects of social psychology can be very effectively taught this way. After interest in the topic has been aroused, readings in psychology books and journals can be recommended for those who wish to pursue an area in more depth, perhaps by way of a project or research paper. Comic books can also be used in comparable ways.

Biographies, Autobiographies, and Journals

Biographies, autobiographies, and journals may be used in similar fashion to novels and science fiction. They have a particular advantage in that they deal with real people and depict actual events and settings that provide more reality and depth to class discussions. In both cases, the teacher needs to be fully familiar with the books assigned so that the content is interpreted in terms of psychological concepts and knowledge.

Another approach in the use of biographies, autobiographies, and journals is to explore the lives of psychologists to introduce and increase interest in the area. Linking research, theories, and concepts to the lives of the psychologists involved builds in a factor of human interest for students of high school age.

Community Guests as Resources for Class Sessions

Many communities have psychologists and/or psychiatrists who are engaged in the practice of such specialties as clinical psychology, family counseling, marriage counseling, and vocational counseling. There may also be psychologists available who are working for alcoholism and/or drug rehabilitation units, community mental health clinics, hospitals, free clinics, or rape crisis centers. School psychologists, personnel managers, and research, industrial, and organizational development psychologists may be found in larger communities. If one is located near a college or university, there are many potential resources among the resident faculty and the visiting psychologists whom they bring to the campus.

All of these people are possible guests for class discussions about potential careers in psychology, practical application of psychological concepts and knowledge, or current research in a particular area. Class sessions with these guests can range from formal talks to open discussion. They can be an opportunity for students to practice interviewing skills learned in previous units.

Classroom Study Groups

Study groups built on a cooperative system can be used for research on subtopics in psychology. These study groups differ from the usual classroom discussion groups in terms of continuity, length, depth, and structure. Each study group pursues a single topic over a period ranging from several days to several weeks. The groups' activities are structured by teacher-prepared handouts that systematically move them through the process of doing research on a topic. Membership of no more than four or five students per group is recommended to promote maximum participation from each person. The topic studied in each group is different but related enough to fit within a common overall theme. The eventual product is either a written report, a brief oral presentation to the class, or both.

Use of Personal Journals

One of the most effective ways of personalizing a course is the use of individual journals. Depending on how the journal is to be used, students may be assigned to keep a daily record of dreams, thoughts, and feelings, or amount of food consumed, incidents observed, and so on. A daily record of food consumption or frequency of a particular behavior is appropriate to illustrate a behavioral approach to self-control. As discussed elsewhere in this chapter, observation of everyday incidents serves as material for class discussion and application of psychological principles. Journals of dreams, thoughts, and feelings are valuable when studying topics such as Jung's theory of personality or as a portion of a unit emphasizing self-understanding.

It is very important that the ground rules be made clear in connection with the use of diaries or journals. Students should know in advance who will be reading the journal, how confidential it will be, and whether it will be used as the basis for class discussion or will be a private communication between student and teacher. Participation should be completely voluntary.

Field Experiences

Most high school teachers are aware of the value of field trips to appropriate settings during the study of a particular topic. Effective at the high school level are field experiences that provide more continuity and considerably more depth than a one-day visit. There are many opportunities for "internships," even in small communities. Agencies such as child-care centers, nursery schools, community recreation centers, senior citizen centers, nursing/convalescent homes, mental health clinics, hospitals, and police headquarters are just a few of the possible direct-service placements that can provide students with opportunities to interact or observe interaction in settings different from their usual contacts. Students may sometimes also be placed as interns with the city council, county government offices, planning commissions, or park and recreation boards, where they can participate in research activities rather than provide direct service.

References and General Resources

Bare, J. K. Psychology: Where to begin. Washington, D. C.: American
    Psychological Association; Boulder, Colo.: ERIC Clearinghouse for
    Social Studies/Social Science Education, 1971. $1.00 paper.

Checklist for a new course in psychology. Washington, D. C.: American
    Psychological Association, undated. Free.

High School Psychology Teacher. Published five times during the academic
    year by the American Psychological Association, Washington, D. C.
    Free.

Johnson, J. M. (Ed.). Instructional strategies and curriculum units for
    secondary behavioral sciences. Plattsburg, N. Y.: State University
    of New York at Plattsburg, 1973. $2.25 paper.

Kasschau, R. A., & Wertheimer, M. Teaching psychology in secondary
    schools. Washington, D. C.: American Psychological Association;
    Boulder, Colo.: ERIC Clearinghouse for Social Studies/Social Science
    Education, 1974. $2.50 paper.

Lewin, K. Field theory in social science. Chicago: University of
    Chicago Press, 1951. $12.50 cloth.

Teaching of Psychology. Published four times during the academic year by
    Division 2 of the American Psychological Association at the Universi-
    ty of Missouri, Columbia. $4.00/year to individuals, $10.00/year to
    institutions.

Watson, G., & Johnson, D. W. Social psychology: Issues and insights
    (2nd ed.). Philadelphia: J. B. Lippincott, 1972. $7.75 paper.

Woods, P. J. (Ed.). Sourcebook on the teaching of psychology. Roanoke,
    Va.: Scholars' Press, 1973. $22.00 cloth. Supplemented annually.

Chapter 11

Ethics and the Teaching of Psychology
in the High School

This chapter presents three sets of guidelines developed by the American Psychological Association to assist high school psychology teachers in safeguarding the rights and welfare of students and experimental subjects while promoting high-quality instruction in psychology. The guidelines pertain to student experimentation and demonstrations with animals, student experimentation and demonstration with humans, and ethical issues faced by the high school psychology teacher.

Student Experimentation and Demonstrations with Animals

A general guideline for animal experimentation in an educational setting like the high school is that invertebrates are to be preferred over vertebrates as subjects for study and that, for vertebrate studies, naturalistic observation is to be preferred over experimental manipulation. <u>Extreme experimental procedures (such as surgery, shock, etc.), if undertaken at all, should be carried out only under strict supervision and in a research setting</u>. When vertebrates are used, the following guidelines should be observed to ensure their humane treatment.

Guidelines for the Use of Animals in School
Science Behavior Projects[1]

Committee on Precautions and Standards in Animal Experimentation[2]

With today's emphasis on the advancement of science, more and more intermediate and secondary students are participating in classroom science projects which involve experiments with live animals. Live animals should be used in classroom situations for their educational value in achieving instructional objectives and not as research contributing new knowledge to human health and welfare, as would be expected from a research facility.

1. In the selection of science behavior projects, students should be strongly urged to select small animals that are easy to maintain or invertebrates as subjects for evaluation.

2. All experiments <u>must</u> be preplanned and conducted in such a manner that respect for basic animal life and all humane considerations are fully understood and carried out by the student.

3. Each student undertaking a science project using animals <u>must have a qualified supervisor</u>. Such a supervisor shall be a person who has

had training and experience in the proper care of small and labora-
tory-type animals. The supervisor <u>must</u> assume the primary responsibility
for all conditions of the experiment. The following requirements must be
fulfilled:
     (a) The student shall research and study the appropriate literature
concerning previous work done in the student's chosen area.
     (b) A written preliminary outline of the student's plan of action
and anticipated outcome for the science project shall be submitted and be
available for evaluation. Such an outline should include the specific
purpose of the research and a justification of the methodology.
     4. Legislation and guidelines for specific care and handling of all
animals do exist. Students, teachers, and supervisors <u>must</u> be cognizant
of such legislation and guidelines. Copies of appropriate humane laws
are available by contacting the local humane organization and the American Humane Association, P. O. Box 1266, Denver, Colorado 80201. Each
state also has specific animal health regulations which must be considered. Copies of animal health regulations are obtainable from the state
veterinarian or state public health office.
     5. No student shall undertake an experiment which includes the use
of drugs, surgical procedures, noxious or painful stimuli such as electric shock, extreme temperature, starvation, malnutrition, ionizing radi-
ation, etc., except under extremely close and rigorous supervision of a
researcher qualified in the specific area of study.
     6. Students using animals <u>must</u> insure for the proper housing, food,
water, exercise, cleanliness, and gentle handling of such animals at all
times. Special arrangements <u>must</u> be made for care during weekend, holi-
day, and vacation periods. The comfort of each animal, by meeting its
basic daily needs, shall be of prime concern. Caution must be taken to
avoid the animals being teased or harmed by other students.
     7. When the research project has been completed and the student does
not wish to maintain the animal(s) as a pet, arrangements shall be made
for proper disposition by the supervisor. <u>Under no circumstances should
the student be allowed to provide "experimental" euthanasia.</u>
     8. Specifications for the detailed treatment of animals are avail-
able from the American Psychological Association, Office of Scientific
Affairs, 1200 Seventeenth Street, N. W., Washington, D. C. 20036.
     9. A copy of these Guidelines shall be posted conspicuously wherever
animals are kept and projects carried out.

Student Experimentation and Demonstrations with Humans

     Studies of fellow humans may be even more intriguing for students
than studies of animals. Again, the approach to be preferred in an educational setting is naturalistic observation or experimental manipulation
that will cause no physical or mental distress. Naturalistic observation
can be used very effectively to help students learn the difference between inference and observation, and the opportunities for conducting it
are abundant: children at play, people on buses or subways, people shop-
ping, etc.

Guidelines for the Use of Human Participants in Research
or Demonstrations Conducted by High School Students[3]

Committee on Psychology in the Secondary Schools[4]

High school students planning to use human participants in research
or demonstrations are strongly urged to become thoroughly acquainted with
the American Psychological Association's Ethical Principles in the Conduct of Research with Human Participants.[5] The potential problems of
such research may not be immediately evident to those doing research for
the first time. Among specific guidelines for the use of human participants in research or demonstrations conducted by high school students are
the following:

1. All research and demonstrations involving human participants
should be properly supervised by a qualified school authority.
    The supervisor should assume the primary responsibility for all con-
ditions of the experiment. The following requirements should be fulfilled:
    a. The supervisor should be familiar with the relevant literature
concerning previous work done in the student's chosen area. When possible, the student should also review and summarize appropriate reading
material.
    b. A written preliminary outline of the student's plan of study, to
include a statement of possible outcomes of the project and a description
of how the student plans to accomplish the objective of the study, should
be submitted and be available for evaluation by relevant school author-
ities. Such an outline should include the general and specific purposes
of the research or demonstration and a justification of the methods to be
employed.

2. Participants should not be exposed to physical or mental risk.
    High school students should not undertake procedures involving human
participants that are likely to harm the participants. Participants
should not be subjected to any risks greater than the ordinary risks of
daily life. To assure compliance with this guideline, high schools are
encouraged to form student-faculty committees that examine all research
or demonstration proposals from the point of view of the APA's Ethical
Principles in the Conduct of Research with Human Participants, to assure
that risks do not exceed the ordinary risks of daily life. Such committees might be constituted at the classroom level, across classes, at the
department level, or school-wide.

3. Agreement to participate should be obtained from all participants.
    The individual conducting the project should obtain each partici-
pant's agreement to participate, based on a full understanding of what
that agreement implies. Obtaining agreement involves providing a full

explanation of the research or demonstration procedures with special emphasis on aspects of the project likely to affect willingness to participate. All questions asked by any prospective participant should be answered directly, honestly, and completely. Participants who are too young or for other reasons cannot comprehend the project should be excluded, or proxy consent should be obtained from parents or guardians; this principle also applies to the siblings of the person conducting the project. A clear and fair agreement that clarifies the responsibilities of both should exist between the individual conducting the project and the participant. All promises and commitments included in that agreement should be honored by the person conducting the project. Such a formal agreement may not be necessary in some studies of public behavior, but in such studies it is especially crucial that participants' rights not be infringed.

4.   Participants should have the right to refuse to participate.
     Potential research participants have the right to refuse to participate and the right to withdraw from participation, for cause, at any time during the course of the research or demonstration procedures. The person conducting the project should explain this right to all potential participants prior to the commencement of the research or demonstration procedures. The person conducting the project should also provide opportunity for withdrawal with minimum discomfort during participation, particularly if a group activity is involved.
     Protection of this right requires special vigilance when the individual conducting the project is in a position of influence over the participant. For example, students in lower grades than the person conducting the project should not be pressured into participating and should not be publicly identified if they decline to participate in a particular experiment, survey, or demonstration. Under no circumstances should potential participants be exposed to ridicule, force, or excessive group pressure.

5.   The student should deal with possible undesirable consequences for participants.
     The supervisor should discuss with the student possible undesirable consequences of the project that should result in at least a temporary halt in the project. In the event that unanticipated undesirable consequences are detected by the individual conducting the project, he or she should halt the project if it is still in progress and notify the supervisor or other appropriate school authorities.

6.   The anonymity of the information gathered should be preserved.
     In certain projects, a participant may not wish the person conducting the project to disclose the results of the study in a way that individually identifies that participant. Only with the participant's full agreement can the person conducting the project disclose identifiable information about that participant to any other individual. A plan for protecting the anonymity of the information gathered should be a part of the procedure for obtaining initial agreement to participate. The person conducting the project should make every effort to maintain anonymity,

but participants should be made aware that in some cases it may be difficult or impossible to maintain full anonymity about all of the information obtained. Formal agreement to participate may not be necessary in
some studies of public behavior, but preservation of anonymity is as important in the observation of public behavior as it is in other research
or demonstrations. In public situations, information should not be collected in such a way that individuals are identifiable.

It is suggested that persons conducting projects encourage potential
participants to read these guidelines. To ensure a careful reading and
adequate understanding of these guidelines, persons conducting projects
may wish participants to sign a statement such as that below.

> I have read the Guidelines for the Use of Human Participants in
> Research or Demonstrations Conducted by High School Students. I
> have received satisfactory answers to my questions concerning
> this research or demonstration. I understand that every effort
> will be made to protect the anonymity of my responses although
> it cannot be guaranteed. I understand that I may withdraw from
> this research or demonstration without penalty at any time.

_____

Name

_____

Signature

_____

Date

Ethical Issues for High School Psychology Teachers

Like other teachers, high school teachers of psychology are bound by
their profession to observe certain general ethical principles in the
conduct of their work. Guidance in the general ethics of teaching is
often provided to teachers as part of their undergraduate preparation.
There also exist published statements pertaining to the general ethics of
teaching (e.g., the National Education Association's Code of Ethics of
the Education Profession). However, general ethics do not always serve
well in specific situations. Where those specific situations are likely
to recur often (because they arise from the particular subject matter
under study, as an example) more detailed guidance for ethical behavior
is desirable. Such is the case with psychology, whose subject matter
deals with intimate phenomena like personality and emotions and whose
procedures may be harmful if safeguards are not observed. The guidelines
below attempt to address ethical problems that are likely to arise in the
teaching of psychology at the high school level.

Ethical Guidelines for High School Psychology Teachers[6]
Committee on Psychology in the Secondary Schools[7]

It is generally recognized that teaching psychology in the high
school is a challenging task, and that experiments, demonstrations, discussions, and other activities can be a valuable part of a psychology
course. Complex ethical issues may be involved in experiments with human
participants, experiments with animal subjects, self-disclosure in class
discussions or activities, and questioning of personal or social values.
This document presents some guidelines for high school psychology teachers. Most of the guidelines are adapted from the American Psychological
Association and National Education Association codes of ethics.

1. Moral, ethical, and legal standards of behavior for any psychology teacher are a personal matter to the same degree as they are for any
other citizen, except as these may compromise the fulfillment of their
professional responsibilities, or reduce the trust in teaching of psychology held by the general public. In addition, teachers can influence
others, and therefore, also should be aware of the possible impact of the
public and ethical behavior that they exhibit in the presence of those
whom they influence.

2. To the extent that high school psychology teachers have not had
the training and experience of professional psychologists specializing in
psychological testing, diagnosis, therapy, or research, they should avoid
representing themselves to students, parents, or colleagues as experts in
these areas. The ethics of teaching psychology require high school
teachers constantly to strive for objectivity, to search for truth, and
to distinguish between scientific principles and generalizations on the
one hand, and personal opinions on the other.

3. High school psychology teachers have simultaneous obligations to
five constituencies: their students, the parents, the school, the community, and the discipline of psychology. Although high school teachers
of psychology should respond appropriately to these five constituencies,
they must, nevertheless, always keep the best interest of their students
in mind. For that reason, high school psychology teachers should not
force students to act against their wills, except as necessary to meet
curriculum requirements or implement effective classroom learning.

4. In planning a course, high school psychology teachers should
evaluate the ethical acceptability of all aspects of the course, taking
these guidelines into account. If the appraisal suggests a deviation
from any guideline, teachers should seek ethical advice from an expert or
an experienced colleague.

5. High school psychology teachers are responsible for the establishment and maintenance of acceptable ethical practice in a course.
They are also responsible for the ethical behavior of co-teachers, student teachers, aides, and students involved in the course. These others,
however, incur parallel ethical obligations. Department heads, principals, other administrators, school boards, and parents are also responsible for ethical practices in schools.

6. A significant part of a high school psychology course is consideration of the ethical aspects of human and animal experimentation. High
school psychology teachers should raise questions about the ethics of

research and treatment methods, applications of research results, and research or demonstrations performed by or on students. It should be made clear that many ethical questions have no simple answers and that thoughtful, well-informed, and well-intentioned individuals often reach different conclusions on ethical issues. Students should be encouraged to exercise ethical judgment and take stands on the ethics of actions that involve them; teachers should respect these stands, especially when the opinions differ from their own.

7. The study of psychology includes value-laden areas of human behavior. At the beginning of a course and throughout it, high school psychology teachers should emphasize that viewpoints on sensitive topics will be presented in addition to those that individual students already hold. Indeed, teachers have a responsibility to help students distinguish among facts, fancies, and values. Teachers should not avoid controversial issues simply because students hold opinions contrary to well-accepted scientific generalizations.

8. High school psychology teachers should protect students from undue psychological discomfort, harm, and danger in a course; students should not be subjected to any risks greater than the ordinary risks of daily life. Procedures that involve a significant possibility of harm to human participants should <u>not</u> be used (this prohibition, however, is not intended to exclude the use of potentially effective laboratory tools such as mild electric shock from a demonstrably safe source). Experiments, discussions, demonstrations, and activities involving personally sensitive topics such as drug use or sexuality may produce undesirable effects. The high school psychology teacher should be aware of the diverse backgrounds of the students, and, when dealing with sensitive topics, treat the material objectively and present it in a manner that takes feelings into account. Teachers should explore alternative possibilities of reaching their intended educational objective and should seek advice on the ethical acceptability of any questionable activities. Students should not be permitted to employ procedures with human participants in areas in which their high school psychology teacher is not adequately trained to offer appropriate supervision. High school teachers of psychology are encouraged to seek the advice and supervision of a qualified scientist in these instances. In all cases, high school psychology teachers should be guided by APA's <u>Ethical Standards of Psychologists</u>[5] and <u>Ethical Principles in the Conduct of Research with Human Participants</u>.[5]

9. It is, of course, important that the quality of relationships between students and the significant persons and social systems in their lives (e.g., family, school, church, and community) not be placed unduly and unnecessarily at risk. High school psychology teachers should not disclose information nor use experiments, demonstrations, discussions, or other activities that involve significant risk to those relationships, without very careful evaluation. For example, relationships could be damaged by the use of deception, including inaccurate or incomplete disclosure of information. On the other hand, even though a unit on the psychology of prejudice might create family problems for a child with a racially bigoted parent, the topic should not be avoided on such grounds alone.

10. Before undertaking an experiment, demonstration, discussion, or other activity, high school psychology teachers should attempt to anticipate undesirable consequences and take precautions to prevent them. In the event that an activity results in unanticipated undesirable consequences for a student or other participant, teachers should be sensitive to and make efforts to correct these consequences, including long-term after-effects, where relevant. When the needs of a student require it, teachers should refer the student to an appropriate professional such as the school psychologist or guidance counselor.

11. Certain events should lead to the discontinuation of an experiment, demonstration, discussion, or other activity. If high school psychology teachers become aware that undue physical or psychological discomfort, harm, or danger to a participant is occurring, or if a participant feels harmed by an activity or challenges its ethical acceptability, teachers should halt the activity immediately and take steps to relieve any harm or to correct any misunderstanding that has occurred. The activity should be resumed or repeated only if there is good reason to believe that the conditions that resulted in the earlier problem no longer exist. Teachers are urged to seek advice, from the participants as well as from colleagues or experts, before resuming or repeating the activity.

12. Students should be free to decline to participate, or to discontinue participation in an experiment, demonstration, discussion, or other activity that might involve undue and severe risk to them. Providing alternative means of fulfilling course requirements is one way of satisfying this guideline. Where possible, students who decline to participate in an activity should not be publicly identified, nor should they be exposed to group pressure or ridicule.

13. Allowing students meaningful freedom to decline to participate in an experiment, demonstration, discussion, or other activity implies that high school psychology teachers have informed students of the features of the activity that might reasonably be expected to influence their decision to participate. It also implies that teachers have answered any questions students may have about the activity. Considerations of class time or educational impact may sometimes prompt teachers not to inform students fully about an activity in advance; if the planned activity is new (without a history of success and safety in similar situations), teachers should seek advice on its ethical acceptability from colleagues and/or students.

14. At the end of a class session involving an experiment or demonstration using student participants, high school psychology teachers should provide the participants (and any observers) with a debriefing that includes a discussion of students' reactions to the activity. A debriefing that fully clarifies the nature of the activity should take place at the end of each experiment or demonstration.

15. High school psychology teachers cannot promise legal confidentiality to students, nor can students promise it to one another. Before an experiment, demonstration, discussion, or other activity, potential participants should be informed whether information that is obtained about or disclosed by them will be anonymous. Information that cannot or will not be anonymous should be kept private to the extent consistent with

student learning. Circumstances under which such information might be disclosed to others, especially persons outside the psychology class, should be the subject of a clear agreement arrived at in advance by the students and the teacher.

16. In situations where there might be a conflict between high school psychology teachers' personal interests and the students' interests--for example, when a teacher is conducting research for outside credit or publication and using the students as subjects--teachers are under special obligation to seek advice on the ethical acceptability of planned activities.

17. In student experiments or demonstrations using animals as subjects, high school psychology teachers should, as a minimum, ensure that students follow APA's Guidelines for the Use of Animals in School Science Behavior Projects.[5] In general, animals used in school experiments or demonstrations should be invertebrates rather than vertebrates, and naturalistic observation of vertebrates is preferable to experimentation on them. Invasive procedures, electric shock, and high stress should be avoided except under those unusual circumstances where a student of extraordinary promise has obtained competent, documented, and sustained supervision. In such cases, the student's experiment or demonstration should conform to the APA Principles for the Care and Use of Animals.[5]

18. In student experiments or demonstrations using human participants, high school psychology teachers should ensure that students follow APA's Guidelines for the Use of Human Participants in Research or Demonstrations Conducted by High School Students.[5] In general, students should obtain agreement to participate from all participants, deal with possible undesirable consequences for participants, and preserve the anonymity of the information gathered. They should not use procedures that expose participants to undue physical or psychological risk. Further, the statements in Guideline #8 on experiments or demonstrations conducted by teachers also apply to experiments or demonstrations conducted by students.

Footnotes

[1]These guidelines were approved by the Board of Scientific Affairs, the Education and Training Board, the Board of Directors, and the Council of Representatives of the American Psychological Association.

[2]Members of the Committee when these guidelines were developed were John Davenport, Bruce Halpern, Daniel Lehrman, Seymour Levine (Chair), William Mason, and Richard Walk.

[3]These guidelines were approved by the Education and Training Board, the Board of Scientific Affairs, the Board of Directors, and the Council of Representatives of the American Psychological Association. They are a condensed version of the APA's official guidelines for the use of human participants in research and represent a distillation of the customary procedures of responsible, experienced research psychologists. Adherence to these principles will provide protection not only to the

participants in research or demonstration projects conducted by high school students, but also to the individuals undertaking or responsible for such research or demonstrations, both students and teachers.

[4]Members of the Committee when these guidelines were developed were John K. Bare (ex officio), Evelyn Frye, Frank B. W. Hawkinshire, Mary Margaret Moffett, Maxine Warnath, and Michael Wertheimer (Chair). The Committee thanks F. Barbara Orlans for pointing out the need for these guidelines and for drafting five of the basic principles that appear in these guidelines.

[5]Copies of all guidelines are available through the APA Clearing-house on Precollege Psychology, 1200 Seventeenth Street, N. W., Washington, D. C. 20036. All are free except Ethical Principles in the Conduct of Research with Human Participants, which is $4.

[6]These guidelines were approved by the Education and Training Board, the Board of Directors, and the Council of Representatives of the American Psychological Association.

[7]Members of the Committee when these guidelines were developed were John K. Bare (ex officio), Evelyn Frye, Frank B. W. Hawkinshire, Linda Meador, Mary Margaret Moffett, Paul Munford, Maxine Warnath, and Michael Wertheimer (Chair).

Appendix A

Publishers' Addresses

Academic Press, Inc., 111 Fifth Avenue, New York, NY 10003
Addison-Wesley Publishing Co., Inc., Reading, MA 01867
Airmont Publishing Co., Inc., 22 East 60th Street, New York, NY 10022
Albion Publishing Co., 1736 Stockton Street, San Francisco, CA 94133
Aldine-Atherton, Inc.--see Aldine Publishing Co.
Aldine Publishing Co., 529 South Wabash Avenue, Chicago, IL 60605
J. A. Allen & Co., Ltd.--distributed by Sporting Book Center, Inc.,
    Canaan, NY 12029
Allyn & Bacon, Inc., 470 Atlantic Avenue, Boston, MA 02210
American Association for the Advancement of Science, 1515 Massachusetts
    Avenue, N. W., Washington, DC 20005
American Book Co., 450 West 33rd Street, New York, NY 10001
American Psychological Association, 1200 Seventeenth Street, N. W.,
    Washington, DC 20036
Animal Welfare Institute, P. O. Box 3650, Washington, DC 20007
Ann Arbor Publishers, 2057 Charlton, Ann Arbor, MI 48103
Annual Reviews, Inc., 4139 El Camino Way, Palo Alto, CA 94306
Apollo Editions, Ten East 53rd Street, New York, NY 10022
Appleton-Century-Crofts, 292 Madison Avenue, New York, NY 10017
Atheneum Publishers, 122 East 42nd Street, New York, NY 10017
Avon Books, 959 Eighth Avenue, New York, NY 10019
Ballantine Books, Inc., 201 East 50th Street, New York, NY 10022
Bantam Books, Inc., 666 Fifth Avenue, New York, NY 10019
Basic Books, Inc., Publishers, Ten East 53rd Street, New York, NY 10022
Beacon Press, 25 Beacon Street, Boston, MA 02108
Behaviordelia, P. O. Box 1044, Kalamazoo, MI 49005
Benjamin/Cummings Publishing Co., Inc., 2727 Sand Hill Road, Menlo Park,
    CA 94025
W. A. Benjamin--see Benjamin/Cummings Publishing Co., Inc.
Benziger--see Benziger Bruce & Glencoe
Benziger Bruce & Glencoe, 17337 Ventura Boulevard, Encino, CA 91316
Bobbs-Merrill Co., 4300 West 62nd Street, Indianapolis, IN 46206
British Book Centre, Fairview Park, Elmsford, NY 10523
Brooks/Cole Publishing Co., 540 Abrego Street, Monterey, CA 93940
William C. Brown Co., Publishers, 2460 Kerper Boulevard, Dubuque, IA
    52001
Canfield Press, Ten East 53rd Street, New York, NY 10022
Chandler Publishing Co., Ten East 53rd Street, New York, NY 10022
Ciba Pharmaceutical Co., 556 Morris Avenue, Summit, NJ 07901
College & University Press, 263 Chapel Street, New Haven, CT 06513
Coward, McCann & Geoghegan, Inc., 200 Madison Avenue, New York, NY 10016
Cowles Book Co., Inc., 114 West Illinois Street, Chicago, IL 60610

CRM Books--see CRM/Random House
CRM/Random House, 201 East 50th Street, New York, NY 10022
Thomas Y. Crowell Co., Inc., Ten East 53rd Street, New York, NY 10022
Crown Publishers, Inc., One Park Avenue, New York, NY 10016
Cummings Publishing Co., Inc.--see Benjamin/Cummings Publishing Co., Inc.
John Day Co., Inc., Ten East 53rd Street, New York, NY 10022
Marcel Dekker, Inc., 270 Madison Avenue, New York, NY 10016
Dell Publishing Co., Inc., One Dag Hammarskjold Plaza, New York, NY 10017
The Dial Press, Inc., One Dag Hammarskjold Plaza, New York, NY 10017
Dickenson Publishing Co., Inc.--see Wadsworth Publishing Co.
Didactic Systems Inc., P. O. Box 457, Cranford, NJ 07016
Dodd, Mead & Co., 79 Madison Avenue, New York, NY 10016
Dorsey Press, 1818 Ridge Road, Homewood, IL 60430
Doubleday & Co., Inc., 245 Park Avenue, New York, NY 10017
Dover Publications, Inc., 180 Varick Street, New York, NY 10014
E. P. Dutton, Two Park Avenue, New York, NY 10016
Educational Testing Service, Princeton, NJ 08541
ERIC Clearinghouse for Social Studies/Social Science Education, 855
     Broadway, Boulder, CO 80302
Farrar, Straus & Giroux, Inc., Nineteen Union Square West, New York, NY
     10003
Fawcett Books, 600 Third Avenue, New York, NY 10016
Fawcett World Library--see Fawcett Books
Fearon ● Pitman Publishers, Inc., Six Davis Drive, Belmont, CA 94002
Fearon Publishers--see Fearon ● Pitman Publishers, Inc.
The Free Press, 866 Third Avenue, New York, NY 10022
W. H. Freeman & Co., Publishers, 660 Market Street, San Francisco, CA
     94104
General Learning Press, 250 James Street, Morristown, NJ 07960
Ginn and Co., 191 Spring Street, Lexington, MA 02173
Greenwood Press, Inc., 51 Riverside Avenue, Westport, CT 06880
Grove Press, Inc., 196 West Houston Street, New York, NY 10014
Grune & Stratton, Inc., 111 Fifth Avenue, New York, NY 10003
Harcourt Brace Jovanovich, Inc., 757 Third Avenue, New York, NY 10017
Harper & Row, Publishers, Ten East 53rd Street, New York, NY 10022
Harper's College Press, Ten East 53rd Street, New York, NY 10022
Hart Publishing Co., Inc., Fifteen West Fourth Street, New York, NY 10012
Harvard Educational Review, Longfellow Hall, 13 Appian Way, Cambridge,
     MA 02138
Harvard University Press, 79 Garden Street, Cambridge, MA 02138
Haworth Press, 149 Fifth Avenue, New York, NY 10010
Hawthorn Books, Inc., 260 Madison Avenue, New York, NY 10016
D. C. Heath & Co., 125 Spring Street, Lexington, MA 02173
Holden-Day, Inc., 500 Sansome Street, San Francisco, CA 94111
Holt, Rinehart & Winston, 383 Madison Avenue, New York, NY 10017
Houghton Mifflin Co., One Beacon Street, Boston, MA 02107
Human Sciences Press, 72 Fifth Avenue, New York, NY 10011
Irvington Publishers, Inc., 551 Fifth Avenue, New York, NY 10017
Richard D. Irwin, Inc., 1818 Ridge Road, Homewood, IL 60430
Jossey-Bass, Inc., Publishers, 433 California Street, San Francisco, CA
     94104

Journal of Biological Psychology, P. O. Box 7590, Ann Arbor, MI 48107
Augustus M. Kelley, Publishers, 300 Fairfield Road, Fairfield, NJ 07006
Key Education Inc., 673 Broad Street, Shrewsbury, NJ 07701
Robert R. Knapp, P. O. Box 7234, San Diego, CA 92107
Alfred A. Knopf, Inc., 201 East 50th Street, New York, NY 10022
R. E. Krieger Publishing Co., Inc., P. O. Box 542, Huntington, NY 11743
Lancer Books, Inc., 1560 Broadway, New York, NY 10036
Life Science Associates, One Fenimore Road, P. O. Box 500, Bayport, NY
     11705
J. B. Lippincott Co., East Washington Square, Philadelphia, PA 19105
Little, Brown & Co., 34 Beacon Street, Boston, MA 02106
Longmans Canada Ltd., 55 Barber Greene Road, Don Mills, Ontario, Canada
     M3C 2A1
The Macmillan Co., 866 Third Avenue, New York, NY 10022
McDougal, Littell & Co., Box 1667, Evanston, IL 60204
McGraw-Hill Book Co., 1221 Avenue of the Americas, New York, NY 10020
David McKay Co., Inc., 750 Third Avenue, New York, NY 10017
Meredith Corp., 750 Third Avenue, New York, NY 10017
Charles E. Merrill Publishing Co., 1300 Alum Creek Drive, Columbus, OH
     43216
The M.I.T. Press, 28 Carleton Street, Cambridge, MA 02142
William Morrow & Co., Inc., 105 Madison Avenue, New York, NY 10016
The C. V. Mosby Co., 11830 Westline Industrial Drive, St. Louis, MO 63141
National Academy of Sciences, National Research Council, 2101
     Constitution Avenue, N. W., Washington, DC 20418
National Press Books, 850 Hansen Way, Stanford Industrial Park, Palo Alto,
     CA 94304
National Textbook Co., 8259 Niles Center Road, Skokie, IL 60076
Natural History Press, 245 Park Avenue, New York, NY 10017
Nelson-Hall Inc., 325 West Jackson Boulevard, Chicago, IL 60606
The New American Library, Inc., 1301 Avenue of the Americas, New York,
     NY 10019
New Directions Publishing Corp., 333 Avenue of the Americas, New York,
     NY 10014
New York University Press, 21 West Fourth Street, New York, NY 10003
W. W. Norton & Co., Inc., 500 Fifth Avenue, New York, NY 10036
Oxford Book Co., Eleven Park Place, New York, NY 10007
Oxford University Press, Inc., 200 Madison Avenue, New York, NY 10016
Pacific Books, Publishers, P. O. Box 558, Palo Alto, CA 94302
Pantheon Books, 201 East 50th Street, New York, NY 10022
Parker Publishing Co., West Nyack, NY 10994
Paulist/Newman Press--see Paulist Press
Paulist Press, 1865 Broadway, New York, NY 10023
F. E. Peacock, Publishers, Inc., 401 West Irving Park Road, Itasca, IL
     60143
Penguin Books, 625 Madison Avenue, New York, NY 10022
Pergamon Press, Inc., Maxwell House, Fairview Park, Elmsford, NY 10523
Philadelphia Book Co., One Brown Street, Philadelphia, PA 19123
Pitman Publishing Corp.--see Fearon ● Pitman Publishers, Inc.
Plenum Publishing Corp., 227 West Seventeenth Street, New York, NY 10011

Pocket Books, 1230 Avenue of the Americas, New York, NY 10020
Praeger Publishers, Inc., 383 Madison Avenue, New York, NY 10017
Precision Media, c/o Behavior Research Co., P. O. Box 3222, Kansas City,
    KS 66103
Prentice-Hall, Inc., Englewood Cliffs, NJ 07632
Press of Case Western University--out of business
Princeton University Press, Princeton, NJ 08540
Principia Press, Inc., 5743 Kimbark Avenue, Chicago, IL 60637
Psychonomic Society Publications, 1108 West 34th Street, Austin, TX 78705
Public Affairs Press, 419 New Jersey Avenue, S. E., Washington, DC 20003
Publishers, Inc., Drawer P, 243 Twelfth Street, Del Mar, CA 92014
G. P. Putnam's Sons, 200 Madison Avenue, New York, NY 10016
Harlan Quist, One Dag Hammarskjold Plaza, New York, NY 10017
Rand McNally & Co., P. O. Box 7600, Chicago, IL 60680
Random House, Inc., 201 East 50th Street, New York, NY 10022
Regent House, 108 North Roselake Avenue, Los Angeles, CA 90026
Rigby, Ltd., Adelaide, Australia
Ronald Press Co., 79 Madison Avenue, New York, NY 10016
Russell Sage Foundation, 230 Park Avenue, New York, NY 10017
Sage Publications, Inc., 275 South Beverly Drive, Beverly Hills, CA 90212
Howard W. Sams & Co., Inc., 4300 West 62nd Street, Indianapolis, IN 46206
W. B. Saunders Co., West Washington Square, Philadelphia, PA 19105
Schocken Books, Inc., 200 Madison Avenue, New York, NY 10016
Scholars' Press, Ltd., P. O. Box 7231, Roanoke, VA 24019
Science Research Associates, 155 Wacker Drive, Chicago, IL 60606 or 1540
    Tang Mill Road, Palo Alto, CA 94304
Scott, Foresman & Co., 1900 East Lake Avenue, Glenview, IL 60025
Charles Scribner's Sons, 597 Fifth Avenue, New York, NY 10017
The Seabury Press, Inc., 815 Second Avenue, New York, NY 10017
Silver Burdett Co., 250 James Street, Morristown, NJ 07960
Simon & Schuster, Inc., 1230 Avenue of the Americas, New York, NY 10020
Peter Smith, Six Lexington Avenue, Magnolia, MA 01930
Social Science Education Consortium, 855 Broadway, Boulder, CO 80302
Social Studies School Service, 10000 Culver Boulevard, Culver City, CA
    90230
Springer Publishing Co., Inc., 200 Park Avenue South, New York, NY 10003
Stanford University Press, Stanford, CA 94305
State University of New York at Plattsburgh, Plattsburgh, NY 12901
Stein & Day, Publishers, Scarborough House, Briarcliff Manor, NY 10510
TAB Books, Blue Ridge Summit, PA 17214
Time-Life Books, Alexandria, VA 22314
United States Government Printing Office, Washington, DC 20402
Universal Publishing & Distributing Corp., 235 East 45th Street, New York,
    NY 10023
University of California Press, 2223 Fulton Street, Berkeley, CA 94720
University of Chicago Press, 5801 Ellis Avenue, Chicago, IL 60637
The University of Michigan Press, Ann Arbor, MI 48106
University of Nebraska Press, 901 North Seventeenth Street, Lincoln, NE
    68588
University of North Carolina Press, P. O. Box 2288, Chapel Hill, NC 27514

University of Oklahoma Press, 1005 Asp Avenue, Norman, OK 73019
University of Pennsylvania Press, 3933 Walnut Street, Philadelphia, PA
    19174
University of Pittsburgh Press, 127 North Bellefield Avenue, Pittsburgh,
    PA 15260
University of Toronto Press, 33 East Tupper Street, Buffalo, NY 14208
Van Nostrand Reinhold Co., 450 West 33rd Street, New York, NY 10001
Vanguard Press, Inc., 424 Madison Avenue, New York, NY 10017
The Viking Press, 625 Madison Avenue, New York, NY 10022
Vocational Guidance Manuals, c/o National Textbook Co., 8259 Niles Center
    Road, Skokie, IL 60076
Wadsworth Publishing Co, 10 Davis Drive, Belmont, CA 94002
Warner Books, Inc., 75 Rockefeller Plaza, New York, NY 10019
Richard West, P. O. Box 6404, Philadelphia, PA 19145
Westinghouse Learning Press, c/o Cambridge Book Co., 488 Madison Avenue,
    New York, NY 10022
Whitston Publishing Co., Inc., P. O. Box 958, Troy, NY 12181
John Wiley & Sons, Inc., 605 Third Avenue, New York, NY 10016
The Williams & Wilkins Co., 428 East Preston Street, Baltimore, MD 21202
Winthrop Publishers, Inc., 17 Dunster Street, Cambridge, MA 02138
Women on Words and Images, 30 Valley Road, Princeton, NJ 08540
World Publishing Co., 110 East 59th Street, New York, NY 10022
Yale University Press, 302 Temple Street, New Haven, CT 06511

NOTES

NOTES

NOTES

NOTES

NOTES